Collins Gem

Italian

Phrase Book

CONSULTANT
Federico Bonfanti

GEM PHRASE BOOKS

DUTCH
FRENCH
GERMAN
GREEK
ITALIAN
PORTUGUESE
SPANISH

Also available Gem Phrase Book CD Packs

First published 1993
This edition published 2003
Copyright © HarperCollins Publishers
Reprint 10 9 8 7 6 5 4 3 2
Printed in Italy by Amadeus S.p.A

www.collins.co.uk

ISBN 0-00-714170-X

Your *Collins Gem Phrase Book* is designed to help you locate the exact phrase you need in any situation, whether for holiday or business. If you want to adapt the phrases, we have made sure that you can easily see where to substitute your own words (you can find them in the dictionary section), and the clear, two-colour layout gives you direct access to the different topics.

The *Gem Phrase Book* includes:

- Over 70 topics arranged thematically. Each phrase is accompanied by a simple pronunciation guide which ensures that there's no problem over pronouncing the foreign words.

- Practical hints and useful vocabulary highlighted in boxes. Where no article (il/la/un/una) is given you will generally see the words written on signs and notices.

WORDS APPEARING IN BLACK ARE ENGLISH WORDS	WORDS APPEARING IN BLUE ARE ITALIAN WORDS

- Possible phrases you may hear in reply to your questions. The foreign phrases appear in blue.

- A clearly laid-out 5000-word dictionary: English words appear in black and Italian words appear in blue.

- A basic grammar section which will enable you to build on your phrases.

It's worth spending time before you embark on your travels just looking through the topics to see what is covered and becoming familiar with what might be said to you.

Whatever the situation, your *Gem Phrase Book* is sure to help!

CONTENTS

PRONOUNCING ITALIAN

Spelling and pronouncing Italian are easy once you know the few basic rules. This book has been designed so that as you read the pronunciation of the phrases, you can follow the Italian. This will help you recognize how Italian is pronounced and give you a feeling for the rythm of the language. Here are a few rules you should know:

ITALIAN	SOUNDS LIKE	EXAMPLE	PRONUNCIATION
■ AU	*ow*	autobus	**ow**-tobus
■ CE	*che*	cena	**chay**na
■ CI	*chee*	cibo	**chee**bo
■ CHE *	*kay*	barche	**bar**kay
■ CHI *	*kee*	chiave	kee-**a**vay
■ GE	*jay*	gelato	jay-**la**to
■ GHE *	*gay*	traghetto	tra-**get**-to
■ GI	*jee*	gita	**jee**ta
■ GHI *	*gee*	ghiaccio	gee**at**-cho
■ GLI	*lyee*	degli	**del**-yee
■ GN	*ny*	ragno	**ran**yo
■ IU	*you*	aiuto	a-**yoo**to
■ SC	*sh*	scena	**shay**na
■ SCH *	*sk*	schermo	**sker**mo

* c and g are hard except when followed by E or I – to make them hard in Italian an H is added.

Double letters SS, TT, LL, etc. are distinctly pronounced – with a slight pause between the two:
posso pos-so, gatto gat-to, pelle pel-lay.

Stress usually falls on the second-to-last syllable. We have indicated the stressed syllable with bold italics in the pronunciation of the phrases.

*Italians can be quite formal in their greeting. If you don't know someone well, the best greeting is **buon giorno** (literally good day). If you are slightly unsure how formal to be **salve** is a good option. **Ciao** is used among family and friends.*

Please	**Thanks (very much)**	**You're welcome!**
Per favore	Grazie (mille)	Prego!
payr fa-**vo**ray	**grats**-yay (**meel**-lay)	**pray**go

Yes	**No**	**Yes, please**	**No, thanks**	**OK!**
Sì	No	Sì, grazie	No, grazie	Va bene!
see	no	see **grats**-yay	no **grats**-yay	va **be**nay

Sir / Mr...	**Madam / Mrs... / Ms...**	**Miss**
Signore / Signor...	Signora	Signorina
seen-**yor** / seen-**yo**ray	seen-**yo**ra	seenyo-**ree**na

Hello	**Goodbye**	**Hi/Bye**	**See you later**
Buon giorno / Salve	Arrivederci	Ciao	A più tardi
bwon **jor**no	ar-reevay-**der**chee	chow	a pyoo **tar**dee

Good evening	**Goodnight**	**See you tomorrow**
Buona sera	Buona notte	A domani
bwona **say**ra	**bwo**na **not**-tay	a do-**ma**nee

Excuse me! / Sorry!	**Excuse me!** (to get past in a crowd)
Scusi! / Mi scusi!	Permesso!
skoozee / mee **skoo**zee	per-**mes**-so

How are you?	**Fine, thanks**	**And you?**
Come sta?	Bene, grazie	E Lei?
komay sta	**be**nay **grats**-yay	ay lay

I don't understand	**I don't speak Italian**
Non capisco	Non parlo italiano
non ka-**pees**ko	non **par**lo eetal-**ya**no

7

KEY PHRASES

the (masculine/feminine)
il / la / l' (+vowel)
eel / la / l'

the (plural masculine/feminine)
i / le
ee / lay

the museum	**the station**	**the shops**	**the houses**
il museo	la stazione	i negozi	le case
eel moo-**zay**o	la stats-**yo**nay	ee ne**gots**-ee	lay **ka**zay

a/one (masculine)
un
oon

(feminine)
una
oona

a ticket / one stamp
un biglietto / un francobollo
oon beel-**yet**-to / oon franko**bol**-lo

a room / one bottle
una camera / una bottiglia
oona **ka**mayra / oona bo-**teel**ya

some (masculine/feminine)
del / della
del / **del**-la

some (plural masculine/feminine)
dei / delle
day / **del**-lay

some wine	**some fruit**	**some biscuits**	**some crisps**
del vino	della frutta	dei biscotti	delle patatine
del **vee**no	**del**-la **froo**t-ta	day bees-**kot**-tee	**del**-lay pa-ta-**tee**nay

Do you have...?
Avete...?
a-**vay**tay...

Do you have a timetable?
Avete un orario?
a-**vay**tay oon or**ar**-yo

Do you have a room?
Avete una camera?
a-**vay**tay oona **ka**-mayra

Do you have milk?
Avete del latte?
a-**vay**tay del **lat**-tay

I'd like...
Vorrei...
vor-**ray**...

We'd like...
Vorremmo...
vor-**rem**-mo...

I'd like an ice cream
Vorrei un gelato
vor-**ray** oon jay**la**to

We'd like to go home
Vorremmo andare a casa
vor-**rem**-mo an**dar**ay a **ka**za

Another/Some more... (singular)	(plural)
Altro(a)...	Altri(e)...
*al*tro(a)...	*al*tree(-ay)...

Some more bread	**Some more glasses**
Altro pane	Altri bicchieri
*al*tro *pa*nay	*al*tree beek-*yer*ee

Another espresso	**Another beer**	**Some more water**
Un altro caffè	Un'atra birra	Ancora dell'acqua
oon *al*tro kaf-*fe*	oon *al*tra *beer*-ra	an*ko*ra del-*lak*wa

How much is it?	**How much does it cost?**
Quant é?	Quanto costa?
kwan-*te*	*kwan*to *kos*ta

large	**small**	**with**	**without**
grandè	piccolo	con	senza
*gran*day	*pee*-kolo	kon	*sent*sa

Where is...?	**Where are...?**	**the nearest**
Dov'é...?	Dove sono...?	il/la piú vicino(a)
dov-*e*...	*do*vay sono...	eel/la pyoo vee-*chee*no(-na)

How do I get...?	**to the museum**	**to the station**	**to Milan**
Per andare...	al museo	alla stazione	a Milano
payr an-*da*ray...	al moo-*zay*o	*al*-la stats-*yo*nay	a mee*la*no

There is...	**There are...**	**There isn't...**	**There aren't any...**
C'è...	Ci sono...	Non c'è...	Non ci sono...
che...	chee sono...	non che...	non chee sono...

When?	**At what time...?**	**today**	**tomorrow**
Quando?	A che ora...?	oggi	domani
*kwan*do	a kay *o*ra...	*od*jee	do-*ma*nee

Can I...?	**smoke**	**taste it**
Posso...?	fumare	provarlo
pos-so...	foo*ma*ray	pro*var*lo

How does this work?	**What does this mean?**
Come funziona?	Che cosa vuol dire questo?
*ko*may foonts-*yo*na	kay *ko*za vwol *dee*ray *kwes*to

9

Ingresso entrance	**Entrata** entrance	**Uscita** exit

APERTO open	**CHIUSO** closed

caldo
hot

freddo
cold

TIRARE pull	**SPINGERE** push

Acqua non potabile
not drinking water

Prego di...
please...

VIETATO
forbidden

libero
free, vacant

occupato
engaged

Attenzione al cane
beware of the dog

UOMINI
gents

DONNE
ladies

Fuori servizio
out of order

CASSA
cash desk

NOLEGGIO for hire / to rent

Divieto di Balneazione
no bathing

in vendità for sale

saldi sale

seminterrato ↓
basement

pianterreno
ground floor

ascensore →
lift

suonare
ring

premere
press

CAMERE
rooms available

COMPLETO
no vacancies

USCITA D'EMERGENZA
emergency exit

Privato
private

Biglietti
tickets

← AI TRENI
to the trains

ALT
stop

convalidare il biglietto qui
validate your ticket

ORARIO
timetable

ARRIVI
arrivals

PARTENZE
departures

BINARIO
platform

DEPOSITO BAGAGLI
left luggage

non fumatori
non-smoking

fumatori
smoking

VIETATO FUMARE
no smoking

11

POLITE EXPRESSIONS

There are two forms of address in Italian: formal (Lei) and informal (tu). You should always stick to the formal until you are invited to use the informal.

The lunch was delicious
Il pranzo era ottimo
eel **pran**tso **e**ra ot-teemo

The dinner was delicious
La cena era ottima
la **chay**na era ot-teema

This is a gift for you
Questo è un regalo per lei
kwesto **e** oon ray-**ga**lo payr lay

Pleased to meet you
Piacere
pee-a-**cher**ay

This is my husband
Questo è mio marito
kwesto **e** **mee**yo ma-**ree**to

This is my wife
Questa è mia moglie
kwesta e **mee**ya **mol**-yay

You have a beautiful home
Avete una bella casa
a-**vay**tay oona **bel**-la **ka**za

You have a beautiful garden
Avete un bel giardino
a-**vay**tay oon bel jar**dee**-no

Thanks for your hospitality
Grazie per l'ospitalità
grats-yay payr lospeetalee-**ta**

We'd like to come back
Vorremmo ritornare
vor-**rem**-mo reetor-**na**ray

Enjoy your holiday!
Buona vacanza!
bwona va**kant**sa

It was nice seeing you again
È stato un vero piacere rivederla
e **sta**to oon **vay**ro pee-a-**cher**ay reeve**der**la

Please come and visit us
Venga a trovarci
venga a tro-**var**chee

I've enjoyed myself very much
Mi è piacuto molto
mee **e** pee-a-**choo**to **mol**to

We must stay in touch
Teniamoci in contatto
ten-**ya**mochee een kon**tat**-to

II'd like to wish you...
Vorrei augurarle (augurarti – informal)...
vor-ray owgoo-rar-lay (owgoo-rar-tee)...

Happy Birthday!
Buon compleanno!
bwon komplay-an-no

Happy Anniversary!
Felice anniversario!
feleechay an-neever-sar-yo

Merry Christmas!
Buon Natale!
bwon na-talay

Happy New Year!
Buon Anno!
bwon an-no

Happy Easter!
Buona Pasqua!
bwona paskwa

Happy festive season!
Buone feste!
bwonay festay

Have a good trip!
Buon viaggio!
bwon veead-jo

Best wishes!
Tanti auguri!
tantee ow-goo-ree

Welcome!
Benvenuti!
benven-ootee

Enjoy your meal!
Buon appetito!
bwon ap-peteeto

Thanks, and the same to you!
altrettanto!
altray-tanto

Cheers!
Salute! or Cin-cin!
sa-lootay / cheen cheen

Congratulations!
Congratulazioni!
kongra-toolats-yonee

see also **MAKING FRIENDS** ▢ **LETTERS**

*In this section we have used the familiar form **tu** for the questions.*

What's your name?
Come ti chiami?
*ko*may tee kee-*amee*

My name is...
Mi chiamo...
mee kee-amo...

How old are you?
Quanti anni hai?
*kwan*tee *an*-nee a-ee

I'm ... years old
Ho ... anni
o ... an-nee

Where are you from?
Di dove sei?
*dee do*vay say

I'm...
Sono...
sono...

Where do you live?
Dove abiti?
*do*vay a-*beetee*

Where do you live? (plural)
Dove abitate?
*do*vay abee-*tatay*

I live in London
Vivo a Londra
*vee*vo a *lon*dra

We live in Glasgow
Viviamo a Glasgow
*veev-yamo a glas*go

I'm at school	I work	I'm retired
Vado a scuola	Lavoro	Sono in pensione
vado a skwola	*la-voro*	*sono een pens-yonay*

I'm...	**married**	**divorced**	**widowed**
Sono...	sposato(a)	divorziato(a)	vedovo(a)
sono...	*spo-zato(a)*	*deevorts-yato(a)*	*vay-dovo(a)*

I have...	**a boyfriend**	**a girlfriend**	**a partner**
Ho...	un ragazzo	una ragazza	un amico(a)
o...	*oon ragats-so*	*oona ragats-a*	*oon a-meeko(a)*

I have ... children	**I have no children**
Ho ... figli	Non ho figli
o ... feel-yee	*non o feel-yee*

I'm here...	**on holiday**	**on business**	**for the weekend**
Sono qui...	in vacanza	per lavoro	per l'weekend
sono kwee...	*een va-kantsa*	*payr la-voro*	*payr lweekend*

What do you do?
Lei che lavoro fa?
lay kay la-**vo**ro fa

Do you like your job?
Le piace il suo lavoro?
lay pee-**a**-chay eel **soo**-o la-**vo**ro

I'm...
Sono...
sono...

a doctor
medico
medeeko

a manager
direttore
deeret-**to**ray

a housewife
casalinga
kasa-**leen**ga

I work in...
Lavoro in...
la-**vo**ro een...

a shop
un negozio
oon neg**ots**-yo

a factory
una fabbrica
oona **fab**-breeka

I work from 9 to 5
Lavoro dalle nove alle cinque
la-**vo**ro **dal**-lay **nov**ay **al**-lay **cheen**-kway

from Monday to Friday
dal lunedì al venerdì
dal loone**dee** al vener-**dee**

I work from home
Lavoro da casa
la-**vo**ro da **ka**za

I'm self-employed
Lavoro in conto proprio
la-**vo**ro een **kon**to **pro**-pree-o

I have been unemployed for...
Sono disoccupato(a) da...
sono deezok-koo-**pa**to(a) da...

months
mesi
mayzee

years
anni
an-nee

It is very difficult to get a job at the moment
È molto difficile trovare un lavoro al momento
e **mol**to deef-**fee**-cheelay tro-**va**ray oon la-**vo**ro al mo-**men**to

What are your hours?
Qual è il suo orario di lavoro?
kwa-**le** eel **soo**-o o**rar**-yo dee la-**vo**ro

How much holiday do you get?
Quante ferie ha all'anno?
kwantay **fer**-yay a al-**lan**-no

What do you want to be when you grow up?
Che cosa vuoi fare quando sarai grande?
kay **ko**za vwoy **fa**ray **kwan**do sa-**ra**-ee **gran**-day

see also **MAKING FRIENDS** ☐ **BUSINESS**

WEATHER

LE PREVISIONI DEL TEMPO *lay pre-veez-yonee*	**WEATHER FORECAST**
TEMPO VARIABILE *tempo varee-abeelay*	**CHANGEABLE WEATHER**
BELLO *bel-lo*	**FINE**
BRUTTO *broot-to*	**BAD**
NUVOLOSO *noovo-loso*	**CLOUDY**

It's sunny
C'è il sole
che eel solay

It's raining
Piove
pee-ovay

It's snowing
Nevica
nay-veeka

It's windy
Tira vento
teera vento

What a lovely day!
Che bella giornata!
kay bel-la jor-nata

What awful weather!
Che brutto tempo!
kay broot-to tempo

What will the weather be like tomorrow?
Come sarà il tempo domani?
komay sa-ra eel tempo do-manee

Do you think it's going to rain?
Pensa che pioverà?
pensa kay pee-ovay-ra

Do I need an umbrella?
Devo prendere l'ombrello?
devo pren-deray lom-brel-lo

When will it stop raining?
Quando smetterà di piovere?
kwando smet-tay-ra dee pee-o-vayray

It's very hot today
Fa molto caldo oggi
fa molto kaldo od-jee

Do you think there will be a storm?
Pensa che ci sarà un temporale?
pensa kay chee sa-ra oon tempo-ralay

Do you think it will snow?
Pensa che nevicherà?
pensa kay neveekay-ra

Will it be foggy?
Pensa che ci sarà la nebbia?
pensa kay chee sa-ra la neb-bya

What is the temperature?
Quanti gradi ci sono?
kwantee gradee chee sono

16

DAVANTI A da-**van**tee a	OPPOSITE
ACCANTO A ak-**kan**to a	NEXT TO
VICINO A vee-**chee**no a	NEAR TO
IL SEMAFORO eel say-**ma**foro	TRAFFIC LIGHTS
L'INCROCIO leen-**kro**cho	CROSSROADS
ALL'ANGOLO (della via) al-**lan**golo (**del**-la **vee**-a)	CORNER (of road)

Excuse me
Scusi
skoozee

how do I get to...?
per andare a/al/alla (etc.)...?
*payr an-**da**ray a/al/**al**-la...*

to the station
alla stazione
*al-la stats-**yo**nay*

to the museum
al museo
*al moo**zay**-o*

to the shops
ai negozi
*a-ee nego**ts**-ee*

We're lost
Ci siamo smarriti
*chee see-**a**mo smar-**ree**tee*

We're looking for...
Cerchiamo...
*cherkee-**a**mo...*

Is this the right way to...?
Questa è la via giusta per...?
*kwesta e la **vee**-a **joo**sta payr...*

Is it far?
È lontano?
*e lon-**ta**no?*

Can I/we walk there?
Si può andare a piedi?
*see pwo an-**da**ray a pee-**e**-dee*

How do I/we get onto the motorway?
Per andare sull'autostrada?
*payr an-**da**ray sool-lowto-**stra**da*

Can you show me on the map?
Mi può indicare sulla cartina?
*mee pwo eendee-**ka**ray **sool**-la kar-**tee**na*

■ **YOU MAY HEAR**

Giri a sinistra / a destra
*jee-ree a see-**nee**stra / a **de**stra*
Turn left / right

Sempre dritto
*sempray **dreet**-to*
Keep straight on

Laggiù
*la-**joo***
down there

dietro / dopo la chiesa
*dee-**e**tro / **do**po la kee-**e**za*
behind / after the church

poi chieda ancora
*po-ee kee-**e**da an-**ko**ra*
then ask again

see also **MAPS & GUIDES**

BUS & COACH

In cities you buy tickets from tobacconists, kiosks and bars. You must punch them in the machine on board the bus or tram. Village buses are referred to as la corriera or il pullman (coach).

Is there a bus / tram to...?
Scusi, c'è un autobus / tram per...?
skoozee che oon ow-toboos / tram payr...

Which bus goes to...?
Quale autobus va a...?
kwalay ow-toboos va a...

Where do I catch the bus / tram to...?
Dove prendo l'autobus / il tram per...?
dovay pren-do low-toboos / eel tram payr...

We're going to...
Andiamo a...
an-dyamo a...

Where can I buy tickets for the bus?
Dove posso prendere i biglietti per l'autobus?
dovay pos-so pren-deray ee beel-yet-tee payr low-toboos

How much is it to go...?
Quanto costa per andare...?
kwanto kosta payr an-daray...

to the centre
al centro
al chentro

to the beach
alla spiaggia
al-la spee-ad-ja

How often are the buses to...?
Ogni quanto ci sono gli autobus per...?
on-yee kwanto chee sono lee ow-toboos payr...

When is the first / the last bus to...?
Quando c'è il primo / l'ultimo autobus per...?
kwando che eel preemo / lool-teemo ow-toboos payr...

Please tell me when to get off
Per favore può dirmi quando devo scendere
payr fa-voray pwo deermee kwando devo shen-deray

Please let me off
Per favore mi fa scendere
payr fa-voray mee fa shen-deray

This is my stop
Questa è la mia fermata
kwesta e la meeya fer-mata

■ **YOU MAY HEAR**

Questa è la sua fermata
kwesta e la soo-a fer-mata
This is your stop

Prenda la metro, è più veloce
prenda la metro e pyoo vel-ochay
Take the metro, it's quicker

see also **METRO** □ **TAXI** □ **LUGGAGE**

Rome and Milan are the only Italian cities with metro systems. Each journey is a flat rate. You save by buying a book of 10 tickets – *un blocchetto di biglietti* (oon blok-**ket**-to dee beel-**yet**-tee).

L'ENTRATA len-**tra**ta	**ENTRANCE**
L'USCITA loo-**shee**ta	**WAY OUT/EXIT**
SETTIMANALE/MENSILE set-tee-men**a**lay/men**see**lay	**WEEKLY/MONTHLY**

A book of tickets, please
Un blocchetto di biglietti, per favore
*oon blok-**ket**-to dee beel-**yet**-tee payr fa-**vo**ray*

A 24-hour ticket
Un biglietto da venti-quattro ore
*oon beel-**yet**-to da ventee-**kwat**-tro oray*

48-hour
da quarantotto ore
*da kwarant-**ot**-to oray*

Where is the nearest metro?
Dov'è la stazione della metropolitana più vicina?
*do-**ve** la stats-yo**nay** **del**-la metro-polee-**ta**na pyoo vee-**chee**na*

How does the ticket machine work?
Come funziona la biglietteria automatica?
*ko**may** foonts-yo**na** la beel-yet-tay**ree**-a owto-**ma**-teeka*

I'm going to...
Vado a...
*va**do** a...*

Do you have a map of the metro?
Avete una piantina della metro?
*a-**vay**tay **oo**na peean-**tee**na **del**-la metro*

How do I get to...?
Per andare a...?
*payr an-**da**ray a...*

Do I have to change?
Devo cambiare?
*de**vo** kamb-**ya**ray*

What is the next stop?
Qual è la prossima fermata?
*kwa-**le** la **pros**-seema fer-**ma**ta*

Excuse me! This is my stop
Scusi! Questa è la mia fermata
*skoo**zee** **kwes**ta e la **mee**ya fer-**ma**ta*

Please let me out
Mi fa scendere
*mee fa **shen**-deray*

see also **BUS & COACH** ☐ **TAXI** ☐ **LUGGAGE**

19

You must get your ticket validated at the small machines situated at the ends of platforms before you get on board. They are not always very obvious. If you don't get your ticket stamped you are liable to be fined. You can see on the ticket where to insert it and get it stamped. You also need to stamp it for the return part of the journey. It means you can buy tickets in advance of your departure date. If you are taking a fast train, check whether there is a supplement to pay.

LOCALE *lo-**ka**lay*	**SLOW STOPPING TRAIN** (stops at all stations)
DIRETTO *dee**ret**-to*	**LOCAL TRAIN** (stops at most stations)
ESPRESSO *es**pres**-so*	**EXPRESS** (stops at main stations)
RAPIDO / INTER CITY **ra**-peedo / **een**tercity	**INTERCITY** (stops at main stations: supplement)
SUPER RAPIDO **soo**per **ra**-peedo	**HIGH-SPEED INTERCITY** (reservations compulsory)
BINARIO *bee-**nar**yo*	**PLATFORM**
BIGLIETTERIA *beel-yet-tay-**ree**-a*	**TICKET OFFICE**
ORARIO *o-**rar**yo*	**TIMETABLE**
RTD *ree**tar**do*	**DELAY** (appears on train noticeboards)
DEPOSITO BAGAGLI *de**poz**eeto ba**gal**yee*	**LEFT LUGGAGE**

Where is the station?
Scusi, dove la stazione?
skoozee dovay la stats-yonay

1 ticket	**2 tickets**	**3 tickets**
un biglietto	due biglietti	tre biglietti
*oon beel-**yet**-to*	*dooay beel-**yet**-tee*	*tray beel-**yet**-tee*

single	**return**	**to...**
solo andata	andata e ritorno	per...
solo** an-**data	*an-**data** ay ree**tor**-no*	*payr...*

first / second class	**smoking / non smoking**
prima / seconda classe	per fumatori / non fumatori
***pree**ma / se**kon**da **klas**-say*	*payr fooma-**to**ree / non fooma-**to**ree*

Is there a supplement to pay?
C'e un supplemento da pagare?
che oon soop-play-mento da pa-garay

I want to book a seat on the super rapido to Rome
Vorrei prenotare un posto per il super rapido per Roma
vor-ray preno-taray oon posto payr eel sooper ra-peedo payr roma

When is the next train to....?
A che ora c'è il prossimo treno per...?
a kay ora che eel pros-seemo trayno payr...

Do I have to change?
Devo cambiare?
devo kamb-yaray

How long is there for the connection?
Quanto tempo c'è per la coincidenza?
kwanto tempo che payr la koeen-chee-dentsa

Which platform does it leave from?
Da quale binario parte?
da kwalay beenar-yo partay

Is this the train for...?
Scusi, questo è il treno per...?
skoozee kwesto e il trayno payr...

Why is the train delayed?
Perché è in ritardo il treno?
payrkay e een ree-tardo eel trayno

When will it leave?
Quando partirà?
kwando partee-ra

Does it stop at...?
Si ferma a...?
see ferma a...

When does it arrive in...?
A che ora arriva a...?
a kay ora ar-reeva a...

Please tell me when we get to...
Per favore mi dica quando arriviamo a...
payr fa-voray mee deeka kwando ar-reev-yamo a...

Is there a restaurant car?
C'è il il vagone ristorante?
che eel vago-nay reesto-rantay

Is this seat free?
È libero questo posto?
e lee-bero kwesto posto

Excuse me! (to get past)
Permesso!
per-mes-so

see also **LUGGAGE**

TAXI

The easiest place to find a taxi stand is at a railway station. Official taxis are generally white (yellow in Rome).

I want a taxi
Vorrei un taxi
*vor-**ray** oon **tak**see*

Where can I get a taxi?
Dove posso trovare un taxi?
***do**vay **pos**-so tro-**var**ay oon **tak**see*

Please order me a taxi...
Per favore mi chiama un taxi...
*payr fa-**vor**ay mee kee-**a**ma oon **tak**see...*

now
subito
soo-beeto

for...(time)
per le...
payr lay...

How much will it cost to go to...?
Quanto verrà a costare per andare a/al/alla (etc.)...?
***kwan**to ver-**ra** a kos-**tar**ay payr an-**dar**ay a/al/**al**-la...*

to the station
alla stazione
***al**-la stats-**yo**nay

to the airport
all'aeroporto
*al-layro-**por**to

to this address
a questo indirizzo
*a **kwes**to een-deer**eets**-so

How much is it?
Quant'è?
*kwan-**te**

Why is it so much?
Come mai è così tanto?
***ko**may ma-ee e ko-**zee** tanto

It's more than on the meter
È più di quanto indicato sul tacchimetro
*e pee-**oo** dee **kwan**to eendee-**ka**to sool tak-**kee**metro

Keep the change
Tenga il resto
***ten**ga eel **res**to

Sorry, I don't have any change
Mi dispiace, non ho moneta
*mee deespee-**a**-chay non o mo-**net**a

I'm in a hurry
Ho fretta
*o **fret**-ta

Can you go a little faster?
Può andare più forte?
*pwo an-**dar**ay pyoo **for**tay

I have to catch...
Devo prendere...
***dev**o **pren**-deray...

a train
il treno
*eel **tray**no

a plane
l'aereo
*la-**e**-rayo

see also **LUGGAGE** □ **BUS** □ **METRO**

You can buy travel cards (**Carta Venezia**) for Venice which allow you to use all the water buses (**vaporetti**).

A Venice card for one day
Una carta Venezia per un giorno
*oo*na **kar**ta ven**et**seeya payr oon **jor**no

two-day
per due giorni
payr dooay **jor**nee

How much is it for an hour on the gondola?
Quanto costa viaggiare in gondola per un'ora?
kwanto **kos**ta veead-**jar**ay een **gon**dola payr oon **ora**

Have you a timetable?
Ha l'orario?
al o**rar**-yo

Is there a car ferry to...?
C'è il traghetto macchine per...?
che eel tra-**get**-to **mak**-keenay payr...

How much is a ticket...?
Quanto costa un biglietto...?
kwanto **kos**ta oon beel-**yet**-to...

single
andata
an-**data**

return
andata e ritorno
an-**data** ay ree-**tor**no

How much is it for a car and ... people?
Quanto costa per un'automobile e ... persone?
kwanto **kos**ta payr oon owto-**mo**beelay ay ... per-**so**nay

Where does the vaporetto leave from?
Da dove parte il vaporetto?
da **dov**ay **par**tay eel vapo**ret**-to

for the Lido
per il Lido
payr eel **lee**do

When is the first / the last boat?
Quando parte il primo / l'ultimo battello?
kwando **par**tay eel **pree**mo / **lool**-teemo bat-**tel**-lo

■ YOU MAY HEAR

Questo è l'ultimo battello
kwesto e **lool**-teemo bat-**tel**-lo
This is the last boat

Oggi non c'è servizio...
od-jee non che ser**veets**-yo...
Today there is no service...

perché c'è lo sciopero
per**kay** che lo **sho**-pero
because there is a strike

23

ARRIVI ar-**ree**vee	**ARRIVALS**
PARTENZE par-**tent**say	**DEPARTURES**
INTERNAZIONALI eenternats-yo**na**ee	**INTERNATIONAL**
NAZIONALI nats-yo**na**ee	**DOMESTIC**
IMBARCO eem-**bar**ko	**BOARDING GATE**

How do I get to the airport?
Scusi, per andare all'aeroporto?
skoozee payr an-**da**ray al-ay-ro-**por**to

Is there a bus to the airport?
C'è l'autobus per l'aeroporto?
che **low**to-boos payr la-ay-ro-**por**to

Where is the luggage for the flight from...?
Scusi, dov'è il bagaglio del volo da...?
skoozee do-**ve** eel ba**gal**-yo del **vo**lo da...

Where can I change some money?
Scusi, dove posso cambiare i soldi?
skoozee **do**vay **pos**-so kamb-**ya**ray ee **sol**dee

How do I/we get into town?
Scusi, come si va in città?
skoozee **ko**may see va een cheet-**ta**

to go into town?
per andare in città?
payr an-**da**ray een cheet-**ta**

How much is it by taxi...?
Quanto costa il taxi...?
kwanto **kos**ta eel **tak**see...

to go to the Hotel...?
per andare all'Hotel...?
payr an-**da**ray al-lo**tel**...

■ YOU MAY HEAR

L'imbarco sarà all'uscita numero...
leem**bar**-ko sa-**ra** al-loo**shee**ta **noo**-mayro...
Boarding will take place at gate number...

Vada subito all'uscita numero...
vada **soo**-beeto al-loo**shee**ta **noo**-mayro...
Go immediately to gate number...

see also **LUGGAGE** ❑ **BUS** ❑ **METRO** ❑ **TAXI**

With the single European Market, EU citizens are subject only to highly selective spot checks and they can go through the blue customs channel (unless they have goods to declare). There will be no restriction, either by quantity or value, on goods purchased by EU travellers in another EU country provided that they are **for their own personal use**. If you are unsure of certain items, check with the customs officials as to whether duty is required.

CITTADINI UE *cheeta-**dee**nee oo-eh*	**EU CITIZENS**
ALTRI PASSAPORTI *altree pas-sa**por**tee*	**OTHER PASSPORTS**
LA CARTA D'IDENTITÀ *la karta deedentee-**ta***	**IDENTITY CARD**
LA DOGANA *la do**ga**na*	**CUSTOMS**

Do I have to pay duty on this?
Devo pagare la dogana per questo?
***dev**o pa-**ga**ray la do-**ga**na payr **kwes**to*

I bought this in ... as a gift
Ho comprato questo a ... per un regalo
*o kom-**pra**to **kwes**to a ... payr oon ray-**ga**lo*

It's for my own personal use
È per uso personale
***e** payr **oo**zo perso-**na**lay*

We are on our way to... *(if in transit through a country)*
Siamo in transito per...
*see-**a**mo een **tran**-zeeto payr...*

The children are on this passport
I bambini sono su questo passaporto
*ee bam-**bee**nee sono soo **kwes**to pas-sa-**por**to*

This is the baby's passport
Questo è il passaporto del bambino / della bambina
***kwes**to **e** eel pas-sa-**por**to del bam-**bee**no / **del**-la bam-**bee**na*

ACCENDERE I FARI

switch on headlights

Deviazione

diversion

PERICOLO

danger

RALLENTARE

slow down

SENSO UNICO

one way

TANGENZIALE

ring road

RACCORDO ANULARE

by-pass

CIRCONVALLAZIONE

by-pass

ZONA PEDONALE

pedestrian zone

PROSSIME USCITE

next exits

AUTOSTRADA

motorway signs are green in Italy

ALT STAZIONE

toll station for motorway

A PEDAGGIO

motorway toll

town centre

all routes

TUTTE LE DIREZIONI

Centro

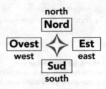

north
Nord

Ovest west

Est east

Sud south

1 ora = 1 hour
The crossed mallets mean work days.
The cross means Sundays.

AUTOSILO

multi-storey car park

DARE LA PRECEDENZA

give way

PARCHEGGIO

parking

TUTTE LE DIREZIONI ➤

all routes

DIVIETO DI SOSTA

no parking

P libero

spaces

P completo

full

LA PATENTE *la pa***ten**-tay	**DRIVING LICENCE**
LA POLIZZA A CASCO *la po***leet**-sa a kasko	**FULLY COMPREHENSIVE INSURANCE**
LA RETROMARCIA *la retro***mar**cha	**REVERSE GEAR**

I want to hire a car
Vorrei noleggiare una macchina
*vor-***ray** *noled-jaray oona mak-keena*

for ... days
per ... giorni
payr ... jornee

with automatic gears
col cambio automatico
*kol **kam**byo owto-ma-teeko*

What cars do you have?
Che tipo di macchina avete?
*kay **tee**po dee **mak**-keena a-**vay**tay*

What are your rates...?
Quanto costa...?
kwanto kosta...

per day
al giorno
*al **jor**no*

per week
per settimana
*payr set-tee-**ma**na*

How much is the deposit?
Quant'è l'anticipo?
*kwan-**te** lantee-cheepo*

Do you take credit cards?
Accettate le carte di credito?
*at-chet-**ta**tay lay **kar**tay dee **kray**-deeto*

Is there a mileage (kilometre) charge?
Si paga per chilometro?
*see **pa**-ga payr kee**lo**-metro*

How much is it?
Quant' è?
*kwan-**te***

Does the price include fully comprehensive insurance?
Il prezzo è inclusivo della polizza a casco?
*eel **prets**-so e eenkloo-**zee**vo **del**-la po-**leet**sa a kasko*

Must I return the car here?
Devo ritornare la macchina qui?
***dev**o reetor-**na**ray la **mak**-keena kwee*

By what time?
Per quando?
*payr **kwan**do*

I'd like to leave it in...
Vorrei lasciarla a...
*vor-**ray** la-**shar**la a...*

How do the controls work?
Come funzionano i comandi
***ko**may foonts-**yo**nano ee ko-**man**dee*

■ **YOU MAY HEAR**

Ritorni la macchina con il serbatoio pieno
*ree-**tor**nee la **mak**-keena kon eel serba-**toyo** pee**yen**o*
Please return the car with a full tank

28

The speed limits in Italy are 50 km/h in built up areas, 90–110 km/h on main roads, 130 km/h on 2-lane motorways and 140 km/h on 3-lane motorways (except in bad weather and at night). On motorways and SS (Strada Statale) roads you must always have your headlights on.

Can I/we park here?
Si può parcheggiare qui?
see pwo parked-jaray kwee

Where is the best place to park?
Dov'è il miglior posto per parcheggiare?
do-ve eel meelyor posto payr parked-jaray

Do I/we need a parking disk?
Si deve avere il disco orario?
see devay a-vayray eel deesko orar-yo

How long can I/we park for?
Per quanto tempo si può parcheggiare qui?
payr kwanto tempo see pwo parked-jaray kwee

We're going to...   **What's the best route?**
Andiamo a...   Qual è la migliore strada?
and-yamo a...   *kwa-le la meel-yoray strada*

How do I get to the motorway?
Scusi, per andare sull'autostrada?
skoozee payr an-daray sool-lowto-strada

Which junction is it for...?
Quale uscita è per...?
kwalay oo-sheeta e payr...

Will the motorway be busy?   **Is the pass open?**
L'autostrada sarà intasata?   Il passo è aperto?
lowto-strada sa-ra eenta-sata   *eel pas-so e a-perto*

Do I/we need snow chains?
Si devono usare le catene per le gomme?
see devono oo-zaray le ka-taynay payr le gom-may

see also **BREAKDOWN □ PETROL**

Many petrol stations are now self-service and you can pay by inserting a banknote into the appropriate slot on the pump.

SUPER **soo**per	**4 STAR**
GASOLIO ga-**zol**yo	**DIESEL**
SENZA PIOMBO **sen**tsa pee-**om**bo	**UNLEADED**

Fill it up, please
Il pieno per favore
*eel pee-***ye***no payr fa-***vo***ray*

Please check the oil / the water
Per favore controlli l'olio / l'acqua
*payr fa-***vo***ray kon***trol***-lee **lol**-yo / **lak**wa*

...30 euros worth of unleaded petrol
...trenta euro di benzina senza piombo
*...***tren***ta ay-***oo***ro dee bend-***zee***na **sen**tsa pee-**om**bo*

Where is...?
Dov'è...?
*do-***ve***...*

the air line
la canna dell'aria
*la **kan**-na del-***lar***-ee-a*

water
la canna dell'acqua
*la **kan**-na del-**lak**wa*

Please fill this with petrol
Per favore riempia questo canestro di benzina
*payr fa-***vo***ray ree-***em***pya **kwes**to ka-***nes***tro dee bend-***zee***na*

Pump number...
Pompa numero...
*pom***pa noo**mayro...*

Where do I pay?
Dove pago?
*do***vay **pa**go*

Can I pay by credit card?
Posso pagare con la carta di credito?
*pos***-so pa-***ga***ray kon la **kar**ta dee **kray**-deeto*

■ YOU MAY HEAR

Manca un po' d'olio / un po' d'acqua
*man***ka oon po **dol**-yo / oon po **dak**wa*
You need some oil / some water

Tutto a posto
*toot***-to a **pos**to*
Everything is OK

see also **BREAKDOWN** ❑ **CAR**

If you break down, the emergency phone number for the Italian equivalent to the AA (ACI – **Automobile Club d'Italia**) is **116**. A garage that does repairs is known as an **autofficina** (owto-of-fee**chee**na).

Can you help me?
Può aiutarmi?
pw**o** a-yoo-**tar**mee

My car has broken down
La mia macchina è in panne
la **mee**ya **mak**-keena **e** een **pan**-nay

I've run out of petrol
Non ho più benzina
non o pyoo bend-**zee**na

The battery is flat
La batteria è scarica
la bat-ter**ee**-a **e** **ska**-reeka

The engine is overheating
Il motore si surriscalda
eel mo-**to**ray see soor-ree-**skal**da

I need water
Ho bisogno di acqua
o beez**on**-yo dee **ak**wa

I've a flat tyre
Ho una foratura
o oona fora-**too**ra

I can't get the wheel off
Non riesco a togliere la ruota
non ree-**es**ko a **tol**-yeray la **rwo**ta

Can you tow me to the nearest garage?
Può trainarmi fino al prossimo garage?
pw**o** tra-ee-**nar**mee **fee**no al **pros**-seemo ga-**razh**

Do you have parts for a (make of car)**...?**
Ha ricambi per la...?
a ree-**kam**bee payr la...

There's something wrong with the...
C'è qualcosa che non va con il/la/i/le (etc.)...
ch**e** kwal-**ko**za kay non va kon eel/la/ee/lay...

Can you replace the windscreen?
Può cambiare il tergicristallo?
pw**o** kamb-**ya**ray eel terjee-kree-**stal**-lo

Can you give me a push please?
Mi dà una spinta per favore?
mee **da** oona **speen**ta payr fa-**vo**ray

see also **CAR PARTS**

CAR PARTS

The ... doesn't work	The ... don't work
Il/La ... non funziona	I/Le... non funzionano
*eel/la ... non foonts-**yo**na*	*ee/lay ... non foonts-**yo**nano*

accelerator	l'acceleratore	*at-chelera-**to**ray*
alternator	l'alternatore	*alterna-**to**ray*
battery	la batteria	*bat-tay-**ree**-a*
bonnet	il cofano	*ko-fano*
brakes	i freni	*fray**nee***
choke	l'aria	*ar-ya*
clutch	la frizione	*freets-**yo**nay*
distributor	il distributore	*deestree-boo-**to**ray*
engine	il motore	*mo-**to**ray*
exhaust	il tubo di scappamento	*toobo dee skap-pa-**men**to*
fuse	il fusibile	*foo**zee**-beelay*
gears	le marce	*marchay*
handbrake	il freno a mano	*fray**no** a mano*
headlights	i fari	*faree*
ignition	l'accensione	*at-chens-**yo**nay*
indicator	la freccia	*frech-cha*
points	le puntine	*poon-**tee**nay*
radiator	il radiatore	*radya-**to**ray*
reverse gear	la retromarcia	*retro-**mar**cha*
seat belt	la cintura di sicurezza	*cheen-**too**ra dee seekoo-**rets**-sa*
spark plug	la candela	*kan-**day**la*
steering	lo sterzo	*stertso*
steering wheel	il volante	*vo-**lan**tay*
tyre	la gomma	*gom-ma*
wheel	la ruota	*rwota*
windscreen	il parabrezza	*para-**bredz**-za*
windscreen washer	il lavacristallo	*lava-kree-**stal**-lo*
windscreen wiper	il tergicristallo	*terjee-kree-**stal**-lo*

see also **BREAKDOWN** ☐ **PETROL**

Bed and breakfast, particularly on farms and in the countryside is becoming very popular. You can find out more about **agriturismo** on **www.agriturismo.com**.

Stanza singola single room	
Stanza doppia double room	
Stanza matrimoniale double-bedded room	
Bagno privato private facilities	
Numero di adulti number of adults	
Numero di bambini number of children	

I'd like to book a room...
Vorrei prenotare una camera...
vor-**ray** preno-**ta**ray oona **ka**-mayra...

	single	**double**
	singola	doppia
	seen-gola	**dop**-pya

Do you have a room for tonight?
Avete una camera per questa notte?
a-**vay**tay oona **ka**-mayra payr **kwes**ta **not**-tay

for one night	**for ... nights**	**from... till...**
per una notte	per ... notti	dal... al...
payr oona **not**-tay	payr ... **not**-tee	dal... al...

with bath	**with shower**	**with a double bed**
con bagno	con doccia	con letto matrimoniale
kon **ban**-yo	kon **dot**-cha	kon **let**-to matree-mon-**ya**lay

twin-bedded	**with an extra bed for a child**
a due letti	con un letto extra per un bambino
a **dooay let**-tee	kon oon **let**-to **ex**tra payr oon bam-**bee**no

cont...

How much is it...?   **per night**   **per week**
Quant'è...?   per notte   per settimana
kwan-te...   *payr not-tay*   *payr set-tee-mana*

Is breakfast included?
La prima colazione è inclusa?
la preema kolats-yonay e een-kloosa

Have you anything cheaper?
Avete qualcosa meno caro?
a-vaytay kwal-koza meno karo

I'd like to see the room
Vorrei vedere la camera
vor-ray vederay la ka-mayra

I will confirm...   **by e-mail**   **by fax**
Confermerò...   per e-mail   con un fax
konfermay-ro...   *payr ee-mail*   *kon oon fax*

Can you suggest somewhere else?
Ci può consigliare un'altro posto?
chee pwo konseel-yaray oon altro posto

■ **YOU MAY HEAR**

Siamo al completo
see-amo al komplay-to
We're full

Per quanti notti?
payr kwantee not-tee
For how many nights?

Il suo nome per favore
eel soo-o nomay payr fa-voray
Your name, please

La prego di confermare...   **per e-mail**   **con un fax**
la praygo dee konfer-maray...   *payr e-mail*   *kon oon fax*
Please confirm...   **by e-mail**   **by fax**

*Many hotels are now signposted in towns. The Italian word for a hotel is **albergo** (al-**ber**go)*

I booked a room...
Ho prenotato una camera...
*o prayno-**ta**to oona **ka**-mayra...*

in the name of...
a nome di...
*a **no**may dee...*

Do you have a room...?
Avete una camera...?
*a-**vay**tay oona **ka**-mayra...*

for tonight
per questa notte
*payr **kwes**ta **not**-tay*

Where can I park the car?
Dove posso parcheggiare la macchina?
***dov**ay **pos**-so parked-**ja**ray la **mak**-keena*

What time is...?
A che ora è...?
*a kay **ora** e...*

dinner
la cena
*la **chay**na*

breakfast
la prima colazione
*la **pree**ma kolats-**yo**nay*

We'll be back late tonight
Questa sera ritorneremo tardi
***kwes**ta **say**ra reetor-ne**ray**mo **tar**dee*

Do you lock the door?
Chiudete la porta d'entrata?
*keeoo-**day**tay la **por**ta den-**tra**ta*

The key, please
La chiave per favore
*la kee-**a**vay payr fa-**vo**ray*

Room number...
Camera numero...
***ka**-mayra **noo**-mayro...*

Are there any messages for me?
C'è un messaggio per me?
*che oon mes-**sad**-jo payr may*

Can I send a fax?
Posso mandare un fax?
***pos**-so man-**da**ray oon fax*

Can you keep this in the safe, please
Potete tenere questo nella cassetta di sicurezza?
*po-**tay**tay te**ne**ray **kwes**to **nel**-la kas-**set**-ta dee see-koo-**ret**-sa*

I'm leaving tomorrow
Parto domani
***par**to do-**ma**nee*

Please prepare the bill
Ci prepara il conto
*chee pre**pa**ra eel **kon**to*

see also **HOTEL (BOOKING)**

CAMPING

LA SPAZZATURA *la* spats-sa**too**ra	**RUBBISH**
ACQUA POTABILE **ak**wa po-ta**beel**ay	**DRINKING WATER**
LA PRESA DI CORRENTE *la* **pres**a dee kor-**ren**tay	**ELECTRIC POINT**

Do you have a list of campsites?
Avete una lista dei campeggi?
a-**vay**tay **oo**na **lees**ta day kam**ped**-jee

Is the campsite sheltered?
Il campeggio è riparato?
eel kam**ped**-jo e reepa-**ra**to

Is the beach far?
La spiaggia è lontana?
la spee-**ad**-ja e lon-**ta**na

Is there a restaurant / a self-service café on the campsite?
C'è un ristorante / un selfservice nel campeggio?
che oon reesto-**ran**tay / oon selfservice nel kam**ped**-jo

Do you have any vacancies?
Avete dei posti?
a-**vay**tay day **pos**tee

How much is it per night?
Quanto costa per notte?
kwanto **kos**ta payr **not**-tay

per tent	**per caravan**	**per person**
per tenda	per roulotte	per persona
payr **ten**da	payr roo**lot**	payr per-**so**na

Does the price include...?
Il prezzo include...?
eel **prets**-so eenk**loo**day...

showers / hot water / electricity
doccia / acqua calda / elettricità
dot-cha / **ak**wa **kal**da / elet-treechee-**ta**

We'd like to stay for ... nights
Vorremmo rimanere per ... notti
vor-**rem**-mo reema-**ne**ray payr ... **not**-tee

Can we camp here overnight?
Possiamo accamparci qui per questa notte?
pos-see-**amo** ak-kam**par**chee kwee payr **kwes**ta **not**-tay

Is there a doctor available?
C'è l'assistenza medica?
che las-sees**ten**za **med**-eeka

Can we have an extra set of keys?
Possiamo avere un altro paio di chiavi?
pos-see-amo a-veray oon altro pa-yo dee kee-avee

When does the cleaner come?
Quando viene la donna di pulizie?
kwando vee-yenay la don-na dee pooleet-seeya

Who do we contact if there are problems?
Chi contattiamo se ci sono dei problemi?
kee kontat-tyamo say chee sono day pro-blemee

How does the heating work?
Come funziona il riscaldamento?
komay foonts-yona eel reeskalda-mento

Is there always hot water?
C'è sempre l'acqua calda?
che sempray lakwa kalda

Where is the nearest supermarket?
Dov'è il supermercato più vicino
do-ve eel soopermerkato pyoo vee-cheeno

Where do we leave the rubbish?
Dove mettiamo la spazzatura?
dovay met-tyamo la spats-satoora

When is the rubbish collected?
Quando vengono a prendere la spazzatura?
kwando vengono a prenderay la spats-satoora

Where is the bottle bank?
Dov'è il posto per il riciclaggio di bottiglie
do-ve eel posto payr eel reechee-kladjo dee bot-teelyay

What are the neighbours called?
Come si chiamano i vicini?
komay see kee-amono ee vee-cheenee

see also **SIGHTSEEING & TOURIST OFFICE**

SHOPPING PHRASES

Opening hours approx. 8.30 am to 12.30 pm and 4 to 7.30 pm Mon. to Sat. Opening hours tend to be longer in summer. Supermarkets are open all day and often have late shopping on Thursday.

Where is...?
Scusi, dov'è...?
skoozee do-**ve**...

Do you have...?
Avete...?
a-**vay**tay...

I'm just looking
Sto solo guardando
sto **solo** gwar-**dan**do

I'm looking for a present for...
Cerco un regalo per...
cherko oon ray-**ga**lo payr...

my mother
mia madre
meeya **ma**dray

a child
un bambino
oon bam-**bee**no

Where can I buy...?
Dove posso comprare...?
dovay **pos**-so kom-**pra**ray...

shoes
delle scarpe
del-lay **skar**pay

gifts
dei regali
day ray-**ga**lee

Can you recommend a good shop for...?
Ci consiglia un buon negozio per...?
chee kon-**seel**ya oon bwon ne**gots**-yo payr...

Do you have anything...?
Avete qualcosa...?
a-**vay**tay kwal-**ko**za...

larger
più grande
pyoo **gran**day

smaller
più piccolo
pyoo **peek**-kolo

It's too expensive for me
È troppo caro per me
e **trop**-po **ka**ro payr me

Can you give me a discount?
Mi può fare uno sconto?
mee pwo **fa**ray oono **skon**to

Is there a market?
C'è un mercato?
con mer-**ka**to

When is the market?
Quando c'è il mercato?
kwando che eel mer-**ka**to

HEAR

Altro?
altro
Anything else?

37

☐ **FOOD** ☐ **CLOTHES** ☐ **POST OFFICE**

SALDI **saldee**		SALE
SCONTO **skonto**		DISCOUNT
CHIUSO PER FERIE **kyoo**zo payr **fer**-yay		CLOSED FOR HOLIDAYS

baker's	PANIFICIO	panee-**fee**cho
bookshop	LIBRERIA	leebray-**ree**-a
butcher's	MACELLERIA	machel-lay-**ree**-a
butcher's (pork)	SALUMERIA	saloomay-**ree**-a
cake shop	PASTICCERIA	pasteechay-**ree**-a
clothes	ABBIGLIAMENTO	ab-beelya-**men**to
DIY	FATELO DA VOI	**fa**-tay-lo da voy
dry-cleaner's	LAVASECCO	lava-**sek**-ko
electrical goods	ELETTRODOMESTICI	aylet-trodo-**may**-steechee
fishmonger's	PESCHERIA	pes-kay-**ree**-a
florist	FIORISTA	feeo-**ree**sta
fruit shop	FRUTTIVENDOLO	frut-tee-**ven**-dolo
furniture	MOBILI	**mo**-beelee
gifts	REGALI	ray-**ga**lee
grocer's	ALIMENTARI	alee-men-**ta**ree
hairdresser's	PARRUCCHIERE	par-rook-**ye**ray
hardware	FERRAMENTA	ferra-**men**ta
jeweller's	GIOIELLERIA	jo-yel-layree-a
launderette	LAVANDERIA	lavan-day**ree**-a
lingerie	BIANCHERIA INTIMA	bee-ankay-**ree**-a **een**-teema
newsagent	GIORNALAIO	jorn-**la**-ayo
optician	OTTICO	**ot**-teeko
perfume shop	PROFUMERIA	pro-foo-may**ree**-a
pharmacy	FARMACIA	farma-**chee**-a
photographic shop	FOTOGRAFO	**fo**to-grafo
shoe shop	CALZATURE	kaltsa-**too**ray
sports shop	ARTICOLI SPORTIVI	ar-**tee**-kolee spor-**tee**vee
stationer's	CARTOLERIA	karto-lay-**ree**a
supermarket	SUPERMERCATO	sooper-mer-**ka**to
tobacconist's	TABACCAIO	tabac-**ka**-yo
toys	GIOCATTOLI	jo**kat**-tolee

see also **SHOPPING PHRASES** ☐ **FOOD** ☐ **CL**

FOOD (GENERAL)

biscuits	i biscotti	bee-**skot**-tee
bread	il pane	panay
bread roll	il panino	pa-**nee**no
bread (brown)	il pane integrale	panay eenteg-**ral**ay
butter	il burro	**boor**-ro
cheese	il formaggio	for**mad**-jo
chicken	il pollo	**pol**-lo
coffee (instant)	il caffè solubile	kaf-**fe** so**loo**-beelay
cream	la panna	**pan**-na
crisps	le patatine	pata-**tee**nay
eggs	le uova	**wov**a
fish	il pesce	**pesh**ay
flour	la farina	fa-**ree**na
ham (cooked)	il prosciutto cotto	pro-**shoot**-to **kot**-to
ham (cured)	il prosciutto crudo	pro-**shoot**-to **kroo**-do
herbal tea	l'infuso di erbe	een-**foo**so dee ayrbay
honey	il miele	mee-**el**ay
jam	la marmellata	marmel-**la**ta
juice, orange	il succo d'arance	**sook**-ko da-**ran**chay
margarine	la margarina	marga-**ree**na
marmalade	la marmellata d'arance	marmel-**la**ta da-**ran**chay
mayonnaise	la maionese	ma-yo-**nez**ay
milk	il latte	**lat**-tay
mustard	la senape	se-**nap**ay
olive oil	l'olio d'oliva	**ol**-yo do-**lee**va
pepper	il pepe	**pep**ay
	il riso	**ree**zo
	il sale	**sal**ay
	...hero	**tsook**-kero
	...lee	

39

ska-tola dee pel-atee *di pelati* ska-tola dee pel-**a**tee
a-chayto
rt yogurt *yogurt*

HES

e also **MEASUREMENTS & QUANTITIES**

■ FRUIT

apples	le mele	*melay*
apricots	le albicocche	albee-**kok**-kay
bananas	le banane	ba-**na**nay
cherries	le ciliegie	cheel-**ye**-jay
grapefruit	il pompelmo	pom-**pel**mo
grapes	l'uva	*oo*va
lemon	il limone	lee-**mo**nay
melon	il melone	mel-**o**nay
oranges	le arance	a-**ran**chay
peaches	le pesche	**pes**kay
pears	le pere	**per**ay
plums	le prugne	**proon**-yay
raspberries	i lamponi	lam-**po**nee
strawberries	le fragole	**fra**-golay
watermelon	l'anguria	ang-**oo**-ree-a

■ VEGETABLES

asparagus	gli asparagi	aspa-**ra**jee
aubergine	la melanzana	melant-**sa**na
carrots	le carote	ka-**ro**tay
cauliflower	il cavolfiore	kavolf-**yo**ray
celery	il sedano	**se**-dano
courgettes	gli zucchini	tsook-**kee**nee
cucumber	il cetriolo	chetree-olo
garlic	l'aglio	**al**-yo
leeks	i porri	**por**-ree
mushrooms	i funghi	**foon**gee
onions	le cipolle	cheepol-**lay**
peas	i piselli	peezel-**lee**
pepper	il peperone	peper-**o**nay
potatoes	le patate	pa-**ta**tay
runner beans	i fagiolini	fajo-**lee**nee
salad	l'insalata	eensa-**la**ta
spinach	gli spinaci	spee-**na**chee
tomatoes	i pomodori	pomo-**do**ree

see also **SHOPPING PHRASES**

CLOTHES

women		men – suits		shoes			
sizes		**sizes**		**sizes**			
UK	EC	UK	EC	UK	EC	UK	EC
8	36	36	46	2	35	7	41
10	38	38	48	3	36	8	42
12	40	40	50	4	37	9	43
14	42	42	52	5	38	10	44
16	44	44	54	6	39	11	45
18	46	46	56				

May I try this on?
Posso provarlo?
pos-so pro-*var*lo

Where can I try this on?
Dove posso provarlo?
*dov*ay *pos*-so pro-*var*lo

Do you have a size...?
Ha una taglia...?
a *oo*na *tal*-ya...

small
piccola
peek-kola

medium
media
med-ya

large
grande
*gran*day

bigger
più grande
pee-*oo gran*-day

smaller
più piccola
pee-*oo peek*-kola

in other colours
in altri colori
een *al*tree ko-*lor*ee

■ **YOU MAY HEAR**

Che taglia porta?
kay *tal*-ya *por*ta
What size *(clothes)* do you take?

Che numero porta?
kay *noo*-mayro *por*ta
What shoe size do you take?

Prego si accomodi
*pray*go see ... dee
Plea...

solo questa taglia
solo *kwes*ta *tal*-ya
...ave this size

belt	la cintura *cheen-*--
blouse	la camicetta *kamee-*--
bra	il reggiseno *red-jee-***sayn**--
coat	il cappotto *kap-**pot**-to*
dress	il vestito *ves-**tee**to*
fleece	la felpa *felpa*
fur coat	la pelliccia *pel-**leet**-cha*
gloves	i guanti *gwantee*
hat	il cappello *kap-**pel**-lo*
jacket	la giacca *jak-ka*
jumper	la maglia *mal-ya*
knickers	le mutandine *mootan-**dee**nay*
nightdress	la camicia da notte *ka-**mee**cha da **not**-tay*
pyjamas	il pigiama *pee-jama*
raincoat	l'impermeabile *eempermay-**a**-beelay*
sandals	i sandali ***san**-dalee*
scarf *(silk)*	il foulard *foo-lar*
scarf *(wool)*	la sciarpa ***sharp**a*
shirt	la camicia *ka-**mee**cha*
shorts	i calzoncini corti *kaltson-**cheen**ee **kort**ee*
skirt	la gonna ***gon**-na*
socks	i calzini *kalt-**seen**ee*
suit *(woman's)*	il tailleur *ta-***yer***
suit *(man's)*	l'abito ***a**-beeto*
swimsuit	il costume da bagno *ko-**stoo**may da **ban**-yo*
tie	la cravatta *kra**vat**-ta*
t-shirt	la maglietta *mal-**yet**-ta*
track suit	la tuta ***too**-ta*
trousers	i pantaloni *panta-**lo**nee*
underpants	le mutande *moo-**tan**day*
vest	la maglietta *mal-**yet**-ta*
zip	la cerniera *chern-**yer**a*

see also **SHOPPING** ▢ **SHOPPING PHRASES** ▢ **PAYING**

Do you have a map...?   of the town   of the region
Avete una piantina...?   della città   della regione
*a-***vay***tay* *oo*na *peean-***tee***na...*   ***del***-la *cheet-***ta***   ***del***-la *ray-***jo***nay*

Can you show me where ... is on the map?
Mi può indicare dov'è ... sulla piantina?
*mee pwo een-dee***ka***ray do-***ve*** ... ***sool***-la *peean-***tee***na*

Do you have a guide to local walks?
Avete una guida delle camminate della zona?
*a-***vay***tay* *oo*na *gwee*da ***del***-lay *kam-mee-***na***tay* ***del***-la *dzo*na*

Could you draw me a map?
Mi può fare una piantina?
mee pwo ***fa***ray* *oo*na *peean-***tee***na*

Do you have a guidebook / a leaflet in English?
Avete una guida / un opuscolo in inglese?
*a-***vay***tay* *oo*na *gwee*da / oon o***poo***-skolo een een-***gle***zay*

I'd like the English-language version *(of a cassette guide)*
Vorrei la versione in inglese (della cassetta)
*vor-***ray*** la vers-***yo***nay een een-***gle***zay (***del***-la kas-***set***-ta)

Do you have any English newspapers / books?
Avete dei giornali / dei libri inglesi?
*a-***vay***tay* day jor-***na***lee / ***lee***bree een-***gle***zee*

When do the English newspapers arrive?
Quando arrivano i giornali inglesi?
kwando ar-***ree***vano ee jorn-***na***lee een-***gle***zee*

Can you reserve *(name newspaper)* **for me?**
Può riservare il ... per me?
*pwo reeser-***va***ray il ... payr me*

Post offices are open approx. 8.30 am to 1.45 pm Mon. to Fri. (8.30 am to 12.45 pm Sat.) and sometimes until 4 pm in large towns. For a quicker service ask for **posta prioritaria** (posta pree-oree-**tary**a). There are special postboxes for **posta prioritaria**.

LA POSTA la **pos**ta	POST OFFICE
I FRANCOBOLLI ee franko-**bol**-lee	STAMPS

Where is the post office?
Scusi, dov'è la Posta?
skoozee do-**ve** la **pos**ta

When does it open?
A che ora apre?
a kay **o**ra **ap**ray

Which is the counter...?
Qual è lo sportello...?
kwa-**le** lo sport-**tel**-lo...

for stamps
per i francobolli
payr ee franko-**bol**-lee

for parcels
per i pacchi
payr ee **pak**-kee

6 stamps for postcards...
Sei francobolli per cartoline...
say franko-**bol**-lee payr karto-**lee**nay...

priority post
posta prioritaria
posta pree-oree-**tar**-ya

for Britain
per l'Inghilterra
payr leengeel-**ter**-ra

for America
per gli Stati Uniti
payr lee **sta**tee oo**nee**tee

for Australia
per l'Australia
payr low-**stra**lya

I want to send this letter registered
Vorrei spedire questa lettera raccomandata
vor-**ray** sped-**ee**ray **kwes**ta **let**-tera rak-koman-**da**ta

I want to send this parcel
Vorrei spedire questo pacco
vor-**ray** sped-**ee**ray **kwes**to **pak**-ko

air / surface mail
via aerea / via normale
vee-a **ay**ray-a / **vee**-a nor-**ma**lay

It's a gift
È un regalo
e oon ray-**ga**lo

The value of contents is ... euro
Il valore del contenuto è di ... euro
eel va-**lo**ray del konten-**oo**to e dee ... ay-**oo**-ro

■ **YOU MAY HEAR**

Può comprare i francobolli dal tabaccaio
pwo kom-**pra**ray ee franko-**bol**-lee dal tabak-**ka**-yo
You can buy stamps at the tobacconist

see also **MONEY ☐ PAYING**

Film can be bought at photographic shops, gift shops or super-markets, but not at pharmacies.

Where can I/we buy tapes for a camcorder?
Dove si possono comprare le cassette per la videocamera?
dovay see pos-sono kom-pray lay kas-set-tay payr la veedayo-kamayra

A colour film...
Un rullino a colori...
oon rool-leeno a ko-loree...

with 24 / 36 exposures
da ventiquattro / trentasei pose
da ventee-kwat-tro / traynta-say pozay

A tape for this camcorder
Una cassetta per questa videocamera
oona kas-set-ta payr kwesta veedayo-kamayra

Do you have batteries for this camera?
Avete le pile per questa macchina fotografica?
a-vaytay lay peelay payr kwesta mak-keena foto-gra-feeka

Can you develop this film?
Può svilupparmi questo rullino?
pwo sveeloop-parmee kwesto rool-leeno

How much will it be?
Quanto costerà?
kwanto kostay-ra

I'd like mat / glossy prints
Vorrei le foto opache / lucide
vor-ray lay foto opakay / loo-cheeday

When will the photos be ready?
Per quando saranno pronte le foto?
payr kwando sa-ran-no prontay lay foto

The film is stuck
La pellicola si è incastrata
la pel-lee-kola see e eenka-strata

Can you take it out for me?
Me la può togliere?
may la pwo tol-yeray

Is it OK to take pictures here?
Si possono fare fotografie qui?
see pos-sono faray foto-gra-fee-ay kwee

Can you take a picture of me / us?
Mi / Ci fa una foto per favore?
mee / chee fa oona foto payr fa-voray

The tourist office is offically called l'Azienda di Turismo
If you are looking for somewhere to stay, they will have details of
hotels, campsites, etc. Most museums are closed on Mondays.

Where is the tourist office?
Scusi, dov'è l'ufficio turistico?
skoozee do-ve loof-feecho too-reesteeko

What can we visit in the area?
Che cosa c'è da vedere in questa zona?
kay koza che da ved-eray een kwesta dzona

in two hours
in due ore
een dooay oray

Have you any leaflets?
Avete degli opuscoli?
a-vaytay del-yee o-pooskolee

When can we visit the...?
Quando possiamo vedere il/la (etc.)...?
kwando pos-see-amo ved-eray eel/la...

When does it close?
A che ora chiude?
a kay ora kyooday

Are there any excursions?
Ci sono delle gite?
chee sono del-lay jeetay

We'd like to go to....
Vorremmo andare a...
vor-rem-mo anda-ray a...

When does it leave? **Where from?** **When does it get back?**
A che ora parte? Da dove parte? Quando ritorna?
a kay ora partay *da dovay partay* *kwando ree-torna*

How much does it cost to get in?
Quanto costa il biglietto d'entrata?
kwanto kosta eel beel-yet-to den-trata

Are there reductions for...? **children** **students**
Ci sono riduzioni per...? i bambini gli studenti
chee sono reedoots-yonee payr... *ee bam-beenee* *lee stoo-dentee*

Are there reductions for over 60s?
Ci sono riduzioni per la terza età?
chee sono reedoots-yonee payr la tertsa e-ta

see also **MAPS & GUIDES** ☐ **LEISURE/INTERESTS**

What is there to do in the evenings?
Che cosa c'è da fare durante la sera?
kay **ko**za che da **fa**ray doo-**ran**tay la **say**ra

Do you have a programme of events?
Avete un programma degli spettacoli?
a-**vay**tay oon pro**gram**-ma **del**-yee spet-**ta**-kolee

Is there anything for children?
Ci sono spettacoli per bambini?
chee sono spet-**ta**-kolee payr bam-**bee**nee

Is there a play park?
C'è un parco giocchi?
che oon **par**-ko **jo**kee

Where can I/we get tickets?
Dove si possono comprare i biglietti?
dovay see **pos**-sono kom-**pra**ray ee beel-**yet**-tee

for tonight
per stasera
payr sta-**say**ra

for the show
per lo spettacolo
payr lo spet-**ta**-kolo

for the match
per la partita
payr la par-**tee**ta

I'd like ... tickets
Vorrei ... biglietti
vor-**ray** ... beel-**yet**-tee

...adults
...adulti
...a**dool**-tee

...children
...bambini
...bam-**bee**nee

Where can I/we go dancing?
Dove si può andare a ballare?
dovay see pwo an-**da**ray a bal-**la**ray

What time does it open?
A che ora apre?
a kay **o**ra **a**pray

How much does it cost to get in?
Quanto costa il biglietto d'entrata?
kwanto **kos**ta eel beel-**yet**-to den-**tra**ta

What do you do at weekends?
Che cosa fa durante l'weekend?
kay **ko**za fa doo-**ran**tay lweek**end**

see also **MUSIC** ☐ **CINEMA** ☐ **THEATRE/OPERA**

Where can I/we go...?
Dove si può andare a...?
*dov*ay see pwo an-*dar*ay a...

fishing
pescare
pes-*ka*ray

walking
camminare
kam-mee-*na*ray

Are there any good beaches near here?
Ci sono delle belle spiagge qui vicino?
chee sono *del*-lay *bel*-lay spee-*ad*-jay kwee vee-*chee*no

Is there a swimming pool?
C'è la piscina?
ch*e* la pee-*shee*na

Where can I/we hire mountain bikes?
Dove si possono noleggiare i rampichini?
*dov*ay see *pos*-sono noled-*ja*ray i rampee-*kee*nee

Do you have cycling helmets?
Avete i caschi per le biciclette?
a-*vay*tay ee *kas*kee payr lay beechee-*klet*-tay

How much is it...?
Quanto costa...?
*kwan*to *kos*ta...

per hour
all'ora
al-*lor*a

per day
al giorno
al *jor*no

What do you do in your spare time?
Qual è il suo hobby?
kwal *e* eel *soo*-o *ob*-bee

I like...
Mi piace...
mee pee-*a*-chay...

(to go) cycling
andare in bicicletta
an-*dar*ay een beechee-*klet*-ta

(playing) sports
fare lo sport
*far*ay lo sport

Are you a member of any clubs?
È membro di un club?
*e mem*bro dee oon klab

Do you like playing...?
Le piace giocare a...?
lay pee-*a*-chay jo-*ka*ray a...

Do you like...? *(familiar)*
Ti piace...?
tee pee-*a*-chay...

see also **SPORT** ☐ **SKIING** ☐ **WALKING**

MUSIC

Are there any good concerts on?
Ci sono dei buoni concerti?
*chee sono day **bwo**nee kon-**cher**tee*

Where can I get tickets for the concert?
Dove posso prendere i biglietti per il concerto?
***dov**ay pos-so **pren**-deray ee beel-**yet**-tee payr eel kon-**cher**to*

Where can we hear some classical music / jazz?
Dove possiamo sentire della musica classica / del jazz?
***dov**ay pos-see-amo sen-**tee**ray **del**-la **moo**-zeeka **klas**-seeka / del jazz*

What sort of music do you like?
Che musica le piace?
*kay **moo**-zeeka lay pee-**a**-chay*

I like...
Mi piace...
*mee pee-**a**-chay...*

Which is your favourite group / singer?
Qual è il suo gruppo / cantante preferito?
*kwa-**le** eel **soo**-o **groop**-po / kan-**tan**tay prefay-**ree**to*

Can you play any musical instruments?
Sa suonare uno strumento?
*sa swo-**na**ray oono stroo-**men**to*

I play...	**the guitar**	**the piano**	**the clarinet**
Io suono...	la chitarra	il piano	il clarinetto
*ee-o **swo**no...*	*la kee**tar**-ra*	*eel pee-**a**no*	*eel klaree-**net**-to*

Have you been to any good concerts?
Ha sentito qualche concerto interessante?
*a sen-**tee**to **kwal**kay kon-**cher**to eenteres-**san**tay*

Do you like opera?
Le piace l'opera?
*lay pee-**a**-chay **lo**-payra?*

Do you like reggae?
Ti piace il reggae? *(familiar)*
*tee pee-**a**-chay eel reggae*

see also **MAKING FRIENDS** □ **ENTERTAINMENT**

In summer villages often organize outdoor showings of films –
cinema all'aperto.

What's on at the cinema (name of cinema) **...?**
Che film danno al cinema...?
*kay feelm dan-no al **chee**-nayma...*

What time does the film start?
A che ora comincia il film?
*a kay **o**ra ko-**meen**cha eel feelm*

Is it dubbed or subtitled?
È doppiato o con i sottotitoli?
*e dop-**pya**to o kon ee sot-to-**tee**tolee*

How much are the tickets?
Quanto costano i biglietti?
***kwan**to **kos**tano ee beel-**yet**-tee*

Two for the (give time of perfomance) **showing**
Due per lo spettacolo **del**-lay...
*dooay payr lo spet-**ta**-kolo **del**-lay...*

What films have you seen recently?
Che film ha visto ultimamente?
*kay feelm a **vees**to ooltee-ma**men**tay*

What is ... called in Italian?
Qual è il titolo del film ... in italiano?
*kwa-**le** eel **tee**tolo del feelm ... een eetal-**ya**no*

Who is your favourite actress?
Quale attrice preferisce?
***kwa**lay at-**tree**chay prayfay-**ree**shay*

Who is your favourite actor?
Quale attore preferisce?
***kwa**lay at-**to**ray prefay-**ree**shay*

see also **ENTERTAINMENT** ❐ **LEISURE/INTERESTS**

LA PLATEA *la plataya*	STALLS
LA GALLERIA *la gal-lereeya*	CIRCLE
IL LOGGIONE *eel lod-jonay*	UPPER CIRCLE
IL PALCO *eel palko*	BOX
IL POSTO *eel posto*	SEAT
IL GUARDAROBA *eel gwarda-roba*	CLOAKROOM

What is on at the theatre?
Che cosa c'è al teatro?
kay koza che al tay-atro

How do I/we get there?
Come si può andarci?
komay see pwo an-darchee

What prices are the tickets?
Quanto costano i biglietti?
kwanto kostano ee beel-yet-tee

I'd like two tickets...
Vorrei due biglietti...
vor-ray dooay beel-yet-tee...

for tonight	for tomorrow night	for the 3rd of August
per stasera	per domani sera	per il 3 di agosto
payr sta-sayra	*payr do-manee sayra*	*payr il tray dee agosto*

How long is the interval?
Quanto dura l'intervallo?
kwanto doora leenter-val-lo

Is there a bar?
C'è un bar?
che oon bar

When does the performance begin / end?
A che ora comincia / finisce lo spettacolo?
a kay ora ko-meencha / fee-neeshay lo spet-ta-kolo

I enjoyed the play
La commedia / tragedia mi è piacuta
la kom-med-ya / tra-jed-ya mee e pee-a-choota

It was very good
Era molto bella
era molto bel-la

■ **YOU MAY HEAR**

Non può entrare, lo spettacolo è iniziato
non pwo en-traray lo spet-ta-kolo e eeneets-yato
You can't go in, the performance has started

Entrerà durante l'intervallo
entray-ra doo-rantay leenter-val-lo
You may enter at the interval

see also **ENTERTAINMENT** ❐ **LEISURE/INTERESTS**

IL TELECOMANDO *eel teleko-***man**do	REMOTE CONTROL
ACCENDERE a**chen**deray	TO SWITCH ON
SPEGNERE **spen**yeray	TO SWITCH OFF
A PUNTATE a poon**ta**-tay	SERIES
LA TELENOVELA la teleno**ve**la	SOAP
IL TELEGIORNALE *eel telejor-***na**lay	NEWS
I CARTONI ANIMATI ee kar-**to**nee aneema-teechee	CARTOONS

Where is the television?
Dov'è la televisione?
do-*ve* la televeez-*yo*nay

How do you switch it on?
Come si accende?
*ko*may see at-*chen*-day

What is on television?
Che cosa c'è alla televisione?
kay *ko*za che al-la televeez-*yo*nay

When is the news?
A che ora c'è il telegiornale?
a kay ora che eel telejor-*na*lay

Do you have any English-language channels?
Ci sono dei canali dove parlano in inglese?
chee sono day ka*na*lee *do*vay *par*lano een een-*gle*zay

When are the children's programmes?
A che ora sono i programmi per i bambini?
a kay *o*ra sono ee pro*gram*-mee payr ee bam-*bee*nee

Do you have any English videos?
Avete delle cassette video in inglese?
a-*vay*tay *del*-lay kas-*set*-tay *vee*-dayo een een-*gle*zay

What is your favourite programme?
Qual è il suo programma preferito?
kwa-*le* eel *soo*-o pro*gram*-ma prefay-*ree*to

Can you video this programme for me?
Mi può registrare sul video questo programma?
mee pwo ray-jeest-*ra*ray sool *vee*-dayo *kwes*to pro*gram*-ma

Where can we play...?
Dove possiamo giocare a...?
*dov*ay pos-see-*a*mo jo-*ka*ray a...

Where can I/we go...?
Dove si può andare a...?
*dov*ay see pwo an-*da*ray a...

swimming
nuotare
nwo-*ta*ray

jogging
fare il footing
*fa*ray eel *foo*ting

Do you have to be a member?
Si deve essere soci?
see *dev*ay *es*-seray *so*chee

How much is it per hour?
Quanto costa per ora?
*kwan*to *kos*ta payr *o*ra

Can we hire...?
Si può noleggiare...?
see pwo noled-*ja*ray...

rackets
le racchette
lay rak-*ket*-tay

golf clubs
le mazze da golf
lay *mat*say da golf

We'd like to see (name team) **play**
Vorremmo vedere giocare...
vor-*rem*-mo ved-*er*ay jo-*ka*ray...

Where can I/we get tickets for the game?
Dove si possono comprare i biglietti per la partita?
*dov*ay see *pos*-sono kom-*pra*ray ee beel-*yet*-tee payr la par-*tee*ta

Which is your favourite football team?
Qual è la sua squadra del pallone preferita?
kwa-*le* la *soo*-a *skwa*dra del pal-*lo*nay prefay-*ree*ta

■ **YOU MAY HEAR**

Non ci sono più biglietti per la partita
non chee sono pyoo beel-*yet*-tee payr la par-*tee*ta
There are no tickets left for the game

Solo i bagarini li vendono
*so*lo ee baga-*ree*nee lee *ven*-dono
Only ticket touts are selling them

La partita è in diretta alla T.V.
la par-*tee*ta e een deer*et*-ta *al*-la tee *voo*
The match is live on television

see also **LEISURE/INTERESTS** ☐ **SKIING** ☐ **WALKING**

LO SCI DI FONDO *lo shee dee **fon**do*		**CROSS-COUNTRY SKIING**
LO SKIPASS *lo **skee**pas*		**SKI PASS**

I want to hire skis
Vorrei noleggiare degli sci
*vor-**ray** noled-**jaray del**-yee shee*

Does the price include...?
Il prezzo comprende...?
*eel **prets**-so kom-**pren**day...*

boots
gli scarponi
*lee skar-**po**nee*

poles
le racchette
*lay rak-**ket**-tay*

How much is a pass...?
Quanto costa lo skipass...?
*kwan*to *kos*ta *lo **skee**-pass...*

daily
giornaliero
*jornal-**ye**ro*

weekly
settimanale
*set-teema-**na**lay*

When is the last ascent?
Quand'è l'ultima salita?
*kwan-**de lool**-teema sa-**lee**ta*

Can you adjust my bindings?
Può regolare i miei attachi?
*pwo rego-**la**ray ee mee-**yay** at-**tak**-kee*

■ **YOU MAY HEAR**

Ha mai sciato prima di adesso?
*a **ma**-ee shee-ato **pree**ma dee a**des**-so*
Have you ever skied before?

Quale misura di sci vuole?
*kwa*lay mee-**zoo**ra dee shee **vwo**lay*
What length skis do you want?

Quale numero di scarponi porta?
*kwa*lay **noo**-mayro dee skar-**po**nee **por**ta*
What is your boot size?

Vuole lezioni di sci?
*vwo*lay lets-**ee**onee dee shee*
Do you want skiing lessons?

see also **LEISURE/INTERESTS** ☐ **SPORT** ☐ **WALKING**   55

WALKING

Are there any guided walks?
Ci sono dei percorsi guidati?
*chee sono day per**kor**see gwee-da**tee***

Do you know any good walks?
Ci può consigliare un buon percorso?
*chee pwo konseel-**ya**ray oon bwon per**kor**so*

How many kilometres is the walk?
Di quanti chilometri è il percorso?
*dee **kwan**tee kee**lo**-metree e eel per**kor**so*

Is it very steep?
È molto in salita?
*e **mol**to een sa-**lee**ta*

How long will it take?
Quanto ci vorrà?
kwan**to chee vor-**ra

Is there a map of the walk?
C'è la piantina del percorso?
*che la peean-**tee**na del per**kor**so*

We'd like to go climbing
Vorremmo andare a fare una scalata
*vor-**rem**-mo an-**da**ray a **fa**ray oona ska**la**ta*

Do you have a detailed map of the area?
Avete una piantina dettagliata della zona?
*a-**vay**tay oona peean-**tee**na det-tal-**ya**ta **del**-la **dzo**na*

Do I/we need walking boots?
Si devono portare gli scarponcini?
*see **de**vono por-**ta**ray lee skarpon-**chee**nee*

Should we take...?
Dobbiamo portare...?
*dob-**bya**mo por-**ta**ray...*

water
acqua
akwa

food
da mangiare
*da man-**ja**ray*

waterproofs
impermeabili
*eempermay-**a**-beelee*

a compass
una bussola
*oona **boos**-sola*

What time does it get dark?
A che ora diventa buio?
*a kay **o**ra dee**ven**-ta **boo**-yaw*

Is there an inn on the way?
C'è il rifugio sul percorso?
*che eel ree-**foo**jo sool per**kor**so*

see also **MAPS & GUIDES** ☐ **SIGHTSEEING**

*The international code for Italy is **00 39** plus the Italian town or area code less the first **0**, e.g., Milan (0)**2**, Rome (0)**6**, Florence (0)**55**. If you are calling the UK from abroad, the UK international code is **00 44** plus the area code less the first **0**. If you are calling within Italy, you must always use the full area code, even for local calls.*

LA SCHEDA TELEFONICA *la **skay**da tele-**fo**neeka*	**PHONECARD**
IL TELEFONINO *eel telefo-**nee**no*	**MOBILE**
LA CELLULARE *la chel-loo-**la**ray*	**MOBILE**

I want to make a phone call
Vorrei fare una telefonata
*vor-**ray** fa*ray *oona telefo-**na**ta*

Where can I buy a phonecard?
Dove posso comprare una scheda telefonica?
***do**vay **pos**-so kom-**pra**ray oona **skay**da tele-**fo**neeka*

A phonecard
Una scheda telefonica
*oona **skay**da tele-**fo**neeka*

for ... euro
da ... euro
*da ... ay-**oo**-ro*

Do you have a mobile?
Avete il telefonino?
*a-**vay**tay eel telefo-**nee**no*

What is the number of your mobile?
Qual è il numero del suo telefonino?
*kwal e eel **noo**-mayro del **soo**-o telefo-**nee**no*

My mobile number is...
Il numero del mio telefonino è...
*eel **soo**-o **noo**-mayro del **mee**yo telefo-**nee**no e...*

Mr Brun, please
Il Signor Brun per favore
*eel seen-**yor** Brun payr fa-**vo**ray*

extension...
interno...
*een**ter**no...*

see also **E-MAIL** □ **INTERNET** □ **FAX** □ **BUSINESS**

I'd like to speak to...
Vorrei parlare con...
vor-ray parlaray kon...

Can I speak to....?
Posso parlare con...?
pos-so parlaray kon...

I'll call back later
Richiamo più tardi
reekee-amo pyoo tardee

I'll call back tomorrow
Richiamo domani
reekee-amo do-manee

This is Mr... / Mrs...
Io sono il Signor... / la Signora...
ee-o sono eel seen-yor... / la seen-yora...

How do I get an outside line?
Come si fa per avere la linea?
komay see fa payr a-vayray la leenay-a

■ YOU MAY HEAR

Pronto	**Chi parla?**	**Sono Angela**
pronto	*kee parla*	*sono Angela*
Hello	Who's calling?	It's Angela

Un momento...
oon mo-mento...
Just a moment...

La sto mettendo in linea
la sto met-tendo een leenay-a
I'm trying to connect you

La linea è occupata
la leenay-a e ok-koo-pata
The line is engaged

Provi più tardi
provee pyoo tardee
Please try later

Vuole lasciare un messaggio?
vwolay la-sharay oon mes-sad-jo
Do you want to leave a message?

...lasciate un messaggio dopo il segnale acustico
...la-shatay oon mes-sad-jo dopo eel sen-yalay a-koo-steeko
...leave a message after the tone

Please switch off all mobile phones
Per favore spegnete i telefonini
payr fa-voray spen-yaytay ee telefo-neenee

SMS is very popular in Italy, where everybody seems to have a mobile phone. It is also a cheaper way to keep in touch with friends. Text messaging is also useful when abroad in a country where phone rates are expensive, as it allows you to tell your relatives at home that your are ok, without having to spend too much money.

I will text you
Ti mando un messaggio
tee **man**do oon mes-**sad**-jo

Can you text me?
Può mandarmi un messaggio?
pwo man**dar**mee oon mes-**sad**-jo

Did you get my message?
Hai rivecuto il mio messaggio?
*a-ee reechay-**voo**to eel **mee**yo mes-**sad**-jo*

Are you there? c6 *(ci sei)*	**Tonight** ss *(stasera)*
Please xf *(per favore)*	**Today** og *(oggi)*
Where are you? d6? *(dove sei?)*	**weekend** we
Why? x' *(perché)*	**Fine** tb *(tutto bene)*
I'll speak to you later tblad *(ti parlo dopo)*	**Do you want to speak** vbla? *(vuoi parlare?)*
Train 3no *(treno)*	**Understood** cpt *(capito)*
See you at my house civecam *(ci vediamo a casa mia)*	**See you at your house** civecat *(ci vediamo a casa tua)*

An informal way of addressing an e-mail is **Ciao...** *and ending it with* **a presto** *(speak to you soon). For more formal e-mails, begin either* **Caro...** *(for a man) and* **Cara...** *(for a woman).*

Nuovo messaggio	New message
A	To
Da	From
Oggetto	Subject
Cc	cc
Ccn	bcc
Allegato	Attachment
Invio	Send

Do you have an e-mail?
Ha un indirizzo e-mail?
*a oon eendee-**reet**-so e-mail*

What is your e-mail address?
Qual è il suo indirizzo e-mail?
*kwal e eel **soo**-o eendee-**reet**-so e-mail*

How do you spell it?
Como si scrive?
***ko**mo see **skree**vay*

All one word
Tutta una parola
***toot**-ta oona pa-**ro**la*

All lower case
Lettere minuscole
*let-**ter**ay mee-**noo**skolay*

My e-mail address is...
Il mio indirizzo e-mail è...
*eel **mee**-yo eendee-**reet**-so e-mail e...*

clare.smith@bit.co.uk
clare punto smith chiocciola bit punto chee oh punto oo kappa
*clare **poon**to smith kee-**yo**chola bit **poon**to o chee oh **poon**to oo **kap**-pa*

Can I send an e-mail?
Posso mandare un'e-mail?
***pos**-so man-**da**ray oon e-mail*

Did you get my e-mail?
Ha ricevuto la mia e-mail?
*a-ee reechay-**voo**to la **mee**ya e-mail*

Most computer terminology tends to be in English and you find the same with the internet.

Are there any internet cafés here?
Ci sono degli internet café qui vicino?
*chee sono **del**-yee **een**ternet ka**fay** kwee vee-**chee**no*

How much is it to log on for an hour?
Quanto costa un'ora in internet?
***kwan**to **kos**ta oon **o**ra een **een**ternet*

Do you have a website?
Avete un sito?
*a-**vay**tay oon **see**to*

The website address is...
L'indirizzo del mio sito è...
*leendee-**reet**-so del **mee**-yo **see**to è...*

www.collins.co.uk
voo voo voo punto collins punto chee oh punto oo kappa
*voo voo voo **poon**to collins **poon**to chee oh **poon**to oo **kap**-pa*

Do you know any good sites?
Conosce dei buoni siti?
*ko-**nosh**ee day **bwo**-nee **see**-tee*

Which is the best search engine to use?
Qual è il miglior sistema di ricerca?
*kwal e eel ee meel**yor** sees-**tema** dee ree-**cher**ka*

Can I book on your website?
Posso prenotare sul vostro sito?
***pos**-so **pren**otaray sool **vos**tro **see**to*

see also **TEXT MESSAGING** ❒ **E-MAIL** ❒ **FAX** ❒ **BUSINESS** 61

FAX

*The code to send faxes to Italy from the UK is **00 39** plus the Italian area code without the first **0**, e.g. Milan (0)**2**, Rome (0)**6**. The code to fax the UK from Italy is **00 44**.*

ADDRESSING A FAX	
A	TO
DA	FROM
DATA	DATE
OGGETTO:	RE:
LE INVIO	PLEASE FIND ATTACHED
UNA COPIA DI...	A COPY OF...
...PAGINE IN TOTALE	...PAGES IN TOTAL

Do you have a fax?
Avete un fax?
*a-**vay**tay oon fax*

I want to send a fax
Vorrei mandare un fax
*vor-**ray** man-**da**ray oon fax*

What is your fax number?
Qual è il suo numero di fax?
*kwa-**le** eel **soo**-o **noo**-mayro dee fax*

My fax number is...
Il mio numero di fax è...
*eel **mee**yo **noo**-mayro dee fax **e**...*

Did you get my fax?
Avete ricevuto il mio fax?
*a-**vay**tay reechay-**voo**to eel **mee**yo fax*

Please resend your fax
Per favore ci rimandi il suo fax
*payr fa-**vo**ray chee ree-**man**dee eel **soo**-o fax*

I can't read it
Non riesco a leggerlo
*non ree-**e**sko a **led**-jerlo*

Your fax is constantly engaged
Il numero del suo fax è sempre occupato
*eel **noo**-mayro del **soo**-o fax **e sem**pray ok-koo-**pa**to*

see also **TEXT MESSAGING** ☐ **INTERNET** ☐ **E-MAIL**

*When writing to a company use **Vostro, Vostra**, etc. When writing specifically to one person use **Suo, Sua**, etc.*

Thursday 16 May 2003   giovedì 16 maggio 2003

Dear Sirs   Spettabile Ditta *(commercial letter)*

Dear Sir / Madam   Egregio Signore / Egregia Signora

Yours faithfully   Distintamente

Dear Mr... / Mrs...   Gent.mo Signor... / Gent.ma Signora...

Yours sincerely   Cordialmente

Dear Paolo / Paola   Caro Paolo / Cara Paola

Best regards   Migliori saluti

Dear Mario / Maria   Caro Mario / Cara Maria

Love   Ciao

What is your address?
Qual è il suo indirizzo?
*kwal e eel **soo**-o eendee-**reet**so*

What is your postcode (zip)?
Qual è il suo codice postale?
*kwal e eel **soo**-o **ko**-deechay post**al**ay*

Thank you for your letter
Grazie per la tua lettera
***grats**-yay payr la **too**-a **let**-tera*

Write soon! *(familiar)*
Scrivi presto!
*skr**ee**vee **prest**o*

Sig.ra/re Galli
via Carbonera, 7
37121 VERONA
Italy

Addressing an envelope

via is the road
postcode and town

see also **INTERNET** ☐ **E-MAIL** ☐ **FAX** ☐ **BUSINESS**   63

*Banks are open approx. 8.30 am to 1.30 pm Mon. to Fri. (and some-times also 3 to 4 pm). The euro is the currency of Italy. Euro cents are known as centesimi (chen-**tes**-eemee).*

LA CARTA DI CREDITO *la karta dee **kray**-deeto*	**CREDIT CARD**
IL BANCOMAT *eel **ban**komat*	**CASH DISPENSER**
LO SCONTRINO *lo skon-**tree**no*	**TILL RECEIPT**

Where can I change some money?
Dove posso cambiare i soldi?
dovay **pos**-so kamb-**ya**ray ee **sol**dee

When does the bank open?
Quando apre la banca
kwando **a**pray la **ban**ka

When does the bank close?
Quando chiude la banca?
kwando kee-**oo**day la **ban**ka

Can I pay with...?	**euros**	**Swiss francs**
Posso pagare con...?	euro	franchi svizzeri
pos-so pa-**ga**ray kon...	ay-**oo**-ro	**fran**kee **zveet**-seree

I want to change these traveller's cheques
Vorrei cambiare questi traveller's cheques
vor-**ray** kamb-**ya**ray **kwes**tee travellers cheques

Where is the nearest cash dispenser?
Dov'è il bancomat più vicino?
do-**ve** eel **ban**komat pyoo vee-**chee**no

Can I use my credit card at the cash dispenser?
Posso usare la mia carta di credito al bancomat?
pos-so oo-**za**ray la **mee**ya **kar**ta dee **kray**-deeto al **ban**komat

Do you have any loose change?
Scusi, ha spiccioli?
skoozee a **speet**-cholee

see also **PAYING**

In Italy it is illegal to leave a shop, bar, etc., without a receipt.

How much is it?
Quanto costa?
kwanto kosta

How much will it be?
Quanto costerà?
kwanto kostay-ra

Can I pay by...?
Posso pagare con...?
pos-so pa-garay kon...

credit card
la carta di credito
la karta dee kray-deeto

cheque
un assegno
oon as-sen-yo

Is service included?
il servizio è compreso?
eel serveets-yo e kom-prayzo

Is tax included?
l'IVA è compresa?
leeva e kom-prayza

Put it on my bill
Lo metta sul mio conto
lo met-ta sool meeyo konto

Where do I pay?
Dove devo pagare?
dovay devo pa-garay

I need a receipt, please
Ho bisogno di una ricevuta, per favore
o beezon-yo dee oona reechay-voota payr fa-voray

Do I pay in advance?
Devo pagare in anticipo?
devo pa-garay een antee-cheepo

Do I need to pay a deposit?
Devo dare un deposito?
devo daray oon day-pozeeto

I'm sorry
Mi dispiace
mee deespee-a-chay

I've nothing smaller *(no change)*
Non ho spiccioli
non o speet-cholee

■ **YOU MAY HEAR**

L'IVA è compresa
leeva e kom-prayza
VAT is included

Il servizio è incluso ma non la mancia
eel serveets-yo e een-klooso ma non la mancha
Service is included but not a tip

Paghi alla cassa
pagee al-la kas-sa
Pay at the till

Prima ritiri lo scontrino alla cassa *(at airport, station bars, etc.)*
preema reetee-ree lo skon-treeno al-la kas-sa
First get a receipt/chit at the till

IL RITIRO BAGAGLI *eel reeteero ba-galyee*	**BAGGAGE RECLAIM**
IL DEPOSITO BAGAGLI *eel day-pozeeto ba-galyee*	**LEFT-LUGGAGE OFFICE**
IL CARRELLO *eel kar-rel-lo*	**LUGGAGE TROLLEY**

My luggage hasn't arrived
Il mio bagaglio non è arrivato
eel meeyo bagal-yo non e ar-reevato

My suitcase has been damaged on the flight
La mia valigia è stata danneggiata durante il volo
la meeya va-leeja e stata dan-ned-jata doo-rantay eel volo

What has happened to the luggage on the flight from...?
Che cos'è successo al bagaglio del volo da...?
kay ko-ze soot-ches-so al bagal-yo del volo da...

Can you help me with my luggage, please?
Può aiutarmi con il mio bagaglio per favore?
pwo a-yoo-tarmee kon eel meeyo bagal-yo payr fa-voray

When does the left-luggage office open / close?
Quando apre / chiude il deposito bagagli?
kwando apray / kyooday eel day-pozeeto bagal-yee

We'd like to leave our luggage here
Vorremmo lasciare qui il bagaglio
vor-rem-mo la-sharay kwee eel bagal-yo

overnight	**for ... hours**
per questa notte	per ... ore
payr kwesta not-tay	*payr ... oray*

Can we leave our luggage?	**We'll collect it at...**
Possiamo lasciare il nostro bagaglio?	Lo ritireremo alle...
pos-see-amo la-sharay eel nostro bagal-yo	*lo reetee-reraymo al-lay...*

■ YOU MAY HEAR

Si può lasciarlo qui fino alle...
see pwo la-sharlo kwee feeno al-lay...
You may leave it here until ... o'clock

see also **TRAIN** ☐ **AIR TRAVEL**

This is broken
Questo è rotto
*kwes*to *e rot*-to

Where can I have this repaired?
Dove posso farlo riparare?
*dov*ay *pos*-so *far*-lo reepa-*ra*ray

Is it worth repairing?
Vale la pena di ripararlo?
*val*ay la *pay*na dee reepa-*rar*lo

Can you repair...? this
Può riparare...? questo
pwo reepa-*ra*ray... *kwes*to

these shoes
queste scarpe
*kwes*tay *skar*pay

my watch
il mio orologio
eel *mee*yo oro-*lo*jo

How much will it be?
Quanto costerà?
*kwan*to ko-*stay*ra

Can you do it straightaway?
Può farlo subito?
pwo farlo soo-beeto

How long will it take?
Quanto ci vorrà?
*kwan*to chee vor-*ra*

When will it be ready?
Per quando sarà pronto?
payr *kwan*do sa-*ra pron*to

Where can I have my shoes reheeled?
Dove posso cambiare il tacco per le mie scarpe?
*dov*ay *pos*-so kamb-*ya*ray eel *tak*-ko payr lay *mee*yay *skar*pay

I need...
Ho bisogno (di)...
o beez*on*-yo (dee)...

some glue
della colla
del-la *kol*-la

some Sellotape®
dello Scotch®
del-lo scotch

Do you have a needle and thread?
Ha un ago e del filo?
a oon *a*-go ay del *fee*lo

The lights have fused
La luce è andata via
la *loo*chay e an-*da*ta *vee*-a

The fuse has gone
Il fusibile è saltato
eel foo-*see*beelay e sal-*ta*to

■ **YOU MAY HEAR**

Mi dispiace ma non si può riparare
mee deespee-*a*-chay ma non see *pwo* reepa-*ra*ray
Sorry, but we can't mend it

see also **BREAKDOWN**   67

LAUNDRY

IL LAVASECCO *eel lava-**sek**-ko*	DRY-CLEANER'S
LA TINTORIA *la **teen**to-reeya*	DRY-CLEANER'S
IL DETERSIVO *eel dayter-**seev**o*	SOAP POWDER
LA CANDEGGINA *la kanday-**jee**na*	BLEACH
LA LAVATRICE *la lava-**tree**chay*	WASHING MACHINE

Where can I wash these clothes?
Dove posso lavare questi panni?
***dov**ay **pos**-so la-**va**ray **kwes**tee **pan**-nee*

Where is the nearest launderette?
Dov'è la lavanderia automatica più vicina?
*do-**ve** la lavan-de**ree**-a owto-**ma**-teeka pyoo vee-**chee**na*

When does it open / close?
A che ora apre / chiude?
*a kay ora **a**pray / **kyoo**-day*

What coins do I need?
Quali monete devo usare?
***kwa**lee mo-**ne**tay **de**vo oo-**za**ray*

Where can I dry my clothes?
Dove posso fare asciugare i miei panni?
***dov**ay **pos**-so **fa**ray ashoo-**ga**ray ee **mee**-yay **pan**-nee*

Do you have a laundry service?
Avete il servizio lavanderia?
*a-**vay**tay eel ser**veets**-yo lavan-de**ree**-a*

How long will it take?
Quanto ci vuole?
***kwan**to chee **vwo**lay*

When will my things be ready?
Quando saranno pronti?
***kwan**do sa-**ran**-no **pron**tee*

Can you iron these clothes?
Può stirare questi indumenti?
*pwo stee-**ra**ray **kwes**tee eendoo-**men**tee*

Can I borrow an iron?
Posso avere un ferro da stiro?
***pos**-so a-**vay**ray oon **fer**-ro da **stee**ro*

This does not work
Questo non funziona
*kwes*to non foonts-*yo*na

It's dirty
È sporco(a)
*e spor*ko(a)

The ... does not work
Il/La/Lo ... non funziona
*eel/la/lo ... non foonts-*yo*na

The ... do not work
I/Le/Gli ... non funzionano
*ee/lay/lee ... non foonts-*yo*nano

light	toilet	heating	air conditioning
la luce	il bagno	il riscaldamento	l'aria condizionata
la *loo*chay	eel *ban*-yo	eel reeskalda-*men*to	*l*arya kondeetsyo-*na*ta

I can't open the window
Non riesco ad aprire la finestra
non ree-*es*ko ad a-*pree*ray la fee-*nes*tra

I can't close the window
Non riesco a chiudere la finestra
non ree-*es*ko a *kyoo*-deray la fee-*nes*tra

I don't like the room...
Non mi piace la camera...
non mee pee-a-chay la *ka*-mayra...

it's noisy
è rumorosa
e roomo-*ro*za

it's too small
è troppo piccola
e trop-po *peek*-kola

It's too hot
È troppo caldo(a)
e trop-po *kal*do(a)

It's too cold
È troppo freddo(a)
e trop-po *fred*-do(a)

To whom should I complain?
A chi potrei rivolgermi per fare un reclamo?
a kee po*tray* reevol-*jer*mee per *fa*ray oon *rek*lamo

I didn't order this
Non ho ordinato questo
non o ordee-*na*to *kwes*to

It's broken
È rotto(a)
e rot-to(a)

I want a refund
Vorrei un rimborso
vor-*ray* oon reem-*bor*so

see also **HOTEL DESK** ❑ **REPAIRS** ❑ **PROBLEMS**

Can you help me?
Può aiutarmi?
pwo a-yoo-tarmee

I speak very little Italian
Parlo molto poco l'italiano
parlo molto poko leetal-yano

Does anyone here speak English?
C'è qualcuno che parla inglese?
che kwal-koono kay parla een-glezay

What's the matter?
Che cosa c'è?
kay koza che

I would like to speak to whoever is in charge of...
Vorrei parlare con chi è incaricato di...
vor-ray par-laray kon kee e eenkaree-kato dee...

I'm lost
Mi sono smarrito(a)
mee sono smar-reeto(a)

How do you get to...
Come si fa per andare a...
komay see fa payr an-daray a...

I missed my train / plane / connection
Ho perso il treno / l'aereo / la coincidenza
o perso eel trayno / la-e-rayo / la koeenchee-dentsa

I've missed my flight because there was a strike
Ho perso l'aereo perché c'era lo sciopero
o perso la-e-rayo per-ke chera lo sho-pero

The coach has left without me
Il pullman è partito senza di me
eel poolman e par-tee-to sentsa dee may

Can you show me how this works, please?
Mi fa vedere come funziona per favore?
mee fa vay-deray komay foonts-yona payr fa-voray

I have lost my money
Ho perso i miei soldi
o perso ee mee-yay soldee

I need to get to...
Devo andare a...
devo an-daray a...

I need to get in touch with the British consulate
Devo contattare il consolato britannico
devo kontat-taray eel konso-lato breetan-neeko

Leave me alone!
Mi lasci in pace!
mee lash-ee een pa-chay

Go away!
Se ne vada!
say nay vada

L'AMBULANZA lamboo-**lan**tsa	AMBULANCE
I CARABINIERI ee karabeen-**yer**ee	MILITARY POLICE
LA POLIZIA la poleet-**see**-a	POLICE
I POMPIERI ee pomp-**yer**ee	FIRE MEN
I VIGILI DEL FUOCO ee **veed**-jeelay del **fwo**ko	FIRE BRIGADE
IL COMMISSARIATO eel kom-mees-ar**ya**to	POLICE STATION
LA QUESTURA la kwes-**too**ra	POLICE STATION

Help!	**Fire!**	**Can you help me?**
Aiuto!	Fuoco!	Può aiutarmi?
a-**yoo**to	**fwo**ko	pwo a-yoo-**tar**mee

There's been an accident!
C'è stato un incidente!
che stato oon eenchee-**den**tay

Someone...	**has been injured**	**has been knocked down**
Qualcuno...	si è fatto male	è stato investito
kwal-**koo**no...	see e **fat**-to **ma**lay	e stato eenves-**tee**to

Please call...	**the police**	**an ambulance**
Per favore chiami...	la polizia	l'ambulanza
payr fa-**vo**ray kee-**a**-mee...	la poleet-**see**-a	lamboo-**lant**sa

Where is the police station?	**I want to report a crime**
Dov'è la questura?	Vorrei denunciare un delitto
do-**ve** la kwes-**too**ra	vor-**ray** denoon-**cha**ray oon day-**lee**to

I've been...	**robbed**	**attacked**
Mi hanno...	derubato(a)	assalito(a)
mee **an**-no...	deroo-**ba**to(a)	as-sa**lee**to(a)

Someone's stolen...	**my bag**	**traveller's cheques**
Mi hanno rubato...	la borsa	i miei traveller's cheques
mee **an**-no roo-**ba**to...	la **bor**sa	ee mee-**yay** travellers cheques

My car has been broken into
Hanno svaligiato la mia macchina
an-no svalee-**ja**to la **mee**ya **mak**-keena

cont...

EMERGENCIES

My car has been stolen
Mi hanno rubato la macchina
mee an-no roo-bato la mak-keena

I've been raped
Mi hanno violentata
mee an-no veeolen-tata

I want to speak to a policewoman
Vorrei parlare con una agente della polizia
vor-ray par-laray kon oona a-jentay del-la poleet-see-a

I need to make a telephone call
Devo fare una telefonata
devo faray oona telefo-nata

I need a report for my insurance
Ho bisogno di un verbale per la mia assicurazione
o beezon-yo dee oon ver-balay payr la meeya as-seekoorats-yonay

I didn't know there was a speed limit
Non sapevo che c'era il limite di velocità
non sa-pevo kay chera eel lee-meetay dee velochee-ta

How much is the fine?
Quant'è la multa?
kwan-te la moolta

Where do I pay it?
Dove pago?
dovay pago

Do I have to pay it straightaway?
Devo pagarla subito?
devo pa-garla soo-beeto

I'm very sorry, officer
Mi dispiace signor agente
mee deespee-a-chay seen-yor a-jentay

LA FARMACIA *la farma-cheeya*	PHARMACY/CHEMIST
LA FARMACIA DI TURNO *la farma-cheeya dee toorno*	DUTY CHEMIST

Can you give me something for...?
Mi dà qualcosa contro il/la *(etc.)*...?
mee da kwal-koza kontro eel/la...

a headache	car sickness	a cough	diarrhoea
il mal di testa	il mal d'auto	la tosse	la diarrea
eel mal dee testa	*eel mal dowto*	*la tos-say*	*la deear-ray-a*

Is it safe for children?
Va bene per bambini?
va benay payr bam-beenee

How much should I give him?
Quanto gliene devo dare?
kwanto lee-nay devo daray

■ YOU MAY HEAR

Tre volte al giorno...	prima	con	dopo	...i pasti
tray voltay al jorno...	*preema*	*kon*	*dopo*	*...ee pastee*
Three times a day...	before	with	after	...meals

■ WORDS YOU MAY NEED

antiseptic	l'antisettico *antee-set-teeko*
aspirin	l'aspirina *aspee-reena*
condoms	i preservativi *preserva-teevee*
cotton wool	il cotone idrofilo *ko-tonay eedro-feelo*
dental floss	il filo interdentale *feelo eenterden-talay*
insect repellant	l'insettifugo *eenset-tee-foogo*
period pains	i dolori mestruali *do-loree mestroo-alee*
plasters	i cerotti *cherot-tee*
sore throat	il mal di gola *mal dee gola*
sunburn	la scottatura solare *skot-ta-toora so-laray*
sweetener	il dolcificante *dolcheefee-kantay*
tampons	gli assorbenti interni *assor-bentee eenternee*
tissues	i fazzoletti di carta *fats-so-let-tee dee karta*
toothpaste	il dentifricio *dentee-freecho*

see also **BODY** ❑ **DOCTOR**

In Italian the possessive (my, his, her, etc.) is generally not used with parts of the body, e.g.

I've broken my **leg**	Ho rotto la gamba
He's hurt his **foot**	Si è fatto male al piede

ankle	la caviglia *ka**veel**-ya*
arm	il braccio ***brat**-cho*
back	la schiena *skee-**e**-na*
bone	l'osso *os-so*
ear	l'orecchio *o**rek**-yo*
eye	l'occhio ***ok**-yo*
finger	il dito ***dee**to*
foot	il piede *pye**day***
hand	la mano *m**a**no*
head	la testa *te**sta***
heart	il cuore *kwo**ray***
hip	l'anca *a**nk**a*
joint	l'articolazione *artee-kolats-yo**nay***
kidney	il rene *re**nay***
knee	il ginocchio *jee**nok**-yo*
leg	la gamba *g**amb**a*
liver	il fegato ***feg**-ato*
mouth	la bocca ***bok**-ka*
muscle	il muscolo *m**oo**-skolo*
neck	il collo ***kol**-lo*
nose	il naso *n**a**zo*
shoulder	la spalla ***spal**-la*
stomach/tummy	lo stomaco/la pancia ***sto**-mako/**pan**cha*
throat	la gola *g**o**la*
thumb	il pollice ***pol**-leechay*
toe	il dito del piede ***dee**to del **pye**day*
wrist	il polso ***pol**so*

see also **DOCTOR** ☐ **PHARMACY**

OSPEDALE *ospay-**day**lay*	**HOSPITAL**
PRONTO SOCCORSO *pronto sok-**kor**so*	**CASUALTY**
USL *oosel*	**LOCAL HEALTH CENTRE**

I need a doctor
Ho bisogno di un medico
*o bee**zon**-yo dee oon **med**-eeko*

I feel ill
Mi sento male
*mee **sen**to **mal**ay*

My son is ill
Mio figlio è malato
*meeyo **feel**-yo e ma-**la**to*

My daughter is ill
Mia figlia è malata
*meeya **feel**-ya e ma-**la**ta*

He/She has a temperature
Ha la febbre
*a la **feb**-bray*

He/She has a pain here...
Ha un dolore qui...
*a oon do-**lo**ray kwee...*

I'm diabetic
Sono diabetico(a)
*sono deea-**be**-teeko(a)*

I'm pregnant
Sono incinta
*sono een**cheen**-ta*

I'm on the pill
Prendo la pillola
*prendo la **peel**-lola*

I'm allergic to penicillin
Sono allergico(a) alla penicillina
*sono al-**ler**-jeeko(a) al-la penee-cheel-**lee**na*

Will he/she have to go to hospital?
Deve andare all'ospedale?
***de**vay an-**da**ray al-lospay-**da**lay*

When are visiting hours?
Qual è l'orario di visita?
*kwa-**le** lo**rar**-yo dee **vee**-zeeta*

Will I have to pay?
Dovrò pagare?
*dov-**ro** pa-**ga**ray*

How much will it cost?
Quanto costerà?
kwan**to kostay-**ra

Can you give me a receipt for the insurance?
Mi dà la ricevuta per l'assicurazione?
*mee **da** la reechay-**voo**ta payr las-seekoorats-**yo**nay*

■ YOU MAY HEAR

Deve andare all'ospedale?
***de**vay an-**da**ray al-lospay-**da**lay*
You will have to go to hospital

Non è grave
*non **e** gravay*
It's not serious

see also **EMERGENCIES** ❑ **PHARMACY** ❑ **BODY**

I need a dentist
Ho bisogno di un dentista
o beezon-yo dee oon den-teesta

He/She has toothache
Ha mal di denti
a mal dee dentee

Can you do a temporary filling?
Può fare un'otturazione provvisoria?
pwo faray oonot-toorats-yonay prov-vee-soree-a

It hurts	**Can you give me something for the pain?**
Fa male	Può darmi qualcosa per calmare il dolore?
fa malay	*pwo darmee kwal-koza payr kalmaray eel do-loray*

Can you repair my dentures?
Può riparare la mia dentiera?
pwo reepa-raray la meeya dent-yera

Do I have to pay?	**How much will it be?**
Devo pagare?	Quanto costerà
devo pa-garay	*kwanto kostay-ra*

Can I have a receipt for my insurance?
Mi dà la ricevuta per la mia assicurazione?
mee da la reechay-voota payr la meeya as-seekoorats-yonay

■ YOU MAY HEAR

Devo fare un'estrazione
devo faray oones-trats-yonay
I'll have to take it out

Le occorre un'otturazione
lay o-kor-ray oonot-toorats-yonay
You need a filling

Questo le potrà fare un po' male
kwesto lay po-tra faray oon po malay
This might hurt a little

see also **PHARMACY**

What facilities do you have for disabled people?
Quali servizi avete per i disabili?
kwalee serveets-ee a-vaytay payr ee dee-zabeelee

Are there any toilets for the disabled?
Ci sono le toilette per i disabili?
chee sono le twalet payr ee dee-zabeelee

Do you have any bedrooms on the ground floor?
Avete delle camere al pian terreno?
a-vaytay del-lay ka-mayray al pyan-ter-reno

Is there a lift?
C'è l'ascensore?
che lashen-soray

Where is the lift?
Dov'è l'ascensore?
do-ve lashen-soray

Can you visit ... in a wheelchair?
Si può visitare ... nella sedia a rotelle?
see pwo vee-zee-taray ... nay-la sed-ya a rotel-lay

Do you have wheelchairs?
Avete delle sedie a rotelle?
a-vaytay del-lay sed-yay a rotel-lay

Where is the wheelchair-accessible entrance?
Dov'è l'accesso per la sedia a rotelle?
do-ve lat-ches-so payr la sed-ya a rotel-lay

Do you have an induction loop?
Avete un auricolare?
a-vaytay oon owree-ko-laray

Is there a reduction for disabled people?
C'è una riduzione per i disabili?
che oona reedoots-yonay payr ee dee-zabeelee

Is there somewhere I can sit down?
Scusi, dove posso sedermi?
skoozee dovay pos-so sed-ermee

see also **HOTEL**

*We have used the familiar **tu** form for these phrases.*

What would you like for breakfast?
Che cosa vuoi per colazione?
*kay **ko**za vwoy payr kolats-**yo**nay*

What would you like to eat?
Che cosa vuoi da mangiare?
*kay **ko**za vwoy da man-**ja**ray*

What would you like to drink?
Che cosa vuoi da bere?
*kay **ko**za vwoy da **be**ray*

Did you sleep well?
Hai dormito bene?
*a-ee dor-**mee**to **ben**ay*

What would you like to do today?
Che cosa vuoi fare oggi?
*kay **ko**za vwoy **fa**ray **od**-jee*

I will pick you up...
Vengo a prenderti...
***ven**go a **pren**-dertee...

at the station
alla stazione
*al-la stats-**yo**nay

at... o'clock
alle...
al-lay...

May I phone home?
Posso chiamare a casa?
***pos**-so kya-**ma**ray a **ka**za*

I like...
Mi piace...
*mee pee-**a**-chay...*

I don't like...
Non mi piace...
*non mee pee-**a**-chay*

Take care
Stai attento
***sta**-ee at-**ten**to*

Thanks for everything
Grazie per tutto
***grats**-yay payr **toot**-to*

Thank you very much
Grazie molto
***grats**-yay **mol**to*

I've had a great time
Mi sono divertito(a) molto
*mee sono deever-**tee**to(ta) **mol**to*

Public transport is free for children under 4. Children between 4 and 12 pay half price.

A child's ticket
Un biglietto per bambini
oon beel-yet-to payr bam-beenee

Is there a reduction for children?
C'è la riduzione per bambini?
che la ree-doots-yonay payr bam-beenee

Do you have a children's menu?
Avete il menù per bambini?
a-vaytay eel menoo payr bam-beenee

Is it OK to take children?
Si possono portare i bambini?
see pos-sono por-taray ee bam-beenee

What is there for children to do?
Che cosa c'è per bambini?
kay koza che payr bam-beenee

Is there a play park near here?
C'è un parco giochi qui vicino?
che oon parko jokee kwee vee-cheeno

Is it safe for children?
È sicuro per bambini?
e see-kooro payr bam-beenee

Do you have...?
Avete...?
a-vaytay...

a high chair
un seggiolone
oon sed-jolonay

a cot
un lettino
oon let-teeno

I have two children
Ho due figli
o dooay feel-yee

Do you have any children?
Ha figli?
a feel-yee

He/She is ... years old
Ha ... anni
a ... an-nee

He/She is 8 years old
Ha otto anni
a ot-to an-nee

see also **PHARMACY** ☐ **DOCTOR**

I'd like to arrange a meeting with...
Vorrei organizzare una riunione con...
vor-**ray** organee-**tsa**ray oona reeoon-**yo**nay kon...

on...
per...
per...

Are you free to meet on...?
È libero per un colloquio per...?
e **lee**-bero payr oon kol-**lok**weeo payr...

the 2nd of May at 3pm
il 2 maggio alle tre
eel dooay **mad**-jo **al**-lay tray

for breakfast
per la prima colazione
payr la **pree**ma kolats-**yo**nay

for lunch
per pranzo
payr **pran**tso

for dinner
per cena
payr **chay**na

I will confirm by e-mail
Confermerò per e-mail
konfermay-**ro** payr e-mail

I will confirm by fax
Confermerò con un fax
konfermay-**ro** kon oon fax

I'm staying at Hotel...
Sono all'Hotel...
sono al-lo**tel**...

What is the best way to get to your office?
Quali mezzi devo prendere per arrivare al suo ufficio?
kwalee **med**zee **de**vo **pren**-deray payr ar-ree-**va**ray al suo oof-**fee**cho

Let Mr ... know that I will be ... minutes late
Dica al Signor ... che arriverò con ... minuti di ritardo
deeka al seen-**yor** ... kay ar-reeva**yro** kon ... mee-**noo**tee dee ree-**tar**do

I have an appointment with...
Ho un appuntamento con...
o oon ap-poonta-**men**to kon...

at ... o'clock
alle...
al-lay...

Here is my card
Ecco il mio biglietto da visita
ek-ko eel **mee**yo beel-**yet**-to da **vee**-zeeta

I'm delighted to meet you at last!
Finalmente, sono molto lieto(a) di incontrarla!
*feenal-**men**tay sono **mol**to **lee**-ayto(a) dee eenkon-**tra**rla*

My Italian is not very good
Parlo poco l'italiano
*parlo **po**ko leetal-**ya**no*

Please speak slowly
La prego di parlare piano
*la **pray**go dee par-**la**ray pee-ano*

I'm sorry I'm late
Mi scusi il ritardo
*mee **skoo**zee eel ree-**tar**do*

My flight was delayed
Il mio volo è arrivato in ritardo
*eel **mee**yo **vo**lo e ar-ree-**va**to een ree-**tar**do*

Can I offer you dinner?
Posso offrirle la cena?
*pos-so of-**freer**lay la **chay**na*

at my hotel
al mio albergo
*al **mee**yo al-**ber**go*

■ **YOU MAY HEAR**

Ha un appuntamento?
*a oon ap-poonta-**men**to*
Do you have an appointment?

...non è in ufficio
*...non **e** een oof-**fee**cho*
...isn't in the office

...arriverà fra due minuti
*...ar-reeve**ra** fra dooay mee-**noo**tee*
...will arrive in two minutes

Prego si accomodi ed attenda
*praygo see ak-**ko**modee ed at-**ten**da*
Please take a seat and wait

see also **TELEPHONE** ☐ **E-MAIL** ☐ **INTERNET** ☐ **FAX**

ALPHABET

J, K, W, X and Y are not native to the Italian language. You will only see these letters in foreign words. Below are the words used for clarification when spelling something out.

How do you spell it?
Come si scrive?
*komay see **skree**vay*

A like Ancona, b like Bari
A come Ancona, b come Bari
*a komay an-**ko**na bee komay **ba**-ree*

A	*a*	Ancona	*an-**ko**na*
B	*bee*	Bari	***ba**-ree*
C	*chee*	Como	***ko**mo*
D	*dee*	Domodossola	*domo-**dos**-sola*
E	*ay*	Empoli	***em**-polee*
F	***ef**-fe*	Firenze	*fee-**rent**say*
G	*jee*	Genova	***je**-nova*
H	***ak**-ka*	Hotel	***o**-tel*
I	*ee*	Imola	***ee**-mola*
L	***el**-le*	Livorno	*lee-**vor**no*
M	***em**-me*	Milano	*mee-**la**no*
N	***en**-ne*	Napoli	***na**-polee*
O	*o*	Otranto	***o**-tranto*
P	*pee*	Palermo	*pa-**layr**mo*
Q	*koo*	Quarto	***kwar**-to*
R	***er**-re*	Roma	***ro**-ma*
S	***es**-se*	Savona	*sa-**vo**na*
T	*tee*	Torino	*to-**ree**no*
U	*oo*	Udine	***oo**-deenay*
V	*voo*	Venezia	*venetseeya*
Z	***dze**-ta*	Zara	***dza**ra*
J	*ee **loon**-ga*		
K	***kap**-pa*		
W	***dop**-pyo voo*		
X	*eex*		
Y	*ee **gre**-ka*		

1 lb = approx. 0.5 kilo	1 pint = approx. 0.5 litre

■ LIQUIDS

1/2 litre of...	mezzo litro di...	*medz*-zo *lee*tro dee...
a litre of...	un litro di...	oon *lee*tro dee...
1/2 bottle of...	mezza bottiglia di...	*medz*-za bot-*teel*-ya dee...
a bottle of...	una bottiglia di...	oona bot-*teel*-ya dee...
a glass of...	un bicchiere di...	oon beek-*yeray* dee...

■ WEIGHTS

100 grams	100 grammi / un etto	*chen*to *gram*-mee / oon *et*-to
1/2 kilo of...	mezzo chilo di...	*medz*-zo *kee*lo dee...
a kilo of...	un chilo di...	oon *kee*lo dee...

■ FOOD

a slice of...	una fetta di...	oona *fet*-ta dee...
a portion of...	una porzione di...	oona ports-*yo*nay dee...
a dozen...	una dozzina di...	oona dodz-*zee*na dee...
a box of...	una scatola di...	oona *ska*-tola dee...
a packet of...	un pacchetto di...	oon pak-*ket*-to dee...
a tin of...	una scatola di...	oona *ska*-tola dee...
a can of...*(beer)*	una lattina di...	oona lat-*tee*na dee...
a jar of...	un vasetto di...	oon va*zet*-to dee...

■ MISCELLANEOUS

...euro worth of...	...euro di...	...ay-*oo*-ro dee...
a quarter	un quarto	oon *kwar*to
20 per cent	il venti per cento	eel *ven*tee payr *chen*to
more than...	più di...	pyoo dee...
less than...	meno di...	*me*no dee...
double	il doppio	eel *dop*-pyo
twice	due volte	dooay *vol*tay

NUMBERS

0	**zero** *dzero*		
1	**uno** *oono*		
2	**due** *dooay*		
3	**tre** *tray*		
4	**quattro** *kwat-tro*		
5	**cinque** *cheen-kway*		
6	**sei** *say*		
7	**sette** *set-tay*		
8	**otto** *ot-to*		
9	**nove** *novay*		
10	**dieci** *dee-e-chee*		
11	**undici** *oon-deechee*		
12	**dodici** *do-deechee*		
13	**tredici** *tray-deechee*		
14	**quattordici** *kwat-tor-deechee*		
15	**quindici** *kween-deechee*		
16	**sedici** *say-deechee*		
17	**diciasette** *deechas-set-tay*		
18	**diciotto** *deechot-to*		
19	**diciannove** *deechan-novay*		
20	**venti** *ventee*		
21	**ventuno** *ven-toono*		
22	**ventidue** *ventee-doo-ay*		
23	**ventitre** *ventee-tray*		
24	**ventiquattro** *ventee-kwat-tro*		
25	**venticinque** *ventee-cheen-kway*		
26	**ventisei** *ventee-say*		
27	**ventisette** *ventee-set-tay*		
28	**ventotto** *vent-ot-to*		
29	**ventinove** *ventee-no-vay*		
30	**trenta** *trayn-ta*		
40	**quaranta** *kwaran-ta*		
50	**cinquanta** *cheenkwan-ta*		
60	**sessanta** *ses-santa*		
70	**settanta** *set-tanta*		
80	**ottanta** *ot-tanta*		
90	**novanta** *no-vanta*		
100	**cento** *chento*		
110	**cento dieci** *chento dee-e-chee*		
1000	**mille** *meel-lay*		
2000	**duemila** *dooay-meela*		
million	**un milione** *oon meel-yonay*		
billion	**un miliardo** *oon meel-yardo*		

1st	**primo** *preemo*
2nd	**secondo** *sekon-do*
3rd	**terzo** *tertso*
4th	**quarto** *kwarto*
5th	**quinto** *kweento*
6th	**sesto** *sesto*
7th	**settimo** *set-teemo*
8th	**ottavo** *ot-tavo*
9th	**nono** *nono*
10th	**decimo** *dechee-mo*

days

LUNEDÌ *loonedee*	MONDAY
MARTEDÌ *martedee*	TUESDAY
MERCOLEDÌ *merkoledee*	WEDNESDAY
GIOVEDÌ *jovedee*	THURSDAY
VENERDÌ *venerdee*	FRIDAY
SABATO *sa-bato*	SATURDAY
DOMENICA *domeneeka*	SUNDAY

seasons

PRIMAVERA *preemavera*	SPRING
ESTATE *es-tatay*	SUMMER
AUTUNNO *owtoono*	AUTUMN
INVERNO *eenverno*	WINTER

months

GENNAIO *jen-na-yo*	JANUARY
FEBBRAIO *feb-ra-yo*	FEBRUARY
MARZO *martso*	MARCH
APRILE *a-preelay*	APRIL
MAGGIO *mad-jo*	MAY
GIUGNO *joon-yo*	JUNE
LUGLIO *lool-yo*	JULY
AGOSTO *a-gosto*	AUGUST
SETTEMBRE *set-tembray*	SEPTEMBER
OTTOBRE *ot-tobray*	OCTOBER
NOVEMBRE *nov-embray*	NOVEMBER
DICEMBRE *deechembray*	DECEMBER

What is today's date?
Qual è la data di oggi?
kwa-le la data dee od-jee

What day is it today?
Che giorno è oggi?
kay jorno e od-jee

It's the 5th of March 2003
È il cinque marzo duemilaetre
e eel cheen-kway martso doo-ay-meela-ay-tray

on Saturday	**on Saturdays**	**every Saturday**
il sabato	tutti i sabati	ogni sabato
eel sa-bato	*toot-tee ee sa-batee*	*on-yee sa-bato*

this Saturday	**next Saturday**	**last Saturday**
questo sabato	sabato prossimo	sabato scorso
kwesto sa-bato	*sa-bato pros-seemo*	*sa-bato skorso*

in June	**at the beginning of June**	**at the end of June**
a giugno	all'inizio di giugno	alla fine di giugno
a joon-yo	*al-leeneets-yo dee joon-yo*	*al-la feenay dee joon-yo*

before summer	**during the summer**	**after summer**
prima dell'estate	durante l'estate	dopo l'estate
preema del-les-tatay	*doo-rantay les-tatay*	*dopo les-tatay*

The 24-hour clock is used a lot more in Italy than in Britain. After 1200 midday, it continues: **1300**–le tredici ; **1400**–le quattordici ; **1500**–le quindici, etc. until **2400**–le ventiquattro.

With the 24-hour clock, the words **quarto** (quarter) and **mezzo** (half) aren't used:

13.15	*le tredici e quindici*
13.30	*le tredici e trenta*
22.45	*le ventidue e quarantacinque*

What time is it, please?
Scusi, che ore sono?
skoozee kay oray sono

It's...	2 o'clock	3 o'clock	6 o'clock (etc.)
Sono...	le due	le tre	le sei
sono...	*lay dooay*	*lay tray*	*lay say*

It's 1 o'clock	It's midday	It's midnight
È l'una	È mezzogiorno	È mezzanotte
e loona	*e medz-zo-jorno*	*e medz-za-not-tay*

9	le nove
	lay novay
9.10	le nove e dieci
	lay novay ay dee-e-chee
quarter past 9	le nove e un quarto
	lay novay ay oon kwarto
9.20	le nove e venti
	lay novay ay ventee
half past 9	le nove e mezza
	lay novay ay medz-za
9.35	le nove e trentacinque
	lay novay ay traynta-cheen-kway
quarter to 10	le dieci meno un quarto
	lay dee-e-chee mayno oon kwarto
5 minutes to 10	le dieci meno cinque
	lay dee-e-chee mayno cheen-kway

When does it open / close?
A che ora apre / chiude?
a kay ora apray / kee-ooday

When does it begin / finish?
A che ora comincia / finisce?
a kay ora ko-meencha / fee-neeshay

at 3 o'clock
alle tre
al-lay tray

before 3 o'clock
prima delle tre
preema del-lay tray

after 3 o'clock
dopo le tre
dopo lay tray

today
oggi
od-jee

tonight
stasera
sta-sayra

tomorrow
domani
do-manee

yesterday
ieri
yeree

the day before yesterday
l'altro ieri
laltro yeree

the day after tomorrow
dopo domani
dopo do-manee

in the morning
di mattina
dee mat-teena

in the afternoon
di pomeriggio
dee pomay-reed-jo

in the evening
di sera
dee sayra

at night
di notte
dee not-tay

this morning
stamattina
stamat-teena

this afternoon
questo pomeriggio
kwesto pomer-eed-jo

this evening/tonight
stasera
sta-sayra

It's nearly 6 o'clock
Sono quasi le sei
sono kwazee lay say

at half past 7
alle sette e mezza
al-lay set-tay ay medz-za

at about 10 o'clock
verso le dieci
verso lay dee-e-chee

in an hour's time
fra un ora
fra oon ora

in half an hour
fra mezz'ora
fra medz-zora

two hours ago
due ore fa
dooay oray fa

soon
fra poco
fra poko

early
presto
presto

late
tardi
tardee

later
più tardi
pyoo tardee

as soon as possible
al più presto possibile
al pyoo presto pos-see-beelay

87

Bar-Caffè

Many bars serve food: generally salads, sandwiches, pasta dishes and pizzas.

Pizzeria

*Pizzas. Take-away food, **da asporto**, is now popular.*

Pasticceria

Cake shop. These sometimes have a café attached where you can sample the cakes.

Trattoria

Generally family-run restaurants that offer local food, but tend to have less choice than a restaurant.

rosticceria

Sells spit-roasted chicken and food to be eaten there (generally standing). Well worth trying.

Ristorante

The menu and prices are usually displayed outside the entrance. Restaurants are open from about mid-day to 2.30 pm and from 7 pm to 10.30 pm.

Paninoteca

Sandwich bar

Bibite

Soft drinks

Toast Farciti

Toasted sandwiches with extra filling such as tomato and gherkin.

Tavola Calda

Self-service type restaurant which is good for a quick meal.

Gelateria

Ice-cream bar which also serves drinks.

If you just ask for **un caffè** *you'll be served* **un espresso**, *a tiny strong black coffee, so specify the type of coffee you want:*

ESPRESSO *es**pres**-so*	**STRONG SMALL BLACK COFFEE**
CAPPUCCINO *kap-poo**chee**no*	**FROTHY WHITE COFFEE**
CAFFÈ AMERICANO *kaf-**fe** amere**eka**no*	**BLACK FILTER COFFEE**
CAFFÈ CORRETTO *kaf-**fe** kor-**ret**-to*	**COFFEE LACED WITH GRAPPA/BRANDY**

a coffee	a lager	an orangeade	...please
un caffè	una birra	un'aranciata	...per favore
oon kaf-**fe**	oona **beer**-ra	oon aran-**chata**	payr fa-**vo**ray

a tea	with milk	with lemon	no sugar
un tè	al latte	col limone	senza zucchero
oon te	al **lat**-tay	kol lee-**mo**nay	**sen**tsa tsook-kayro

for two	for me	for him/her	for us	with ice
per due	per me	per lui/lei	per noi	con ghiaccio
payr **doo**ay	payr me	payr **loo**-ee/lay	payr noy	kon **gyat**-cho

a bottle of mineral water	sparkling	still
una bottiglia d'acqua minerale	gassata	naturale
oona bot-**teel**-ya **dak**wa meenay-**ra**lay	gas-**sa**ta	natoo-**ra**lay

Would you like to have a drink?	What will you have?
Prende qualcosa da bere?	Che cosa prende?
pren-day kwal-**ko**za da **be**ray	kay **ko**za **pren**-day

I'm very thirsty	It's my round!	I'm paying!
Ho molta sete	Offro io!	Pago io!
o **mol**ta **se**tay	**of**-fro **ee**-o	**pa**go **ee**-o

■ OTHER DRINKS TO TRY

analcolico *non-alcoholic, slightly bitter drink served as apéritif*

chinotto *fizzy soft drink with taste of bitter orange*

cioccolata calda *rich-tasting hot chocolate*

crodino *slightly bitter, non-alcoholic apéritif*

lemonsoda *fizzy drink with taste of real lemons*

spremuta di... *freshly-squeezed juice:* **pompelmo** – *grapefruit*

see also **IN A RESTAURANT**

READING THE MENU

*If you were planning to eat a full Italian meal, you would begin with **antipasto** (starter), then **primo** (often pasta), then **secondo** (meat or fish), and end with fruit or **dolci** (dessert). This requires some time, so people often skip one or two of the courses.*

Pane – Coperto	Cover charge (*pane* is bread)
Menù Turistico 7 € ⁵⁰	Tourist menu often including wine
Menù a prezzo fisso (solo pranzo)	Set-price menu (lunch only)
PIATTI DA ASPORTO	TAKE-AWAY DISHES

Menù	**Menu**
Pane – Coperto	Cover charge
Antipasti	Starters (often cold meats)
Primi Piatti	First Course (often pasta)
Secondi Piatti	Main Course (meat or fish)
Contorni	Vegetables
Formaggi	Cheese
Frutta	Fruit
Dolci	Sweet

For those who are vegetarian, or who prefer vegetarian dishes, turn to the VEGETARIAN topic on p. 92 for further phrases.

Where can we have something to eat?   not too expensive
Dove possiamo mangiare qualcosa?   non troppo caro
dovay pos-see-amo man-jaray kwal-koza   *non **trop**-po **ka**ro*

Can you recommend a good local restaurant?
Ci può consigliare un buon ristorante locale?
chee pwo konseel-yaray oon bwon reesto-rantay lo-kalay

I'd like to book a table for ... people
Vorrei prenotare un tavolo per ... persone
vor-ray preno-taray oon ta-volo payr ... per-sonay

for tonight...   **for tomorrow night...**   **at 8 o'clock**
per questa sera...   per domani sera...   alle otto
payr kwesta sayra...   *payr do-manee sayra...*   *al-lay ot-to*

The menu, please   **What is the dish of the day?**
Il menù per favore   Qual è il piatto del giorno?
eel menoo payr fa-voray   *kwa-le eel pyat-to del jorno*

Do you have a tourist menu?   **at a set price?**
Avete il menù turistico?   a prezzo fisso?
a-vaytay eel menoo too-reesteeko   *a prets-so fees-so*

What is the speciality of the house?
Qual è la specialità della casa?
kwa-le la spetchalee-ta del-la kaza

Can you tell me what this is?   **I'll have this**
Mi può spiegare che cos'è questo?   Prendo questo
mee pwo spyay-garay kay ko-ze kwesto   *prendo kwesto*

Could we have some more bread / more water, please?
Ci dà ancora un po' di pane / un po' di acqua per favore?
chee da an-kora oon po dee panay / oon po dee akwa payr fa-voray

The bill, please   **Is service included?**
Il conto per favore   Il servizio è incluso?
eel konto payr fa-voray   *eel serveets-yo e een-klooso*

Don't expect great things – Italians love good meat.

Are there any vegetarian restaurants here?
Ci sono dei ristoranti per vegetariani?
*chee sono day reesto-**ran**tee payr ved-jay-tar-**ya**nee*

Do you have any vegetarian dishes?
Avete dei piatti per vegetariani?
*a-**vay**tay day **pyat**-tee payr ved-jay-tar-**ya**nee*

Which dishes have no meat / fish?
Quali piatti non hanno carne / pesce?
*kwalee **pyat**-tee non **an**-no **kar**-nay / **pay**shay*

What fish dishes do you have?
Quali piatti di pesce avete?
*kwalee **pyat**-tee dee **pay**shay a-**vay**tay*

I'd like pasta as a main course
Vorrei un piatto di pasta come secondo
*vor-**ray** oon **pyat**-to dee **pas**ta **ko**may se**kon**do*

I don't like meat
Non mi piace la carne
*non mee pee-**a**-chay la **kar**-nay*

What do you recommend?
Che cosa mi consiglia?
*kay **ko**za mee kon-**seel**ya*

Is it made with vegetable stock?
È fatto con dadi vegetariani?
*e **fat**-to kon **da**dee ved-jay-tar-**ya**nee*

■ **POSSIBLE DISHES**

insalata mista *mixed salad (lettuce, tomato, peppers, etc.)*
insalata tricolore *mozzarella, tomato and fresh basil*
minestrone *thick vegetable soup*
pasta al sugo/al pomodoro *pasta with tomato sauce*
pasta al pesto *pasta with basil, garlic and pinenut sauce*
peperonata *sweet pepper and tomato stew*
pizza (margherita, ai funghi, vegetariana) *various pizzas*
polenta uncia *maize pudding with butter, garlic and cheese*
riso in bianco *boiled rice with butter, garlic, black pepper*

The wine list, please   **white wine**   **red red**
La lista dei vini per favore   vino bianco   vino rosso
la **lees**ta day **vee**nee payr fa-**vo**ray   **vee**no **byan**-ko   **vee**no **ros**-so

Can you recommend a good local wine?
Ci può consigliare un buon vino locale?
chee puo konseel-**ya**ray oon bwon **vee**no lo-**ka**lay

A bottle...   **A carafe...**   **of house wine**
Una bottiglia...   Una caraffa...   di vino della casa
oona bot-**teel**-ya...   oona ka-**raf**-fa...   dee **vee**no **del**-la **ka**za

■ **WINES**

Asti Spumante sparkling sweet or semi-sweet white wine often drunk for celebrations. Produced in the Asti district of Piedmont

Barbaresco dry, full-bodied red wine from Piedmont

Barbera dry, spicy red wine from Piedmont

Bardolino light, dry red or rosé wine from the Veneto

Barolo good, full-bodied red wine from Piedmont

Brunello di Montalcino superior, powerful red wine from Tuscany

Chianti full, fruity red wine from Tuscany

Chiaretto light, rosé-style white wine from the Veneto

Cinqueterre dry, light and fragrant white wines from Liguria

Est! Est! Est! crisp, fruity white wine from region near Rome

Frascati crisp, fresh, dry to off-dry white wine from near Rome

Lacrima christi full-bodied wine from Campania and Sicily

Lambrusco slightly sparkling wines from Emilia-Romagna

Marsala dark dessert wine from Sicily

Merlot good, dry red wine from NE Italy

Montepulciano dry or sweet red wine from Tuscany

Moscato sweet, aromatic white wine from NW Italy

Nebbiolo light, red wine from Piedmont

Orvieto crisp, smooth, dry white wine from Umbria

Pinot bianco dry white wine from NE Italy

Savuto dry red wine from Calabria

cont...

WINES & SPIRITS

Soave *dry white wine from the Veneto*
Valpolicella *light, fruity red wine from the Veneto*
Verdicchio *fresh, dry white wine from the Marches*
Verduzzo *dry, tangy white wine from NE Italy*
Vernaccia di San Gimignano *dry white wine from Tuscany*
Vino da tavola *table wine*
Vino della casa *house wine*
Vin Santo *golden, scented wine ranging from sweet to dry*

■ SPIRITS & LIQUEURS

What liqueurs do you have?
Quali liquori avete?
kwalee lee-kworee a-vaytay

Amaretto *strong, sweet almond-flavoured liqueur*
Cynar *strongly flavoured artichoke-based digéstif*
Digestivo *slightly bitter, herb-flavoured liqueur to help digestion*
Grappa *strong spirit from grape pressings, often laced in coffee*
Sambuca *aniseed liqueur, served with coffee beans and set alight*
Strega *stong herb-flavoured liqueur*
Vecchia Romagna *Italian cognac*

see also **IN A BAR/CAFÉ**

A

abbacchio suckling or milk-fed lamb, usually eaten at Easter. Roasted with garlic and rosemary
  abbacchio alla cacciatora lamb cooked in olive oil, garlic and rosemary

acciughe anchovies: fresh, salted or in olive oil
  acciughe ripiene fresh anchovies filled with salted anchovy fillets and cream cheese and fried in oil

aceto vinegar
  aceto balsamico balsamic vinegar

acqua brillante tonic water

acqua cotta traditional Tuscan soup made from onions, peppers, celery and tomato. Beaten eggs and parmesan are added just before serving

acqua minerale mineral water; this can be still (*naturale*), with gas (*effervescente*), or with artificial gas (*gassata*)

affettato misto selection of cold meats: ham, salami, mortadella, etc

affogato poached
affogato al caffè vanilla ice cream with hot espresso coffee poured over it

affumicato smoked

aglio garlic
  aglio, olio e peperoncino garlic, olive oil and hot chilli sauce

agnello lamb
  agnello al forno roast lamb with vegetables
  agnello all'arrabbiata lamb cooked in a tomato and chilli sauce
  agnello arrosto roast lamb

agnollotti pasta squares filled with white meat and cheese, usually served with bolognese sauce

agoni small fish, usually marinated in vinegar and herbs

agrodolce sweet and sour sauce made from sugar, water, vinegar, wine, pine-nuts and sultanas; served with vegetables or meat such as rabbit or duck

ai ferri grilled

al, alla etc means with, or in the style of: eg *pasta al sugo* is pasta with tomato sauce, and *pollo alla cacciatora* is chicken hunter-style

albicocche apricots
albicocche ripiene stuffed apricots

alici anchovies, often served dipped in flour and fried

alloro bayleaf

amarene dark morello cherries

amaretti macaroons, biscuits with a strong almond flavour

Amaretto di Saronno almond liqueur

amaro bitter liqueur drunk as a *digestivo* (to aid digestion)

amatriciana, ...all' bacon, tomato and onion sauce

analcolico non-alcoholic, slightly bitter drink served as an aperitif

ananas pineapple

anatra duck
anatra di Palmina duck cooked in wine

anatra in porchetta roast duck stuffed with its liver and ham

anelletti baked squid or cuttlefish rings

anguille eel
anguille alla comácchio stewed eel
anguille carpionate fried eels
anguille in umido eel stewed in tomato sauce

anguria watermelon

anice aniseed liqueur

anisetta powerful aniseed liqueur

antipasto starters/appetizers
antipasto misto selection of cold starters such as ham, salami, russian salad and pickles

aperitivo aperitif

Aperol aperitif made with the essence of various plants

aragosta crayfish
aragosta allo spiedo crayfish cooked kebab-style

arance oranges

aranciata orangeade

arancini di riso rice croquettes filled with minced veal and peas

arrabbiata, ...all' tomato sauce with bacon, onion, tomatoes and hot chillies

arrosto roast meat, usually cooked in casserole with wine and herbs

arrosto di maiale roast pork

arrosto di manzo roast beef

arrosto di vitello roast veal

asparagi asparagus

asparagi alla parmigiana lightly boiled asparagus baked with parmesan

astice lobster

B

baccalà salt cod

baccalà alla fiorentina salt cod cooked in tomato sauce

baccalà alla vicentina salt cod cooked in milk with anchovies, onion, garlic, parsley and herbs

baccalà alla livornese salt cod cooked in a tomato sauce

baccalà alla milanese Milanese salt cod fritters, served with lemon

bagna cauda hot garlic and anchovy dip

banana banana

basilico basil

Bel Paese soft, creamy mild cheese

ben cotto well done

besciamella béchamel sauce

bianco, in literally it means white, pasta or rice served with melted butter, garlic, sage and parmesan

bietola beetroot

birra lager-type beer; draught beer is *birra alla spina*

biscotti biscuits

bistecca steak

bistecca alla fiorentina thickly cut, charcoal-grilled steak

bistecca alla pizzaiola fried steak in a tomato and herb sauce

bistecchini di cinghiale wild boar steaks in a sweet and sour sauce

bitter non-alcoholic, bitter drink served as an aperitif

bocconcini di vitello pieces of veal cooked in wine and butter

bollito boiled

bollito misto different kinds of meat and vegetables cooked together

bolognese, ...alla with tomato and minced meat sauce, served with parmesan

bomba doughnut with custard filling

bonet chocolate pudding with caramel

borlotti dried red haricot beans

boscaiola, ...alla with mushroom and ham sauce

bottarga preserved tuna or mullet roes, served in thin slices as a starter (Sardinian speciality)

brace, ...alla grilled

braciola rib steak/chop

braciole al ragù chops cooked in tomato sauce

brasato beef stew

bresaola dried cured beef, cut finely and served with black pepper and olive oil

broccoletti leafy green vegetable similar to turnip tops

broccoli broccoli

brodetto di pesce fish soup made with different kinds of fish

brodo bouillon or broth often served with meat-stuffed pasta such as ravioli (*in brodo*)

bruschetta thickly-sliced bread rubbed with garlic and olive oil, often served topped with tomato

bucatini thick spaghetti-like with a hole running through it

budino a blancmange-type pudding

budino di ricotta pudding made from ricotta cheese

buridda famous Genoese fish soup using a variety of fish

burrini a creamy cheese from Basilicata

burro butter

burro, ...al fried in butter, usually wih garlic and sage

burro e salvia butter and sage sauce

busecca rich tripe and cheese soup

C

cacciatora, ...alla meat or game, hunter-style – cooked with tomato, herbs, garlic and wine

cachi persimmons

caciocavallo cow's cheese, quite strong when mature

caffè coffee – if you ask for *un caffè* you'll be served *un espresso* (small, strong and black)

caffè americano black filter coffee

caffè corretto coffee laced with *grappa* or any strong spirit

caffè doppio a large coffee (twice normal size)

caffèllatte milky coffee

calamaretti imbottiti baby squid stuffed with breadcrumbs and anchovies

calamari squid

calamari fritti squid rings dipped in batter and fried

calzone folded over pizza with filling. There are lots of local variations

camomilla camomile tea

Campari bitter-tasting aperitif made with herbs and fruit

canederli tirolesi Tyrolean dumplings made with bacon and sausage

cannella cinnamon

cannellini small white beans

cannelloni meat-filled pasta tubes covered with béchamel sauce and baked. Vegetarian options are filled with spinach and ricotta

cannoli fried pastries stuffed with ricotta, candied fruit and bitter chocolate from Sicily

cantucci nutty biscuits

capocello smoked salami preserved in olive oil

caponata Sicilian dish of aubergines cooked in a

sweet and sour sauce

cappelletti literally 'little hats' filled with ricotta cheese, can be served with bolognese meat sauce

capperi capers

cappon magro an elaborate cold seafood and cooked vegetable salad

cappuccino frothy white coffee

caprese tomato and mozzarella salad with basil

capretto baby goat (kid)
capretto arrosto oven-roasted kid with vegetables and wine

caprino soft goat's cheese, usually eaten with a sprinkling of olive oil and freshly ground black pepper

caramelle sweets

carbonade beef cooked in wine; polenta is the classic accompaniment

carbonara, ...alla smoked bacon, egg, cream and parmesan

carciofi globe artichokes

carciofi alla Giudia young globe artichokes, flattened and deep-fried

carciofi alla romana globe artichokes stuffed with breadcrumbs, parsley and anchovies

carciofi ripieni artichokes stuffed with mozarella, parmesan and anchovies

carciofini artichoke hearts

cardi cardoons (similar to fennel)

carne meat

carote carrots

carpaccio raw sliced lean beef eaten with lemon juice, olive oil and thickly grated parmesan cheese

carpione carp

carpione, in pickled in vinegar, wine and lemon juice. Fish is often served this way and fried

casalinga, ...alla home-made

cassata layers of ice cream with candied fruits
cassata siciliana sponge dessert with ricotta and candied fruits

cassola pork, cabbage and vegetable casserole

castagnaccio chestnut cake

castagne chestnuts

cavolatte rich custard pudding

cavolfiore cauliflower

cavolo cabbage

ceci chickpeas

céfalo grey mullet

cena dinner

Centerbe herbal liqueur

cervelle calves' brains usually fried

cetriolo cucumber

China bitter liqueur

chinotto fizzy, bitter-orange soft drink

cialzons alla carnia pasta squares filled with spinach, chocolate and cinnamon

ciambella ring-shaped fruit cake

ciambellini ring-shaped aniseed biscuits

cicoria chicory

ciliege cherries

cinghiale wild boar

Cinzano popular aperitif

cioccolata calda rich hot chocolate, often served with cream

cioccolatini chocolates

cioccolato chocolate

ciociara, ...alla with mushroom, cream and ham sauce

cipolle onions

cipolle ripiene stuffed onions

coccio a yeast cake with dried fruit

cocco coconut

cocomero watermelon

coda di bue oxtail

coda alla vaccinara famous Roman dish of oxtail stewed with tomatoes and herbs

conchiglie shell-shaped pasta

confetti sugared almonds

congelato frozen

coniglio rabbit

coniglio all'ischiana rabbit stewed in wine

coniglio in umido rabbit stew

contorni vegetable side dishes

cornetto a croissant filled with jam, custard or chocolate

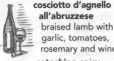

cosciotto d'agnello all'abruzzese braised lamb with garlic, tomatoes, rosemary and wine

cotechino spicy pork sausage usually cooked with lentils

cotoletta cutlet/chop

cotoletta al prosciutto veal cutlet with a slice of Parma ham

cotoletta alla bolognese veal cutlet topped with ham and cheese

cotoletta alla milanese veal cutlet dipped in egg and breadcrumbs then fried

cotoletta alla valdostana breaded veal chop stuffed with cheese

cotoletta di vitello veal cutlet

cotolette di abbacchio lamb chops

cotolette di agnello alla brace marinated, grilled lamb chops

cotto cooked

cozze mussels

cozze arraganate grilled mussels

crema di... cream soup or sauce/custard

crêpe pancake

crespolina stuffed pancake

crocchette di patate potato croquettes

crodino slightly bitter, non-alcoholic aperitif

crostata tart, usually filled with fruit and glazed

crostata di frutta fruit tart

crostini di fegatini chicken liver pâté on toast

crudo raw

Cynar bitter aperitif (made from artichokes)

D

dente, ...al pasta cooked so it is still quite firm

dèntice sea bream

digestivo slightly bitter, herb-flavoured liqueur to aid digestion

dolce dessert

dolcelatte soft, creamy blue cheese

dragoncello tarragon

E

entrecote steak

F

fagiano pheasant
fagiano con funghi pheasant with porcini mushrooms
fagiano in salmì pheasant stewed in wine

fagioli type of bean
fagioli al tonno haricot beans with tuna fish in olive oil
fagioli con cotiche bean stew with pork
fagioli nel fiasco haricot beans cooked in a flask

fagiolini runner beans

faraona guinea fowl

farcito stuffed

farfalle butterfly-shaped pasta

farsu magru veal stuffed and rolled in wine, cooked in wine (Sicilian speciality)

fave broad beans
fave al guanciale broad beans cooked with bacon and onion

fegatini di pollo chicken livers

fegato liver (mainly calves')
fegato alla veneziana calves' liver fried in butter and onion

ferri, ...ai grilled without oil

fettuccine fresh ribbon pasta

ficatu all'agru e duci calves' liver in sweet and sour sauce (Sicilian)

fichi figs
fichi d'India prickly pears

filetto fillet steak
filetto di tacchino alla bolognese turkey breast served with a slice of ham and cheese

Filu Ferru very strong *grappa* from Sardinia

finanziera, ...alla with chicken livers, mushrooms and wine sauce

finocchio fennel

fiori di zucchini courgette flowers fried in batter

focaccia flat bread brushed with garlic, salt and olive oil, sprinkled with herbs or onions

fonduta al parmigiano cheese fondue made with Fontina cheese, eggs, butter and truffles. Eaten with crusty bread

fontina mild to strong cow's milk cheese

formaggio cheese

forno, ...al cooked in the oven

fragole strawberries

frittata omelette, usually with different ingredients

fritto fried

fritto misto platter of deep-fried food including different kinds of meat and vegetables

fritto misto di mare fried/grilled selection of seafood

frullato di frutta milk shake made with fruits

frutta fruit

frutti di mare shellfish/seafood

funghi mushrooms – very popular and varied in Italy. In autumn many Italians take to the woods in search of the prized porcini

funghi trifolati sliced mushrooms fried with garlic and parsley

Fuoco dell'Etna very strong liqueur from Sicily

fusilli spiral-shaped pasta

G

gamberi prawns

gamberoni giant prawns

gazzosa fizzy bottled lemonade

gelato ice cream

gelato misto a selection of different flavoured ice creams

gioddu yoghurt

girasole sunflower

gnocchi small dumplings made from potato and flour, can be made with spinach. Boiled and served with tomato sauce or ragù

gnocchi alla romana dumplings made from semolina, butter and parmesan, oven-baked

gnocchi verdi spinach and cheeese dumplings, usually cooked in butter, garlic and sage

Gorgonzola a strong blue cows'-milk cheese

granchio crab

grana hard cows'-milk cheese; generic name given to Parmesan cheese

granita flavoured crushed ice drink
granita di caffè coffee drink with crushed ice and cream
granita di limone lemon drink with crushed ice
granceola large crab
grappa strong spirit from grape pressings, often added to coffee
grattugiato grated
griglia, ...alla grilled
grigliata di cervo grilled venison steaks
grigliata mista mixed grill consisting of various barbecued meats
grissini breadsticks
guanciale streaky bacon made from pig's cheek
gulasch spicy beef stew

I

impepata di cozze peppery mussels
insalata salad
insalata caprese tomato, basil and mozarella salad
insalata di mare mixed seafood salad

insalata di pomodori tomato salad
insalata di riso rice salad

insalata mista mixed salad
insalata russa russian salad
insalata verde green salad
involtini rolls of veal or pork stuffed with chicken liver, pork sausage and parmesan
italiana, ...alla platters with mixed cured meats/cheeses, olives and savouries

L

lamponi raspberries
lasagne layers of pasta with bolognese and béchamel sauces, baked
lasagne verdi layers of green pasta filled with bolognese (or ricotta) and béchamel sauces.
latte milk
lattuga lettuce
lemonsoda fizzy lemon drink
lenticchie lentils usually cooked with pork sausage

lepre hare
   lepre in salmì hare stewed in wine
latte milk
lesso boiled
limonata bottled lemon drink
limone lemon
limoncello lemon liqueur
lingua tongue
linguine thin strips of pasta
lombata di maiale pork chop
lonza type of salami
luccio pike
lumache snails

M

maccheroni macaroni
   maccheroni ai quattro formaggi pasta with four cheeses
   maccheroni alla chitarra square-shaped pasta often served with lamb in chilli and tomato sauce
macedonia (con panna) fresh fruit salad (with cream)
macinata mince

magro, di a meatless dish (often a fish alternative)
maiale pork
maionese mayonnaise
mandorle almonds
manzo beef
marmellata jam
Marsala dark dessert wine from Sicily
Martini famous Italian aperitif
mascarpone rich cream cheese used in desserts such as *tiramisù*
mela apple
melanzane aubergines
   melanzane alla Parmigiana layers of aubergine baked with tomato sauce, parma ham, parmesan and mozzarella
   melanzane ripiene stuffed aubergines
melagrana pomegranate
melone melon
menta mint
merengata meringue and ice cream dessert
merluzzo cod
miele honey

milanese, ...alla normally applied to veal cutlets dipped in egg and breadcrumbs before frying

minestra soup

minestra calanchina vegetable and rice soup served with cheese

minestrone vegetable, bean and pasta soup

minestrone al pesto minestrone flavoured with pesto sauce

missultitt grilled dried fish, often eaten with *polenta*

misto di funghi mushroom stew

more blackberries

mortadella type of salami

mostarda pickled fruit. Served with *bollito* (boiled meats)

mozzarella buffalo-milk cheese

mozzarella in carozza mozarella sandwiched in bread, dipped in egg and breadcrumbs and fried

mugnaia, ...alla usually fish dusted in flour then fried in butter

N

nocciole hazelnuts

nocciole d'agnello noisette of lamb

nocepesca nectarine

noci walnuts

norma, ...alla tomatoe and aubergines Sicilian sauce

O

olio oil

olio d'oliva olive oil

olive olives

orecchiette ear-shaped pasta

orecchiette ai broccoli pasta with broccoli

origano oregano

orzata cool, milky drink made from barley

ossobuco marrow-bone veal steak cooked in tomato and wine sauce

ostriche oysters

P

paglia e fieno green and plain ribbon pasta cooked with mushrooms, sausage and cream

pan pepato sweet loaf with mixed nuts

pancetta streaky bacon

pandoro yeast cake, traditionally eaten at Christmas

pane bread
pane e coperto cover charge
pane integrale wholemeal bread

panettone cork-shaped yeast cake with dried fruit, traditionally eaten at Christmas

panforte a hard, dried-fruit and nut cake

panino bread roll or sandwich

panna cream

pansôti (di Rapallo) pasta squares filled with spinach and egg and served in a walnut and parmesan sauce

panzerotti ravioli stuffed with mozzarella, salami and ham, usually fried

paparelle e fegatini chicken livers with pasta

pappardelle wide ribbon-shaped pasta
pappardelle al sugo di lepre wide ribbon pasta with hare, wine and tomato sauce

parmigiana, ...alla with parmesan cheese
parmigiana di melanzane aubergine layers, oven-baked with tomato sauce and parmesan cheese

parmigiano parmesan cheese. A hard cow's milk cheese used extensively in Italian cooking.

pasta the dry variety takes 10–15 minutes to cook, the fresh just 3 or 4
pasta al forno pasta baked with minced meat, eggs, tomato and cheese
pasta all'uovo fresh pasta made from flour and eggs
pasta asciutta pasta served with a sauce such as *spaghetti al sugo* and not in a soup form such as *ravioli in brodo* (ravioli in bouillon)
pasta con le sarde a baked dish of layers of pasta and fried sardines

pasta e fagioli pasta with beans

pasta fresca fresh pasta

pasticcio pie

pastina in brodo pasta pieces in clear broth

patate potatoes

patate fritte chips

patatine crisps

patatine fritte chips

pecorino hard tangy cheese made from ewe's milk, used in *pesto*

penne quill-shaped pasta

penne rigate ribbed quill-shaped pasta

pepe pepper

peperonata sweet peppers cooked with tomatoes and olive oil

peperoncino hot chilli pepper

peperoni peppers

peperoni ripieni stuffed peppers

pere pears

pesca peach

pesce fish

pesce arrosto baked fish

pesce persico perch

pesce spada swordfish, often grilled or served in a tomato sauce

pesce spada alla siciliana swordfish cooked with orange and lemon juice

pesto sauce of pounded basil, garlic, pine-nuts, olive oil and pecorino

petto di pollo chicken breast

pezzenta variety of salad

piatto dish

piatto del giorno dish of the day

piatti tipici regional dishes

piccatine al limone tender thinly sliced veal in butter and lemon

pietanze main courses

pinoli pine nuts

piselli peas

pistacchio pistachio

pizza originally from Naples, cooked in wood-burning ovens

pizza ai funghi mushroom pizza

pizza alla Siciliana pizza with tomato, anchovy, black olives and capers

pizza capricciosa pizza with baby artichoke, ham and egg

pizza cardinale pizza with ham and olives

pizza frutti di mare pizza with seafood

pizza margherita named after the first queen of a united Italy; symbolising the Italian flag's colours: red (tomatoes), green (basil) and white (mozarella)

pizza marinara tomato and garlic pizza

pizza Napoli/ Napoletana pizza with tomato, cheese, anchovy, olive oil and oregano

pizza quattro formaggi a pizza divided into four sections, each with a different cheese topping

pizza quattro stagioni pizza divided into four sections with a selection of toppings on each

pizzaiola, ...alla cooked with tomatoes, garlic and herbs

pizzetta small cheese and tomato pizza

pizzoccheri buckwheat pasta noodles, oven-baked with cabbage, potatoes and cheese

polenta coarse corn or maize meal solidified porridge. A perfect accompaniment to stews. Can be dipped in egg, breadcrumbs, grated parmesan and then fried

polenta e osei polenta with song birds.

polenta uncia polenta cooked with butter, garlic and Fontina cheese

pollame poultry/fowl

pollo chicken

pollo alla diavola chicken grilled with herbs and chilli pepper

pollo alla marengo chicken cooked in wine, served with eggs and prawns

pollo alla romana chicken with tomatoes and peppers

pollo arrosto roast chicken

polpette beef meatballs made with parmesan and parsley

polpo octopus, served in salad (cold) or tomato sauce

polpo affogato octopus cooked in tomato sauce

pomodoro tomato
pomodoro, ...al tomato sauce (same as *sugo*)
pomodori da sugo plum tomatoes
pomodori ripieni stuffed tomatoes

pompelmo grapefruit

porceddu suckling pig

porchetta roast suckling pig

porcini prized cep mushrooms, often dried

porri leeks

pranzo lunch

prezzemolo parsley

prima colazione breakfast

primo first course

prosciutto ham
prosciutto cotto boiled ham
prosciutto crudo cured Parma ham which is sliced off the bone
prosciutto di cinghiale cured ham made from wild boar
prosciutto e melone Parma ham and melon slices

Prosecco sparkling dry white wine

provolone creamy cow's milk cheese, mild to strong

prugne plums

puttanesca, ...alla tomato, garlic, hot chilli, anchovies and capers

Q

quaglie quails

R

radicchio red-leaf lettuce

ragù, ...al minced meat, tomato and garlic (same as *bolognese*)

rana pescatrice monkfish

rane frogs' legs

ravioli pasta cushions filled with meat or cheese and spinach

ribes blackcurrants

riccio di mare sea urchin

ricotta soft white cheese used as filling for pasta as well as in desserts

111

rigatoni ribbed tubes of pasta

ripieno stuffed

risi e bisati rice cooked with eel, a traditional Venetian dish

risi e bisi thick rice and pea soup (almost liquid risotto) cooked with bacon

riso rice

riso alla pilota rice cooked with sausage, nutmeg and cinnamon

risotto rice cooked in broth with different ingredients added

risotto ai funghi risotto with porcini mushrooms

risotto al nero di seppie risotto made with cuttlefish and its ink

risotto alla milanese rich yellow risotto flavoured with saffron, parmesan and butter, and cooked in meat broth

risotto alla pescatora seafood rice

risotto alle seppie risotto cooked with squid (Venetian speciality). Its ink turns the rice black

risotto con le quaglie quails with risotto

robiola creamy cheese with a mild taste

rognone kidney

rosmarino rosemary

rospo monkfish

S

salame salami (there are many types)

sale salt

salmone salmon

salsa sauce

salsa verde sauce made of olive oil, breadcrumbs, anchovies, hard boiled egg and parsley, usually served with boiled meat or fish

salsicce sausages: there are many regional variations but they are mainly thick pork sausages which can be boiled or grilled

saltimbocca alla romana veal cooked in white wine with parma ham

salvia sage

Sambuca aniseed liqueur, served with coffee beans and set alight

sampiero John Dory
(type of fish)

sangue, ...al rare

sarde sardines
  sarde e beccafico sardines
  stuffed with breadcrumbs,
  anchovies, sultanas and
  pine-nuts
  sarde in saour sardines
  marinated in vinegar,
  sultanas and pine nuts

sartù di riso rice and meat
timbale (rather like a pie)

scaloppine veal escalopes
  scaloppine al limone veal
  escalopes cooked in lemon
  juice
  scaloppine al marsala veal
  escalopes cooked in marsala
  scaloppine alla milanese
  veal escalopes dipped in
  egg, breadcrumbs and
  fried in butter, served with
  wedges of lemon

scamorza a cheese similar
to mozzarella but smoked

scampi scampi

secondo main dish, usually
meat or fish

sedano celery

selz soda water

semifreddo
chilled dessert
made with ice
cream

senape mustard

seppie coi piselli
squid cooked with peas

servizio compreso service
included

sfogliatelle frolle puff
pastry cakes filled with
ricotta cheese

sgavecio fried fish served
cold with vinegar and
seasonings

sgombro mackerel

soffritto pig's offal with
tomatoes and spices

sogliola sole

sopa cauda soup made
from bread and pigeon

soppressata type of salami,
with pistachio

sott'olio in olive oil

spaghetti spaghetti
  **spaghetti aglio, olio e
  peperoncino** spaghetti
  with garlic, chilli pepper
  and olive oil sauce
  spaghetti all'amatriciana
  spaghetti with bacon, onion
  and tomato sauce

113

spaghetti alle vongole spaghetti with clams

spaghettini aromatici fine spaghetti in a sauce of anchovies, garlic, black olives and capers

speck type of smoked cured ham from mountain regions

spezzatino stew, usually with tomato sauce

spiedini meat kebabs

spiedo, ...allo spit-roasted, or on skewer

spinaci spinach
spinaci alla piemontese spinach cooked with anchovies and garlic

spremuta freshly squeezed fruit juice
spremuta di pompelmo fresh grapefruit juice

spumante sparkling wine

stoccafisso stoccafisso (*bacalà*, as opposed to *baccalà*) is dried, not salted cod and needs still more soaking before cooking

stracciatella consommé with egg stirred in and grated parmesan

stracotto braised beef slow-cooked with vegetables. Often served with polenta

Strega strong herb-flavoured liqueur

succo di frutta bottled fruit juice

sugo sauce, often refers to the basic tomato, basil and garlic sauce (same as *al pomodoro*)

surgelato frozen

T

tacchino turkey

tagliatelle ribbon-like pasta often served in cream sauce

Taleggio soft, creamy cheese similar to Camembert

tartine canapés

tartufo truffles: black (*nero*) and white (*bianco*) are used extensively in risotto and game dishes
tartufo di cioccolato rich chocolate ice cream shaped like a truffle

tè tea. Normally served with lemon (*al limone*). If you want it with milk you must ask for *tè al latte*

teglia earthenware casserole dish

tiella di sardine baked sardines with cheese

timballo a baked dish
timballo di melanzane baked aubergines, egg, cheese and parma ham

timo thyme

tinche tench

tiramisù dessert made with mascarpone, sponge, coffee and marsala

tónica tonic water

tonno tuna fish
tonno, ...al with a sauce made of tuna fish and tomatoes
tonno e fagioli tuna and bean salad

torrone nougat, traditionally eaten at Christmas

torta cake/flan/tart

tortellini meat-filled pasta cushions
tortellini panna e prosciutto tortellini cooked with cream and ham

tortine al tartufo little savoury tarts with truffles

tramezzini sliced white bread with mixed fillings

trenette long thin strips of pasta, traditionally served with pesto sauce

triglie red mullet
triglie alla livornese red mullet fried with chillies in tomato sauce
triglie alla siciliana a Sicilian dish of red mullet cooked in white wine and orange peel

trippa tripe, often cooked with tomatoes and onions

trota trout
trote alla panna acida trout in soured cream

U

ucelli scappati pork kebabs

umido, in stewed

uova eggs
uova alla fiorentina poached eggs on spinach tarts

uva grapes

uva passa raisins

115

V

vaniglia vanilla

Vecchia Romagna Italian cognac

verdure vegetables

vermicelli very thin pasta

Vermut very popular aperitif made from herbs and wine

verza Savoy (green) cabbage

vino wine
vin bianco white wine
vin dulce sweet wine
vin rosato rosé wine
vin rosso red wine
vin secco dry wine

vitello veal

vongole clams
vongole, ...alle clam, parsley, garlic and olive oil

W

wurstel Frankfurter sausages

Y

yogurt yoghurt

Z

zabaglione frothy dessert made with egg yolks and sugar beaten with marsala over heat

zafferano saffron, used in *risotto alla milanese*

zampone spicy sausage in the shape of a pig's trotter, sliced and served hot

zucca marrow

zucchero sugar

zucchini courgettes

zuccotto rich cream and nut pudding in a pumpkin shape

zuppa soup
zuppa di cozze mussel and tomato soup
zuppa di fagioli bean soup
zuppa di pesce seafood soup with many delicious regional variations
zuppa inglese dessert similar to trifle laced with whisky or *Vermut*
zuppa pavese a bread soup with broth and poached eggs, topped with grated cheese

A

a(n) un/una/uno

abbey l'abbazia *(f)*

able: to be able (to) essere capace (di)

abortion l'aborto *(m)*

about su ; circa
a book about... un libro su...
about ten o'clock circa le dieci

above sopra

abroad l'estero *(m)*
to go abroad andare all'estero

abscess l'ascesso *(m)*

accelerator l'acceleratore *(m)*

accent l'accento *(m)*

to accept accettare

access l'accesso *(m)*
wheelchair access l'accesso per disabili

accident l'incidente *(m)*

accident & emergency department il pronto soccorso

accommodation l'alloggio *(m)*

to accompany accompagnare

account *(bill)* il conto
(in bank) il conto in banca

account number il numero del conto

to ache fare male
it aches fa male

acid l'acido *(m)*

actor *(m/f)* l'attore/l'attrice

adaptor *(electrical appliance)* il riduttore

address l'indirizzo *(m)*
what is the address? qual è l'indirizzo?

address book la rubrica

admission charge/fee il biglietto d'ingresso

to admit *(to hospital)* ricoverare

adult l'adulto(a)
for adults per adulti

advance: in advance in anticipo

advertisement la pubblicità
(in newspaper) l'annuncio *(m)*

to advise consigliare

A&E il pronto soccorso

aeroplane l'aeroplano *(m)*

aerosol l'aerosol *(m)*

afraid: to be afraid avere paura

after dopo

afternoon il pomeriggio
this afternoon oggi pomeriggio
tomorrow afternoon domani pomeriggio
in the afternoon di pomeriggio

aftershave il dopobarba

again ancora ; di nuovo

against contro

A

age l'età *(f)*

agency l'agenzia *(f)*

ago fa
a week ago una settimana
fa

to agree essere d'accordo

agreement l'accordo *(m)*

AIDS l'AIDS *(m)*

airbag l'airbag *(m)*

airbed il matarasso
gonfiabile

air-conditioning l'aria
condizionata *(f)*

air freshener il deodorante
per l'ambiente

airline la linea aerea

air mail: by air mail per
via aerea

airplane l'aeroplano *(m)*

airport l'aeroporto *(m)*

airport bus l'autobus per
l'aeroporto *(m)*

air ticket il biglietto d'aereo

aisle il corridoio

alarm l'allarme *(m)*

alarm clock la sveglia

alcohol l'alcool *(m)*

alcohol-free analcolico(a)

alcoholic alcolico(a)

all tutto(a)

allergic to allergico(a) a
I'm allergic to... sono
allergico(a) a...

allergy l'allergia *(f)*

to allow permettere

all right *(agreed)* va bene
are you all right? sta bene?

almost quasi

alone solo(a)

Alps le Alpi

already già

also anche

altar l'altare *(m)*

aluminium foil la carta
stagnola

always sempre

a.m. del mattino

am: *I am* sono

amber *(light)* il giallo

ambulance l'ambulanza *(f)*

America l'America *(f)*

American americano(a)

anaesthetic l'anestetico *(m)*
local anaesthetic
l'anestetico locale
general anaesthetic
l'anestetico generale

anchor l'ancora *(f)*

ancient antico(a)

and e

angina l'angina pectoris *(f)*

angry arrabbiato(a)

animal l'animale *(m)*

ankle la caviglia

anniversary l'anniversario *(m)*

to announce annunciare

announcement l'annuncio *(m)*

annual annuale
another un altro/un'altra
  another beer un'altra birra
  another coffee un altro caffè
answer la risposta
to answer rispondere
answerphone la segreteria telefonica
antacid l'antiacido (m)
antibiotic l'antibiotico (m)
antifreeze l'antigelo (m)
antihistamine l'antistaminico (m)
antiques i pezzi d'antiquariato
antique shop il negozio d'antiquariato
antiseptic l'antisettico (m)
any dei/delle/degli (di)
  I haven't any money non ho soldi
  have you any apples? ha delle mele?
anyone qualcuno ; chiunque
anything qualcosa ; qualsiasi cosa
apartment l'appartamento (m)
appendicitis l'appendicite (f)
apple la mela
application form il modulo di domanda
appointment l'appuntamento (m)
  I have an appointment ho un appuntamento

approximately circa
April aprile
architect m/f l'architetto
architecture l'architettura (f)
are sono
arm il braccio
armbands (swimming) i braccioli
armchair la poltrona
to arrange sistemare
to arrest arrestare
arrivals (plane, train) gli arrivi
to arrive arrivare
art l'arte (f)
art gallery la galleria d'arte ; la pinacoteca
arthritis l'artrite (f)
artificial finto(a) ; artificiale
artist m/f l'artista
ashtray il portacenere
to ask (question) domandare (for something) chiedere
asleep: he/she is asleep dorme
aspirin l'aspirina (f)
asthma l'asma (f)
  I have asthma ho l'asma
at a
  at home a casa
  at 8 o'clock alle otto
  at once subito
  at night di notte
to attack aggredire
attractive attraente

A

auction l'asta *(f)*
audience il pubblico
August agosto
aunt la zia
au pair la ragazza alla pari
Australia l'Australia *(f)*
Australian australiano(a)
author *m/f* l'autore/l'autrice
automatic automatico(a)
automatic car la macchina con cambio automatico
auto-teller il Bancomat®
autumn l'autunno *(m)*
available disponibile
avalanche la valanga
avenue il viale
average medio(a)
to avoid evitare
awake: to be awake essere sveglio(a)
away via
awful terribile
axle *(car)* l'asse *(m)*

B

baby il/la bambino(a)
baby food gli alimenti per bambini
baby milk il latte per bambini
baby wipes le salviettine per bambini

baby's bottle il biberon
babyseat *(in car)* il seggiolino per bambini
babysitter il/la babysitter
back *(of body)* la schiena
backpack lo zaino
bacon la pancetta
bad *(food)* andato(a) a male *(weather, news)* brutto(a)
badminton il badminton
bag la borsa
baggage i bagagli
baggage allowance il peso consentito di bagaglio
baggage reclaim il ritiro bagagli
bait *(for fishing)* l'esca *(m)*
baked al forno
baker's la panetteria ; il panificio
balcony il balcone
bald *(person)* calvo(a) *(tyre)* liscio(a)
ball *(large)* il pallone *(small)* la pallina
ballet il balletto
balloon il palloncino
banana la banana
band *(musical)* la banda
bandage la benda
bank la banca *(river)* la riva
bank account il conto in banca

banknote la banconota

bankrupt fallito(a)

bar il bar

bar of chocolate la tavoletta di cioccolato

barbecue il barbecue
  to have a barbecue fare il barbecue

barber il barbiere

to bark abbaiare

barn il granaio

barrel *(wine/beer)* il barile

basement il seminterrato

basil il basilico

basket il cestino

basketball la palacanestro

bat *(baseball, etc)* la mazza

bath il bagno
  to have a bath fare un bagno

bathing cap la cuffia

bathroom il bagno
  with bathroom con bagno

battery *(radio, etc)* la pila
  (car) la batteria

bay *(along coast)* la baia

B&B la pensione familiare

to be essere

beach la spiaggia
  private beach la spiaggia privata
  sandy beach la spiaggia con sabbia
  nudist beach la spiaggia di nudisti

beach hut la cabina

bean il fagiolo

beard la barba

beautiful bello(a)

beauty salon l'istituto di bellezza *(m)*

because perché

to become diventare

bed il letto
  double bed il letto matrimoniale
  single bed il letto a una piazza
  sofa bed il divano letto
  twin beds i letti gemelli

bed and breakfast la pensione familiare

bed clothes le coperte e lenzuola

bedroom la camera da letto

bee l'ape *(f)*

beef il manzo

beer la birra
  draught beer la birra alla spina

before prima di
  before breakfast prima di colazione

to begin cominciare

behind dietro di

beige beige

to believe credere

bell *(church)* la campana
  (doorbell) il campanello

B

to belong to appartenere a
it belongs to... appartiene a...
below sotto
belt la cintura
bend *(in road)* la curva
berth *(train, ship)* la cuccetta
beside *(next to)* accanto a
beside the bank accanto alla banca
best: *the best* il/la migliore
bet la scommessa
to bet scommettere
better (than) meglio (di)
between fra
to beware of stare attento(a) a
beyond oltre
bib *(baby's)* il bavaglino
bicycle la bicicletta ; la bici
by bicycle in bicicletta
bicycle repair kit il kit per riparare la bici
bidet il bidet
big grande
bigger (than) più grande (di)
bike *(pushbike)* la bici
(motorbike) la moto
bike lock il lucchetto della bici
bikini il bikini
bill *(hotel, restaurant)* il conto
(for work done) la fattura
(gas, telephone) la bolletta

bin *(dustbin)* il bidone
bin liner il sacco della spazzatura
binoculars il binocolo
bird l'uccello *(m)*
biro la biro
birth la nascita
birth certificate il certificato di nascita
birthday il compleanno
happy birthday! auguri! buon compleanno
my birthday is on... il mio compleanno è il...
birthday card il biglietto d'auguri di compleanno
birthday present il regalo di compleanno
biscuits i biscotti
bit il pezzo
a bit un po'
bite *(of insect)* la puntura
(of dog) la morsicatura
a bite to eat qualcosa da mangiare
to bite *(animal)* mordere
(insect) morsicare
bitten morso(a)
(by insect) morsicato(a)
bitter *(taste)* amaro(a)
black nero(a)
black ice il ghiaccio sulla strada
blanket la coperta
bleach la candeggina

to bleed sanguinare

blender il frullatore

blind *(person)* cieco(a)

blind *(window)* l'avvolgibile *(f)*

blister la vescica

block of flats il palazzo ;
la palazzina

blocked *(pipe, sink)*
tappato(a)
(road) bloccato(a)

blond *(person)* biondo(a)

blood il sangue

blood group il gruppo
sanguigno

blood pressure la pressione
sanguigna

blood test l'analisi del
sangue *(f)*

blouse la camicetta

to blow-dry asciugare con
il fon

blue *(light)* azzurro(a)
dark blue blu scuro
light blue azzurro(a)

blunt *(knife, blade)* non taglia

boar il cinghiale

to board *(plain, train, etc)*
imbarcarsi su

boarding card/pass la carta
d'imbarco

boarding house la pensione

boat la barca ; il battello
(rowing) la barca a remi

boat trip la gita in battello

body il corpo
(dead) il cadavere

to boil bollire

boiler la caldaia

boiled bollito(a)

bomb la bomba

bone l'osso *(m)*
fish bone la spina di pesce

bonfire il falò

bonnet *(car)* il cofano

book il libro
book of tickets il
blocchetto di biglietti

to book prenotare

booking la prenotazione

booking office *(train)*
la biglietteria

bookshop la libreria

boots *(long)* gli stivali
(ankle) gli stivaletti

border *(of country)* la frontiera

boring noioso(a)

born: to be born essere
nato(a)

to borrow prendere in
prestito

boss il capo

both tutti e due

bottle la bottiglia
a bottle of wine una
bottiglia di vino
a half-bottle una mezza
bottiglia

B

bottle opener l'apribottiglie

bowl (cereal, soup) la scodella

bow tie la cravatta a farfalla

box la scatola

box office il botteghino

boxer shorts i boxer

boy (young child) il bambino (teenage) il ragazzo

boyfriend il ragazzo

bra il reggiseno

bracelet il braccialetto

brain il cervello

to brake frenare

brake fluid il liquido dei freni

brake light il fanalino dello stop

brake pads le pastiglie dei freni

brakes i freni

branch (of tree) il ramo (of bank, etc) la succursale

brand (make) la marca

brass l'ottone (m)

brave coraggioso(a)

bread il pane
  brown bread il pane integrale
  French bread il filoncino
  sliced bread il pancarré

bread roll il panino

to break rompere

breakable fragile

breakdown (car) il guasto (nervous) l'esaurimento nervoso (m)

breakdown van il carro attrezzi

breakfast la (prima) colazione

breast il seno

to breast-feed allattare

to breathe respirare

brick il mattone

bride la sposa

bridegroom lo sposo

bridge il ponte

briefcase la cartella

Brillo-pad la paglietta

to bring portare

Britain la Gran Bretagna

British britannico(a)

broccoli i broccoli

brochure l'opuscolo (m)

broken rotto(a)

broken down (car, etc) guasto(a)

bronchitis la bronchite

bronze il bronzo

brooch la spilla

broom (brush) la scopa

brother il fratello

brother-in-law il cognato

brown marrone

bruise il livido

brush la spazzola

bubble bath il bagnoschiuma

bucket il secchiello

buffet car il vagone ristorante

to build costruire

building l'edificio (m)

bulb *(lightbulb)* la lampadina

bumbag il marsupio

bumper *(on car)* il paraurti

bunch *(of flowers)* il mazzo di fiori

(of grapes) il grappolo d'uva

bungee jumping il bungee jumping

bureau de change l'agenzia di cambio (f)

burger l'hamburger (m)

burglar il/la ladro(a)

burglar alarm l'antifurto (m)

to burn bruciare

bus l'autobus (m)

bus pass la tessera dell'autobus

bus station la stazione delle autolinee

bus stop la fermata (dell'autobus)

bus ticket il biglietto d'autobus

business gli affari

on business per affari

business card il biglietto da visita

business class la business class

businessman/woman l'uomo/la donna d'affari

business trip il viaggio d'affari

busy occupato(a) ; impegnato(a)

but ma ; però

butcher's il macellaio

butter il burro

button il bottone

to buy comprare

by *(next to)* accanto a

(via) via

by bus in autobus

by car in macchina

by train in treno

by ship in battello

bypass *(road)* la circonvallazione

C

cab *(taxi)* il taxi

cabaret il cabaret

cabin *(on boat)* la cabina

cabin crew l'equipaggio di bordo (m)

cablecar la funivia

café il bar

internet café il cyber-café

cafetière la caffettiera

cake *(big)* la torta

(small) il pasticcino

cake shop la pasticceria

calculator la calcolatrice

calendar il calendario

C

call *(phone call)* la chiamata
to call chiamare
  (phone) chiamare per
  telefono
calm calmo(a)
camcorder la videocamera
camera la macchina
  fotografica
camera case la custodia
  della macchina fotografica
to camp campeggiare
camping gas il camping gas
camping stove il fornellino
  da campeggio
campsite il campeggio
can il barattolo ; la scatola
to can *(to be able)* potere
  I can posso
  we can possiamo
  I cannot non posso
  we cannot non possiamo
  can I...? posso...?
  can we...? possiamo...?
Canada il Canada
Canadian canadese
canal il canale
to cancel cancellare ;
  annullare
cancellation la cancellazione
cancer il cancro
candle la candela
canoe la canoa
to canoe andare in canoa
can opener l'apriscatole *(m)*

126

cap *(hat)* il berretto
  (diaphragm) il diaframma
capital *(city)* la capitale
car la macchina
car alarm l'antifurto *(m)*
car ferry il traghetto
car hire l'autonoleggio *(m)*
car insurance l'assicurazione
  della macchina *(f)*
car keys le chiavi della
  macchina
car park il parcheggio
car parts i pezzi di ricambio
car radio l'autoradio *(f)*
car seat *(for children)*
  il seggiolino per bambini
carwash l'autolavaggio *(m)*
carafe la caraffa
caravan la roulotte
carburettor il carburatore
card *(greetings)* il biglietto
  d'auguri
  (business) il biglietto da
  visita
  (playing cards) le carte
  da gioco
cardboard il cartone
cardigan il cardigan
careful attento(a)
  to be careful fare
  attenzione
carpet *(fitted)* la moquette
  (rug) il tappeto
carriage *(railway)* il vagone

carrots le carote
to carry portare
carton il cartone
case *(suitcase)* la valigia
cash i contanti
to cash *(cheque)* incassare
cash desk la cassa
cash dispenser il Bancomat®
cashier il/la cassiere(a)
cashpoint il Bancomat®
casino il casinò
casserole dish la casseruola
cassette la cassetta
cassette player il registratore
castle il castello
casualty department
il pronto soccorso
cat il gatto
cat food il cibo per gatti
catacombs le catacombe
catalogue il catalogo
to catch *(train, etc)* prendere
cathedral il duomo
Catholic cattolico(a)
cave la grotta
cavity *(in tooth)* la carie
CD il CD
CD player il lettore CD
ceiling il soffitto
cellar la cantina
cellphone il cellulare
cemetery il cimitero
centimetre il centimetro

central centrale
central heating il
riscaldamento
central locking *(car)*
la chiusura centralizzata
centre il centro
century il secolo
ceramics la ceramica
cereal *(for breakfast)* i cereali
certificate il certificato
chain la catena
chair la sedia
chairlift la seggiovia
chalet lo chalet
challenge la sfida
chambermaid la cameriera
Champagne lo Champagne
change il cambio
(small coins) gli spiccioli
(money returned) il resto
to change: *to change
money* cambiare soldi
to change clothes cambiarsi
to change train cambiare
treno
changing room
lo spogliatoio
Channel *(English)* la Manica
chapel la cappella
charcoal il carbone
charge *(fee)* la tariffa
to charge addebitare
charge it to my account
lo metta sul mio conto

C

charger *(for battery)* il caricabatterie

charter flight il volo charter

cheap economico(a)
cheaper più economico(a)

cheap rate *(phone)* la tariffa economica

to check controllare

to check in *(airport)* fare il check-in
(at hotel) firmare il registro

check-in il check-in

cheek la guancia

cheers! salute! ; cin-cin!

cheese il formaggio

chef il cuoco

chemist's la farmacia

cheque l'assegno *(m)*

cheque book il libretto degli assegni

cheque card la carta assegni

cherries le ciliegie

chess gli scacchi

chest *(of body)* il petto

chewing gum la gomma da masticare

chicken il pollo

chicken breast il petto di pollo

chickenpox la varicella

child il/la bambino(a)

children *(small)* i bambini
(older children) i ragazzi
for children per bambini

child safety seat *(car)* il seggiolino di sicurezza per bambini

chimney il camino

chin il mento

china la porcellana

chips *(french fries)* le patatine fritte

chocolate la cioccolata

chocolates i cioccolatini

choir il coro

choice la scelta

to choose scegliere

chop *(meat)* la costoletta

chopping board il tagliere

christening il battesimo

Christian name il nome di battesimo

Christmas il Natale
Merry Christmas! Buon Natale!

Christmas card il biglietto d'auguri natalizi

Christmas Eve la vigilia di Natale

church la chiesa

cigar il sigaro

cigarette la sigaretta

cigarette lighter l'accendino

cigarette papers le cartine

cinema il cinema

circle *(theatre)* la galleria

circuit breaker il salvavita

circus il circo

cistern la cisterna
  (of toilet) il serbatoio
  dell'acqua
city la città
city centre il centro città
class: *first class* prima classe
  second class seconda
  classe
clean pulito(a)
to clean pulire
cleaner *(person)* l'addetto(a)
  alle pulizie
cleanser il detergente
clear chiaro(a)
client il/la cliente
cliff *(on coast)* la scogliera
  (mountain) la rupe
to climb scalare
climbing l'alpinismo *(m)*
climbing boots gli scarponi
  da montagna
Clingfilm® la pellicola per
  alimenti
clinic la clinica
cloakroom il guardaroba
clock l'orologio *(m)*
to close chiudere
closed *(shop, etc)* chiuso(a)
cloth il panno
clothes i vestiti
clothes peg la molletta
clothes shop il negozio
  d'abbiglia-mento
cloudy nuvoloso(a)

club il club
clutch *(car)* la frizione
coach il pullman
coach station la stazione
  dei pullman
coach trip la gita in pullman
coal il carbone
coast la costa
coastguard il guardacoste
coat il cappotto
coat hanger la gruccia
cockroach lo scarafaggio
cocktail il cocktail
cocoa il cacao
code il codice
coffee *(espresso)* il caffè
  black coffee il caffè
  americano
  white coffee il caffellatte
  cappuccino il cappuccino
  decaffeinated coffee il
  decaffeinato
coil *(IUD)* la spirale
coin la moneta
Coke® la Coca®
colander lo scolapasta
cold freddo(a)
  I'm cold ho freddo
  it's cold fa freddo
cold *(illness)* il raffreddore
  I have a cold ho il
  raffreddore
cold sore l'herpes *(m)*
Coliseum il Colosseo

C

collar il colletto
collar bone la clavicola
colleague il/la collega
to collect raccogliere
  (to collect someone) andare a prendere
collection *(of stamps)* la collezione
  (of letters) la levata
  (of rubbish) la rimozione
colour il colore
colour-blind daltonico(a)
colour film *(for camera)* la pellicola a colori
comb il pettine
to come venire
  (to arrive) arrivare
to come back tornare
to come in entrare
  come in! avanti!
comedy la commedia
comfortable comodo(a)
company *(firm)* la ditta
compartment lo scompartimento
compass la bussola
to complain fare un reclamo
complaint il reclamo
complete completo(a)
to complete *(finish)* finire
  (form) riempire
compulsory obbligatorio(a)
computer il computer
computer disk il dischetto

computer game il videogioco
computer program il programma di computer
concert il concerto
concert hall la sala da concerti
concession la riduzione
concussion la commozione cerebrale
condensed milk il latte condensato
conditioner il balsamo
condoms i preservativi
conductor *(on bus)* il bigliettaio
cone il cono
conference il congresso
to confirm confermare
confirmation *(of flight, etc)* la conferma
confused confuso(a)
congratulations le congratulazioni
connection *(train, etc)* la coincidenza
constipated stitico(a)
consulate il consolato
to consult consultare
to contact mettersi in contatto con
contact lens cleaner il liquido per lenti a contatto
contact lenses le lenti a contatto
to continue continuare

contraceptive l'anticoncezionale

contract il contratto

convenient: *is it convenient?* va bene?

convulsions le convulsioni

to cook cucinare

cooked cotto(a)

cooker la cucina

cookies i biscotti

cool fresco(a)

cool-box *(picnic)* la borsa termica

copper il rame

copy la copia

to copy copiare

cork il tappo

corkscrew il cavatappi

corner l'angolo *(m)*

cornflakes i cornflakes

corridor il corridoio

cosmetics i cosmetici

to cost costare
how much does it cost? quanto costa?

costume *(swimming)* il costume da bagno

cot il lettino

cottage il cottage

cotton il cotone

cotton bud il cotton fioc®

cotton wool il cotone idrofilo

couchette la cuccetta

cough la tosse

to cough tossire

cough mixture lo sciroppo per la tosse

cough sweets le pasticche per la tosse

counter *(in shop, etc)* il banco

country *(not town)* la campagna *(nation)* il paese

countryside la campagna

couple *(two people)* la coppia
a couple of... un paio di...

courgettes le zucchine

courier service il corriere

course *(of meal)* il piatto *(of study)* il corso

cousin il/la cugino(a)

cover charge il coperto

cow la mucca

crafts l'artigianato *(m)*

craftsperson l'artigiano(a)

cramps i crampi

crash *(car)* lo scontro

to crash *(car)* avere un incidente

crash helmet il casco

cream *(lotion)* la crema *(dairy)* la panna
soured cream la panna acida
whipped cream la panna montata

credit card la carta di credito

D

crime il reato
crisps le patatine
croissant la brioche
to cross (road) attraversare
cross la croce
cross-country skiing lo sci di fondo
crossing (sea, lake) la traversata
crossroads l'incrocio (m)
crossword puzzle il cruciverba
crowd la folla
crowded affollato(a)
crown la corona
cruise la crociera
crutches le grucce
to cry (weep) piangere
crystal (made of) di cristallo
cucumber il cetriolo
cufflinks i gemelli
cul-de-sac il vicolo cieco
cup la tazza
cupboard l'armadio (m)
curlers i bigodini
currant la sultanina
currency: (foreign) currency la valuta (estera)
current la corrente
curtain la tenda
cushion il cuscino
custom (tradition) il costume
customer il/la cliente

customs (duty) la dogana
cut il taglio
to cut tagliare
cutlery le posate
to cycle andare in bicicletta
cycle track la pista ciclabile
cycling il ciclismo
cyst la cisti
cystitis la cistite

D

daily (each day) ogni giorno ; quotidiano(a)
dairy produce i latticini
dam la diga
damage il danno
damp umido(a)
dance il ballo
to dance ballare
danger il pericolo
dangerous pericoloso(a)
dark (colour) scuro(a)
  (night) buio(a)
  after dark a notte fatta
date la data
date of birth la data di nascita
daughter la figlia
daughter-in-law la nuora
dawn l'alba (f)
day il giorno
  per day al giorno

every day ogni giorno
(span of time) la giornata
dead morto(a)
deaf sordo(a)
dear caro(a)
debts i debiti
decaffeinated
decaffeinato(a)
have you decaff coffee?
ha del decaffeinato?
December dicembre
deckchair la sedia a sdraio
to declare dichiarare
nothing to declare niente
da dichiarare
deep profondo(a)
deep freeze il surgelatore
deer il cervo
to defrost scongelare
to de-ice sbrinare
delay il ritardo
how long is the delay?
di quant'è il ritardo?
delayed: to be delayed
(flight) subire un ritardo
delicatessen il negozio di
specialità gastronomiche
delicious delizioso(a)
demonstration la
manifestazione
dental floss il filo
interdentale
dentist il/la dentista
dentures la dentiera

deodorant il deodorante
to depart partire
department il reparto
department store il grande
magazzino
departure la partenza
departure lounge la sala
partenze
deposit il deposito
to describe descrivere
description la descrizione
desk la scrivania
(information, etc) il banco
dessert il dolce
details i dettagli
detergent il detersivo
detour la deviazione
to develop *(photos)*
sviluppare
diabetes il diabete
diabetic diabetico(a)
I'm diabetic sono
diabetico(a)
to dial fare il numero
dialect il dialetto
dialling code il prefisso
telefonico
dialling tone il segnale
di libero
diamond il diamante
diapers i pannolini
diaphragm il diaframma
diarrhoea la diarrea
diary l'agenda *(f)*

D

dice il dado

dictionary il dizionario ;
   il vocabolario

to die morire

diesel il gasolio

diet la dieta
   I'm on a diet sono a dieta
   special diet una dieta
   specifica

different diverso(a)

difficult difficile

to dilute diluire

dinghy *(rubber)* il canotto

dining room la sala da
   pranzo

dinner *(evening meal)* la cena
   to have dinner cenare

dinner jacket lo smoking

direct *(train, etc)* diretto(a)

directions
   to ask for directions
   chiedere la strada

directory *(telephone)*
   l'elenco telefonico *(m)*

directory enquiries il
   servizio informazioni

dirty sporco(a)

disability il handicap

disabled *(person)* disabile ;
   handicap-pato(a)

to disagree non essere
   d'accordo

to disappear scomparire

disaster il disastro

disco la discoteca

discount lo sconto

to discover scoprire

disease la malattia

dishtowel lo strofinaccio dei
   piatti

dishwasher la lavastoviglie

disinfectant il disinfettante

disk *(floppy disk)* il disco

to dislocate *(joint)* lussarsi

disposable *(camera)* usa e
   getta

distance la distanza

distilled water l'acqua
   distillata *(f)*

district *(of town)* il quartiere

to disturb disturbare

to dive tuffarsi

diversion la deviazione

diving i tuffi

divorced divorziato(a)

DIY shop il negozio di
   bricolage

dizzy: *to be dizzy* avere
   il capogiro

to do fare

doctor il medico/la
   dottoressa

documents i documenti

dog il cane

dog food il cibo per cani

dog lead il guinzaglio

doll la bambola

dollars i dollari

domestic *(flight)* nazionale

donor card la tessera dell'A.I.D.O.

door la porta

doorbell il campanello

double doppio(a)

double bed il letto matrimoniale

double room la camera doppia

down: *to go down* scendere

downstairs giù ; dabbasso

drain lo scarico

draught *(of air)* la corrente (d'aria)
there's a draught c'è corrente

draught lager la birra alla spina

drawer il cassetto

drawing il disegno

dress il vestito

to dress *(oneself)* vestirsi

dressing *(for food)* il condimento
(for wound) la fasciatura

dressing gown la vestaglia

drill *(tool)* il trapano

drink *(soft)* la bibita

to drink bere

drinking water l'acqua potabile *(f)*

to drive guidare

driver *(of car)* l'autista *(m/f)*

driving licence la patente

drought la siccità

to drown affogare

drug *(medicine)* il farmaco
(narcotics) la droga

drunk ubriaco(a)

dry secco(a) ; asciutto(a)

to dry asciugare

dry-cleaner's la tintoria ; il lavasecco

dummy *(for baby)* la tettarella

during durante

dust la polvere

duster lo straccio

dustpan and brush lo scopino e la paletta

duty-free esente da dogana

duvet il piumino

duvet cover il copripiumone

dye la tinta

dynamo la dinamo

E

each ogni

ear l'orecchio *(m)*

earache il mal d'orecchi

earlier più presto

early presto

E

to earn guadagnare

earphones le cuffie

earplugs i tappi per le orecchie

earrings gli orecchini

earth la terra

earthquake il terremoto

east l'est (m)

Easter la Pasqua
Happy Easter! Buona Pasqua!

easy facile

to eat mangiare

economy (class) la classe turistica

egg l'uovo (m)
eggs le uova
fried egg l'uovo fritto
hard-boiled egg l'uovo sodo
scrambled eggs le uova strapazzate
soft-boiled egg l'uovo alla coque

either ... or o ... o

elastic band l'elastico (m)

Elastoplast il cerotto

elbow il gomito

electric elettrico(a)

electric blanket la coperta elettrica

electrician m/f l'elettricista

electricity l'elettricità (f)

electricity meter il contatore dell'elettricità

electric razor il rasoio elettrico

electric shock la scossa

elevator l'ascensore (m)

e-mail la posta elettronica ; l'e-mail (f)
to e-mail s.o. mandare un'e-mail a qualcuno

e-mail address l'indirizzo di posta elettronica (m)

embassy l'ambasciata (f)

emergency l'emergenza (f)

emergency exit l'uscita d'emergenza (f)

emery board la limetta per le unghie

empty vuoto(a)

end la fine

engaged (to be married) fidanzato(a)
(phone, toilet, etc) occupato(a)

engine il motore

England l'Inghilterra (f)

English inglese
(language) l'inglese (m)

to enjoy divertirsi
(to like) piacere
I enjoyed the trip la gita mi è piaciuta
I enjoy swimming mi piace nuotare
enjoy your meal! buon appetito!

enough abbastanza
  that's enough basta così

enquiry desk il banco informazioni

to enter entrare

entertainment il divertimento

entrance l'entrata *(f)* ; l'ingresso *(m)*

entrance fee il biglietto d'ingresso

envelope la busta

epileptic epilettico(a)

epileptic fit la crisi epilettica

equal uguale ; pari

equipment l'attrezzatura *(f)*

eraser la gomma da cancellare

error l'errore *(m)*

eruption l'eruzione *(f)*

escalator la scala mobile

to escape fuggire

essential essenziale

estate agent's l'agenzia immobiliare *(f)*

euro l'Euro *(m)*

eurocheque l'eurocheque *(m)*

Europe l'Europa *(f)*

European europeo(a)

European Union l'Unione Europea *(f)*

eve la vigilia

evening la sera
  this evening stasera

tomorrow evening domani sera
  in the evening la sera

evening dress l'abito da sera *(m)*

evening meal la cena

every ogni ; ciascuno ; tutti

everyone tutti

everything tutto

everywhere dappertutto

examination l'esame *(m)*

example: *for example* per esempio

excellent ottimo(a)

except salvo

excess baggage il bagaglio in eccedenza

to exchange cambiare

exchange rate il cambio

exciting emozionante

excursion l'escursione *(f)*

to excuse scusare

excuse me! *(sorry)* mi scusi! *(when passing)* permesso!

exercise l'esercizio *(m)*

exhaust pipe il tubo di scappamento

exhibition la mostra

exit l'uscita *(f)*

expenses le spese

expensive costoso(a) ; caro(a)

expert l'esperto(a)

to expire *(ticket, etc)* scadere

E

to **explain** spiegare

explosion l'esplosione (f)

to **export** esportare

express (train) l'espresso (m)

express (parcel, etc)
espresso(a)

extension (electrical)
la prolunga

extra (spare) in più
(more) supplementare
an extra bed un letto in
più

eye l'occhio (m)

eyebrows le sopracciglia

eye drops il collirio

eyelashes le ciglia

eye shadow l'ombretto (m)

F

fabric la stoffa

face la faccia

face cloth il guanto di spugna

facial la pulizia del viso

facilities (leisure facilities)
le attrezzature

factory la fabbrica

to **fail** fallire

to **faint** svenire

fainted svenuto(a)

fair (just) giusto(a)
(blond) biondo(a)

fair (trade) la fiera
(funfair) il luna park

fake falso(a)

fall (autumn) l'autunno (m)

to **fall** cadere
he/she has fallen
è caduto(a)

false teeth la dentiera

family la famiglia

famous famoso(a)

fan (hand-held) il ventaglio
(electric) il ventilatore
(football) il/la tifoso(a)

fan belt la cinghia della
ventola

fancy dress il costume ;
la maschera

far lontano(a)
is it far? è lontano?

fare la tariffa

farm la fattoria

farmer l'agricoltore (m)

farmhouse la fattoria

fashionable alla moda

fast veloce
too fast troppo veloce

to **fasten** (seatbelt, etc)
allacciare

fat grasso(a)
(noun) il grasso
saturated fats i grassi
saturi
unsaturated fats i grassi
insaturi

father il padre

father-in-law il suocero

fault *(defect)* il difetto
  it's not my fault non è
  colpa mia

favour il favore

favourite preferito(a)

fax il fax
  by fax per fax

to fax mandare un fax

February febbraio

to feed dare da mangiare

to feel sentire ; sentirsi
  I don't feel well non mi
  sento bene
  I feel sick ho la nausea

feet i piedi

felt-tip pen il pennarello

female femmina ; femminile

ferry il traghetto

festival la festa

to fetch *(bring)* portare
  (to go and get) andare a
  prendere

fever la febbre

few pochi
  a few alcuni

fiancé(e) il/la fidanzato(a)

field il campo

to fight combattere ; lottare

file *(folder)* il raccoglitore
  (computer) l'archivio *(m)*

to fill riempire

to fill in *(form)* compilare

fill it up! *(petrol)* il pieno!

fillet il filetto

filling *(dental)* l'otturazione *(f)*

film *(at cinema)* il film
  (for camera) la pellicola

Filofax® l'agenda *(f)*

filter il filtro

to find trovare

fine *(to be paid)* la multa

finger il dito

to finish finire

finished finito(a)

fire il fuoco ; l'incendio *(m)*
  fire! al fuoco!

fire alarm l'allarme
  antincendio *(m)*

fire brigade i vigili del fuoco

fire engine l'autopompa *(f)*

fire escape la scala
  antincendio

fire extinguisher l'estintore

fireplace il caminetto

fireworks i fuochi d'artificio

firm *(company)* l'azienda *(f)* ;
  la ditta

first primo(a)

first aid il pronto soccorso

first aid kit la cassetta di
  pronto soccorso

first class la prima classe

first name il nome di
  battesimo

fish il pesce

to fish pescare

fisherman il pescatore

F

fishing permit la licenza di pesca

fishing rod la canna da pesca

fishmonger's la pescheria

to fit *(clothes)* andare bene
it doesn't fit non va bene

fit *(seizure)* l'attacco *(m)*

to fix riparare ; sistemare
can you fix it? può ripararlo?

fizzy gassato(a)

flag la bandiera

flame la fiamma

flash *(for camera)* il flash

flashlight la pila

flask *(thermos)* il thermos

flat l'appartamento *(m)*

flat piatto(a)
flat battery la batteria scarica
flat tyre la gomma a terra

flavour il gusto
what flavour? che gusto?

flaw il difetto

fleas le pulci

flesh la carne

flex il filo flessibile

flight il volo

flip flops gli infradito

flippers le pinne

flood l'alluvione *(f)*
flash flood l'inondazione *(f)*

floor *(of building)* il piano
(of room) il pavimento

which floor? a che piano?

on the ground floor al pianterreno

on the first floor al primo piano

on the second floor al secondo piano

floorcloth lo straccio per pavimenti

Florence Firenze

florist's shop il fioraio

flour la farina

flowers i fiori

flu l'influenza *(f)*

fly la mosca

to fly volare

flysheet *(tent)* il sopratetto

fog la nebbia

foggy nebbioso(a)

foil *(silver paper)* la carta stagnola

to fold ripiegare

to follow seguire

food il cibo

food poisoning l'intossicazione alimentare *(f)*

foot il piede
on foot a piedi

football il calcio ; il pallone

football match la partita di calcio

football pitch il campo di calcio

football player il calciatore

footpath il sentiero

for per
for me/us per me/noi
for him/her per lui/lei
for you per te/lei/voi

forbidden proibito(a)

forehead la fronte

foreign straniero(a)

foreigner lo/la straniero(a)

forest la foresta

forever per sempre

to forget dimenticare

fork *(for eating)* la forchetta
(in road) il bivio

form *(document)* il modulo

fortnight quindici giorni

forward avanti

foul *(football)* il fallo

fountain la fontana

four-wheel drive con quattro ruote motrici

fox la volpe

fracture la frattura

fragile fragile

fragrance la fragranza

frame *(picture)* la cornice

France la Francia

free *(not occupied)* libero(a)
(costing nothing) gratis

freezer il congelatore

French francese
(language) il francese

French fries le patatine fritte

frequent frequente

fresh fresco(a)

fresh water l'acqua dolce *(f)*

Friday il venerdì

fridge il frigorifero

fried fritto(a)

friend l'amico(a)

friendly amichevole

frog la rana

from da
from Scotland dalla Scozia
from England dall'Inghilterra

front davanti
in front of... di fronte a...

front door la porta d'ingresso

frost la brina

frozen *(food)* surgelato(a)

fruit la frutta
dried fruit la frutta secca

fruit juice il succo di frutta

fruit salad la macedonia

to fry friggere

frying-pan la padella

fuel *(petrol)* la benzina

fuel gauge la spia della benzina

fuel pump la pompa

fuel tank il serbatoio della benzina

full pieno(a)
(occupied) completo(a)

F

full board la pensione completa
fumes *(of car)* i gas di scarico
fun il divertimento
funeral il funerale
funfair il luna park
funny *(amusing)* divertente
fur il pelo
furnished ammobiliato(a)
furniture i mobili
fuse il fusibile
fuse box la scatola dei fusibili
future il futuro

G

gallery la galleria
game il gioco
  (meat) la selvaggina
garage *(private)* il garage
  (for repairs) l'autofficina *(f)*
  (for petrol) la stazione di servizio
garden il giardino
garlic l'aglio *(m)*
gas il gas
gas cooker la cucina a gas
gas cylinder la bombola del gas
gastritis la gastrite
gate il cancello
  (airport) l'uscita *(f)*
gay *(person)* gay

142

gear *(car)* la marcia
  first gear la prima
  second gear la seconda
  third gear la terza
  fourth gear la quarta
  neutral folle
  reverse la retromarcia
gearbox il cambio
generous generoso(a)
gents' *(toilet)* la toilette (per uomini)
genuine *(leather, silver)* vero(a)
  (antique, etc) autentico(a)
German tedesco(a)
  (language) il tedesco
German measles la rosolia
Germany la Germania
to get *(obtain)* ottenere
  (to receive) ricevere
  (to fetch) prendere
to get in/on *(vehicle)* salire in/su
to get off *(bus, etc)* scendere da
gift il regalo
gift shop il negozio di souvenir
girl *(young child)* la bambina
  (teenage) la ragazza
girlfriend la ragazza
to give dare
to give back restituire
glacier il ghiacciaio
glass *(substance)* il vetro
  (for drinking) il bicchiere

a glass of water un bicchiere d'acqua

a glass of wine un bicchiere di vino

glasses *(specs)* gli occhiali

glasses case la custodia degli occhiali

gloves i guanti

glue la colla

to go andare

I'm going to... vado a...

we're going to... andiamo a...

to go back ritornare

to go in entrare in

to go out *(leave)* uscire

goat la capra

God Dio

goggles gli occhialini
(for skiing) gli occhiali da sci

gold l'oro *(m)*

golf il golf

golf ball la pallina da golf

golf clubs le mazze da golf

golf course il campo di golf

good buono(a)
(pleasant) bello(a)
very good ottimo(a)

good afternoon buon giorno
(after 5pm) buona sera

goodbye arrivederci

good day buon giorno

good evening buona sera

good morning buon giorno

good night buona notte

goose l'oca *(f)*

gram il grammo

grandchild il/la nipote

granddaughter la nipotina

grandfather il nonno

grandmother la nonna

grandparents i nonni

grandson il nipotino

grapes l'uva *(f)*

grass l'erba *(f)*

grated grattugiato(a)

grater la grattugia

greasy grasso(a)

great *(big)* grande
(wonderful) fantastico(a)

Great Britain la Gran Bretagna

green verde

green card *(car insurance)* la carta verde

greengrocer's il fruttivendolo

greetings card il biglietto d'auguri

grey grigio(a)

grill la griglia

to grill cuocere alla griglia

grilled alla griglia

grocer's il negozio di alimentari

ground la terra

G

ground floor il pianterreno
 on the ground floor a
 pianterreno
groundsheet il telone
 impermeabile
group il gruppo
guarantee la garanzia
guard *(on train)* il capotreno
guest *(house guest)* l'ospite
 (m/f)
 (in hotel) il/la cliente
guesthouse la pensione
guide *(tourist)* la guida
guidebook la guida
guided tour la visita guidata
guitar la chitarra
gun *(pistol)* la pistola
 (rifle) il fucile
gym *(place)* la palestra
gym shoes le scarpe da
 ginnastica

H

haemorrhoids le emorroidi
hail la grandine
hair i capelli
hairbrush la spazzola per
 capelli
haircut il taglio di capelli
hairdresser il parrucchiere/
 la parrucchiera
hair dryer il fon
hair dye la tintura per capelli

hair gel il gel per capelli
hairgrip la molletta per
 capelli
hair mousse la spuma
hair spray la lacca per capelli
half la metà
 a half bottle of... una
 mezza bottiglia di...
 half an hour mezz'ora
half board mezza pensione
half fare il ridotto
half-price metà prezzo
ham *(cooked)* il prosciutto
 cotto
 (cured) il prosciutto crudo
hamburger l'hamburger *(m)*
hammer il martello
hand la mano
handbag la borsa
handicapped disabile ;
 handicappato(a)
handkerchief il fazzoletto
handle il manico
handlebars il manubrio
hand luggage il bagaglio a
 mano
hand-made fatto a mano
hands-free phone il telefono
 viva voce
handsome bello(a)
hanger *(coat hanger)* la gruccia
 per abiti
hang gliding il volo con
 deltaplano

hangover i postumi della sbornia

to happen succedere
what happened? cos'è successo?

happy felice
happy birthday! buon compleanno!

harbour il porto

hard duro(a)
(difficult) difficile

hardware shop il negozio di ferramenta

to harm nuocere

harvest il raccolto ; la vendemmia

hat il cappello

to have avere
I have... ho...
I don't have... non ho...
we have... abbiamo...
we don't have... non abbiamo...
do you have...? ha/hai/avete...?

to have to dovere

hay fever il raffreddore da fieno

he egli ; lui

head la testa

headache il mal di testa
I have a headache ho mal di testa

headlights i fari

headphones la cuffia

health la salute

health-food shop l'erboristeria *(f)*

healthy sano(a)

to hear sentire

hearing aid l'apparecchio acustico *(m)*

heart il cuore

heart attack l'infarto *(m)*

heartburn il bruciore di stomaco

to heat up *(food)* riscaldare

heater il termosifone

heating il riscaldamento

heavy pesante

heel il tallone

heel bar il banco del calzolaio

height l'altezza *(f)*

helicopter l'elicottero *(m)*

hello! salve! ; ciao!
(on telephone) pronto

helmet il casco

help! aiuto!

to help aiutare
can you help me? può aiutarmi?

hem l'orlo *(m)*

hepatitis l'epatite *(f)*

her il/la suo(a)
her passport il suo passaporto
her room la sua camera

herb l'erba aromatica *(f)*

H

herbal tea la tisana

here qui
here is... ecco...
here is my passport ecco il mio passaporto

hernia l'ernia *(f)*

hi! ciao!

to hide nascondere

high alto(a)
(speed) forte

high blood pressure la pressione alta

high chair il seggiolone

hill la collina

hill-walking il trekking

him lui ; lo ; gli

hip l'anca *(f)*

hip replacement la protesi dell'anca

hire il noleggio
car hire il noleggio auto
bike hire il noleggio bici
boat hire il noleggio barche
ski hire il noleggio sci

to hire noleggiare

hired car la macchina a noleggio

his il/la suo(a)
his passport il suo passaporto
his room la sua camera

historic storico(a)

history la storia

to hit colpire

to hitchhike fare l'autostop

hobby il passatempo

to hold tenere
(to contain) contenere

hold-up *(traffic)* l'ingorgo *(m)*

hole il buco

holiday la festa
on holiday in vacanza

holiday rep il/la rappresentante dell'agenzia di viaggio

home la casa
at home a casa

homesick: to be homesick avere nostalgia di casa
I'm homesick ho nostalgia di casa

homosexual omosessuale

honest onesto(a)

honey il miele

honeymoon la luna di miele

hood *(on jacket)* il cappuccio

hook *(for fishing)* l'amo *(m)*

to hope sperare
I hope so/not spero di sì/no

hors d'œuvre l'antipasto *(m)*

horse il cavallo

horse racing l'ippica *(f)*

to horse-ride andare a cavallo

hosepipe la canna dell'acqua

hospital l'ospedale *(m)*

hostel l'ostello *(m)*

hot caldo(a)

I'm hot ho caldo
it's hot (weather) fa caldo

hot-water bottle la borsa dell'acqua calda

hotel l'albergo (m) ; l'hotel (m)

hour l'ora (f)
half an hour mezz'ora
1 hour un'ora
2 hour due ore

house la casa

housewife la casalinga

house wine il vino della casa

housework i lavori di casa

how? (in what way) come?
how much? quanto(a)?
how many? quanti(e)?
how are you? come sta?

hungry: to be hungry avere fame

hunt la caccia

to hunt andare a caccia

hunting permit la licenza di caccia

hurry: I'm in a hurry ho fretta

to hurt fare male
that hurts fa male

husband il marito

hut (bathing/beach) la cabina (mountain) la baita

hydrofoil l'aliscafo (m)

hypodermic needle l'ago ipodermico (m)

I io

ice il ghiaccio
with ice con ghiaccio
without ice senza ghiaccio

ice box il freezer

ice cream il gelato

iced coffee il caffè freddo

iced tea il tè freddo

ice lolly il ghiacciolo

ice rink la pista di pattinaggio su ghiaccio

to ice skate pattinare sul ghiaccio

ice skates i pattini da ghiaccio

idea l'idea (f)

identity card la carta d'identità

if se

ignition l'accensione (f)

ignition key la chiave dell'accensione

ill malato(a)
I'm ill sto male

illness la malattia

immediately subito

immersion heater lo scaldabagno elettrico

immigration l'immigrazione (f)

immunisation l'immunizzazione (f)

to import importare

I

important importante

impossible impossibile

to improve migliorare

in in
  in 2 hours in due ore
  in London a Londra

in front of davanti a

included compreso(a) ;
  incluso(a)

inconvenient scomodo(a)

to increase aumentare
  to increase volume alzare
  il volume

indicator (in car) la freccia

indigestion l'indigestione (f)

indigestion tablets le
  compresse per digerire

indoors dentro ; al chiuso

infection l'infezione (f)

infectious contagioso(a)

informal (clothes) sportivo(a)

information le informazioni

information office l'ufficio
  informazioni (m)

ingredients gli ingredienti

inhaler l'inalatore (m)

injection l'iniezione (f) ;
  la puntura

to injure ferire

injured ferito(a)

injury la lesione

ink l'inchiostro (m)

inn la locanda

inner tube la camera d'aria

inquiries le informazioni

insect l'insetto (m)

insect bite la puntura
  d'insetto

insect repellent l'insettifugo

inside dentro

instant coffee il caffè
  solubile

instead of invece di

instructor l'istruttore/
  l'istruttrice

insulin l'insulina (f)

insurance l'assicurazione (f)

insurance certificate il
  certificato di assicurazione

to insure assicurare

insured: *to be insured*
  essere assicurato(a)

to intend to avere
  intenzione di

interesting interessante

international internazionale

internet l'Internet (m)

internet café il cyber-café

interpreter l'interprete (m/f)

interval l'intervallo (m)

interview l'intervista (f)

into in
  into town in città
  into the centre in centro

to introduce someone to
  presentare qualcuno a

invitation l'invito (m)

to invite invitare

invoice la fattura

Ireland l'Irlanda *(f)*

Irish irlandese

iron *(for clothes)* il ferro da stiro
(metal) il ferro

to iron stirare

ironing board l'asse da stiro

ironmonger's il negozio di ferramenta

is è

island l'isola *(f)*

it lo/la

Italian italiano(a)
(language) l'italiano *(m)*

Italy l'Italia *(f)*

to itch prudere
my leg itches mi prude la gamba
my eyes itch mi prudono gli occhi

item *(on bill)* la voce

itemised bill il conto dettagliato

J

jack *(for car)* il cric

jacket la giacca
waterproof jacket il giaccone impermeabile

jam *(food)* la marmellata

jammed bloccato(a)

January gennaio

jar *(honey, jam, etc)* il vaso

jaundice l'itterizia *(f)*

jaw la mascella

jealous geloso(a) ; invidioso(a)

jeans i blue jeans

jelly *(dessert)* la gelatina

jellyfish la medusa

jet ski l'acqua-scooter *(m)*

jetty il molo

jeweller's la gioielleria

jewellery i gioielli

Jewish ebreo(a)

job il lavoro

to jog fare jogging

to join *(club)* iscriversi a

to join in *(game)* participare a

joint *(hip, etc)* l'articolazione *(f)*

joke lla barzelletta
(practical) lo scherzo *(m)*

to joke scherzare

journalist il/la giornalista

journey il viaggio

judge il/la giudice *(m/f)*

jug la brocca

juice il succo
a carton of juice un cartone di succo di frutta

July luglio

to jump saltare

jumper il maglione

jump leads *(for car)* i cavi per far partire la macchina

J

junction (road) l'incrocio (m)

June giugno

just: just two solamente due
  I've just arrived sono
  appena arrivato(a)

K

to keep (retain) tenere
  keep the change! tenga il
  resto

kennel il canile

kettle il bollitore

key la chiave
  card key il passe-partout

keyboard la tastiera

keyring il portachiavi

to kick dare calci a

kid (child) il bambino

kidneys (in body) i reni

to kill uccidere

kilo il chilo
  a kilo of apples un chilo
  di mele
  2 kilos due chili

kilogram il chilogrammo

kilometre il chilometro

kind (sort) il tipo

kind (person) gentile

king il re

kiosk l'edicola (f)

kiss il bacio

to kiss baciare

kitchen la cucina

kitchen paper la carta
  assorbente da cucina

kite l'aquilone (m)

knee il ginocchio

knee highs i gambaletti

knickers le mutandine

knife il coltello

to knit lavorare a maglia

to knock (on door) bussare

to knock down (car)
  investire

to knock over (glass, vase)
  rovesciare

knot il nodo

to know (facts) sapere
  (to be acquainted with)
  conoscere
  I don't know non lo so

to know how to sapere
  to know how to swim
  saper nuotare

kosher kasher

L

label l'etichetta (f)

lace il pizzo

laces (shoe) i lacci

ladder la scala

ladies' (toilet) la toilette
  (per signore)

lady la signora

lager la birra (bionda)

lake il lago

lamb l'agnello *(m)*
lame zoppo(a)
lamp la lampada
lamppost il lampione
lampshade il paralume
land la terra
to land *(plane)* atterrare
landlady la padrona di casa
landlord il padrone di casa
landslide la frana
lane la stradina
  (of motorway) la corsia
language la lingua
language school la scuola
  di lingue
laptop il laptop
large grande
last ultimo(a) ; scorso(a)
  the last bus l'ultimo
  autobus
  the last train l'ultimo treno
  last night ieri notte
  last week la settimana
  scorsa
  last year l'anno scorso
  last time l'ultima volta
late tardi
  the train's late il treno è
  in ritardo
  sorry we're late scusi il
  ritardo
later più tardi
to laugh ridere
launderette la lavanderia
  automatica

laundry il bucato
lavatory la toilette
lavender la lavanda
law la legge
lawn il prato inglese
lawyer *(m/f)*
  l'avvocato/l'avvocatessa
laxative il lassativo
layby la piazzola di sosta
lazy pigro(a)
lead *(electric)* il filo
lead *(metal)* il piombo
lead-free senza piombo
leaf la foglia
leak *(of gas, liquid)* la perdita
  (in roof) il buco
to leak: *it's leaking* perde
to learn imparare
lease *(rental)* l'affitto *(m)*
leather il cuoio ; la pelle
to leave *(leave behind)*
  lasciare
  (train, bus, etc) partire
  when does the bus leave?
  quando parte l'autobus?
  *when does the train
  leave?* quando parte il
  treno?
left la sinistra
  on/to the left a sinistra
left-handed mancino(a)
left-luggage il deposito
  bagagli

L

left-luggage locker
l'armadietto per
despositare i bagagli *(m)*
leg la gamba
lemon il limone
lemonade la limonata
to lend prestare
length la lunghezza
lens *(camera)* l'obiettivo *(m)*
(contact lens) la lente a
contatto
lenses le lenti
lesbian lesbica
less meno
less than meno di
lesson la lezione
to let *(allow)* permettere
(to hire out) affittare
letter la lettera
letterbox la cassetta delle
lettere
lettuce la lattuga
level crossing il passaggio
a livello
library la biblioteca
licence il permesso
(driving) la patente
lid il coperchio
to lie mentire
lie *(untruth)* la bugia
to lie down sdraiarsi
life belt il salvagente
lifeboat la scialuppa di
salvataggio

lifeguard il bagnino
life insurance l'assicurazione
sulla vita *(f)*
life jacket il giubbotto
salvagente
life raft la zattera di
salvataggio
lift *(elevator)* l'ascensore *(m)*
(in car) il passaggio
light *(not heavy)* leggero(a)
(colour) chiaro(a)
light la luce
have you a light? ha da
accendere?
light bulb la lampadina
lighter l'accendino *(m)*
lighthouse il faro
lightning il fulmine
like come
to like piacere
I like coffee mi piace il
caffè
I don't like... non mi piace...
I'd/we'd like... vorrei/
vorremmo...
lilo il materassino
lime *(fruit)* il cedro
line *(row, queue)* la fila
(telephone) la linea
linen il lino
lingerie la biancheria intima
da donna
lip reading la labiolettura
lips le labbra

lip salve il burro di cacao

lipstick il rossetto

liqueur il liquore

list l'elenco *(m)* ; la lista

to listen (to) ascoltare

litre il litro
  a litre of milk un litro di latte

litter *(rubbish)* i rifiuti

little *(small)* piccolino(a)
  a little… un po' di…

to live vivere ; abitare
  I live in London vivo a
  Londra
  he lives in a flat abita in
  un appartamento

liver il fegato

living room il salotto

loaf of bread la pagnotta

local locale

to lock chiudere a chiave

lock la serratura
  the lock is broken
  la serratura è rotta

locker l'armadietto *(m)*

locksmith il fabbro

log book *(car)* il libretto
  di circolazione

logs i ceppi

lollipop il lecca lecca

London Londra
  in/to London a Londra

long lungo(a)
  for a long time molto
  tempo

long-sighted presbite

to look after prendersi cura di

to look at guardare

to look for cercare

loose *(not fastened)* slegato(a)
  it's come loose (knot) si è
  allentato(a)

lorry il camion

to lose perdere

lost *(object)* perso(a)
  I've lost my… ho perso il/la…
  I'm lost mi sono smarrito(a)
  we're lost ci siamo
  smarriti(e)

lost property office l'ufficio
  oggetti smarriti *(m)*

lot: a lot molto

lottery la lotteria

loud forte

lounge *(in hotel)* il salone
  (in house) la sala
  (in airport) la sala d'attesa

love l'amore *(m)*

to love *(person)* amare
  I love you ti amo
  I love swimming mi piace
  nuotare

lovely bellissimo(a)

low basso(a)
  (standard, quality) scadente

low-alcohol a basso
  contenuto alcolico

to lower volume abbassare
  il volume

low-fat magro(a)

L

luck la fortuna
lucky fortunato(a)
luggage i bagagli
luggage rack il portabagagli
luggage tag l'etichetta (f)
luggage trolley il carrello
lump (swelling) il gonfiore
lunch il pranzo
lunch break l'intervallo del pranzo (m)
lung il polmone
luxury di lusso

M

machine la macchina
mad (insane) matto(a)
(angry) arrabbiato(a)
magazine la rivista
maggot il verme
magnet la calamita
magnifying glass la lente d'ingrandimento
maid (in hotel) la cameriera
maiden name il nome da ragazza
mail la posta
main principale
main course (meal) il secondo
main road la strada principale

to make (generally) fare
(meal) preparare
make-up il trucco
male maschio ; maschile
mallet la mazza
man l'uomo (m)
to manage (be in charge of) dirigere
manager il direttore ; il gerente
manual (gear change) manuale
many molti(e)
map (of country) la carta geografica
(city) la piantina
marble il marmo
March marzo
margarine la margarina
marina il porticciolo
mark (stain) la macchia ; il segno
(brand) la marca
market il mercato
where is the market?
dov'è il mercato?
when is the market?
quando c'è il mercato?
marmalade la marmellata d'arancia
married sposato(a)
I'm married sono sposato(a)
are you married?
è sposato(a)?

marry: *to get married*
sposarsi

marsh la palude

mascara il mascara

mass *(in church)* la messa

mast l'albero *(m)*

masterpiece il capolavoro

match *(game)* la partita

matches i fiammiferi

material il materiale
(cloth) il tessuto

to matter importare
it doesn't matter non
importa
what's the matter? cosa
c'è?

mattress il materasso

May maggio

mayonnaise la maionese

mayor il/la sindaco(a)

maximum il massimo

me me ; mi

meal il pasto

to mean *(signify)* voler dire
what does it mean? cosa
vuol dire?

measles il morbillo

to measure misurare

meat la carne

mechanic il meccanico

medical insurance
l'assicurazione medica *(f)*

medical treatment le cure
mediche

medicine la medicina

Mediterranean
il Mediterraneo

medium rare *(steak)* poco
cotto(a)

to meet incontrare
pleased to meet you!
piacere!

meeting la riunione
(by chance) l'incontro *(m)*

meeting point il meeting
point

to melt sciogliere

member *(of club, etc)*
il/la socio(a)

membership card la tessera

memory la memoria
(memories) i ricordi

men gli uomini

to mend riparare

meningitis la meningite

menu il menù
set menu il menù a prezzo
fisso ; il menù turistico
à la carte menu il menù
alla carta

message il messaggio

metal il metallo

meter il contatore

metre il metro

metro *(underground)*
la metropolitana

metro station la stazione
del metrò

microwave oven il forno a microonde

midday il mezzogiorno
at midday a mezzogiorno

middle il mezzo

middle-aged di mezz'età

midge il moscerino

midnight la mezzanotte
at midnight a mezzanotte

migraine l'emicrania *(f)*
I have a migraine ho l'emicrania

Milan Milano

mild dolce ; mite

milk il latte
fresh milk il latte fresco
hot milk il latte caldo
long-life milk il latte a lunga conservazione
powdered milk il latte in polvere
whole milk il latte intero
semi-skimmed milk il latte parzialmente scremato
soya milk il latte di soia
with/without milk con/senza latte

milkshake il frappé ; il frullato

millimetre il millimetro

mince *(meat)* la carne macinata

mind: do you mind? le dà fastidio?
I don't mind non mi dà fastidio

mineral water l'acqua minerale *(f)*

minibar il minibar

minimum il minimo

minister *(church)* il sacerdote
(political) il ministro

minor road la strada secondaria

mint *(herb)* la menta

mint tea il tè alla menta

minute il minuto

mirror lo specchio

to misbehave comportarsi male

miscarriage l'aborto spontaneo *(m)*

to miss *(train, etc)* perdere

Miss Signorina

missing *(thing)* smarrito(a)
(person) scomparso(a)

mistake l'errore *(m)*

misty nebbioso(a)

misunderstanding il malinteso

to mix mescolare

mobile phone il cellulare

modem il modem

modern moderno(a)

moisturizer l'idratante *(m)*

mole *(on skin)* il neo

moment: just a moment un momento

monastery il monastero

Monday il lunedì

money i soldi
I have no money non ho soldi

money belt il marsupio

money order il vaglia

month il mese
this month questo mese
last month il mese scorso
next month il mese prossimo

monthly mensilmente

monument il monumento

moon la luna

mooring l'ormeggio *(m)*

mop lo straccio da terra

moped il motorino

more (than) più (di)
more than 3 più di tre
more wine ancora un po' di vino

morning la mattina
in the morning di mattina
this morning stamattina
tomorrow morning domani mattina

morning-after pill la pillola del giorno dopo

mosquito la zanzara

mosquito net la zanzariera

mosquito repellent lo zanzarifugo

most il/la più ; il massimo

moth *(clothes)* la tarma

mother la madre

mother-in-law la suocera

motor il motore

motorbike la moto

motorboat il motoscafo

motorway l'autostrada *(f)*

mould la muffa

mountain la montagna

mountain bike la mountain bike

mountain rescue il soccorso alpino

mountaineering l'alpinismo *(m)*

mouse il topo
(computer) il mouse

moustache i baffi

mouth la bocca

mouthwash il colluttorio

move muoversi
it isn't moving non si muove

movie il film

Mr Signor

Mrs Signora

Ms Signora

much molto
too much troppo

muddy *(ground)* fangoso(a)

mugging lo scippo

mumps gli orecchioni

muscle il muscolo

museum il museo

mushrooms i funghi

music la musica

musical il musical

mussels le cozze

M

must *(to have to)* dovere
 I must devo
 we must dobbiamo
 I mustn't non devo
 we mustn't non dobbiamo

mustard la senape

my il/la mio(a)
 my passport il mio passaporto
 my room la mia camera

N

nail *(metal)* il chiodo
 (fingernail) l'unghia *(f)*

nailbrush lo spazzolino per le unghie

nail clipper il tagliaunghie

nail file la limetta per le unghie

nail polish/varnish lo smalto per le unghie

nail polish remover l'acetone *(m)*

nail scissors le forbicine

name il nome
 my name is... mi chiamo...
 what is your name? come si chiama?

nanny la bambinaia

napkin il tovagliolo

Naples Napoli

nappies i pannolini

narrow stretto(a)

national nazionale

national park il parco nazionale

nationality la nazionalità

natural naturale

nature la natura

nature reserve la riserva naturale

navy blue blu marino

near to vicino(a)
 is it near? è vicino?
 near the bank vicino alla banca

necessary necessario(a)

neck il collo

necklace la collana

nectarine la nocepesca

to need avere bisogno di...
 I need... ho bisogno di...
 we need... abbiamo bisogno di...

needle l'ago *(m)*
 a needle and thread un ago e filo

negative *(photo)* il negativo

neighbour il/la vicino(a)

nephew il nipote

net la rete
 the Net l'Internet *(m)*

never mai
 I never drink wine non bevo mai il vino

new nuovo(a)

news le notizie
 (on television) il telegiornale

newsagent's il giornalaio

newspaper il giornale

newsstand l'edicola *(f)*

New Year il Capodanno
happy New Year! buon
Anno!

New Year's Eve la notte
di San Silvestro ; l'ultimo
dell'anno *(m)*

New Zealand la Nuova
Zelanda

next prossimo(a)
next to accanto(a) a
next week la settimana
prossima
the next bus il prossimo
autobus
the next train il prossimo
treno
the next stop la prossima
fermata

nice piacevole
(person) simpatico(a)

niece la nipote

night la notte
at night di notte
last night ieri notte
per night a notte
tomorrow night domani
sera
tonight stasera

nightclub il nightclub

nightdress la camicia da
notte

night porter il portiere
notturno

no no
no entry vietato l'ingresso
no smoking vietato fumare
no thanks no, grazie
(without) senza
no sugar senza zucchero
no ice senza ghiaccio
no problem non c'è
problema

nobody nessuno

noise il rumore

noisy rumoroso(a)
it's very noisy è molto
rumoroso(a)

non-alcoholic analcolico(a)

none nessuno(a)

non-smoker non-fumatore

non-smoking per non-
fumatori

north il nord

Northern Ireland l'Irlanda
del Nord *(f)*

nose il naso

not non
I do not know non lo so

note *(bank note)*
la banconota
(letter) il biglietto

note pad il bloc-notes

nothing niente
nothing else nient'altro

notice l'avviso *(m)*

notice board la bacheca

novel il romanzo

November novembre

N

now adesso

nowhere da nessuna parte

nuclear nucleare

nudist beach la spiaggia nudista

number il numero

number plate *(car)* la targa

nurse l'infermiera/ l'infermiere *(f/m)*

nursery *(children's)* l'asilo *(m)* *(for plants)* il vivaio

nursery slope la pista per principianti

nut *(to eat)* la noce *(for bolt)* il dado

O

oars i remi

oats l'avena *(f)*

to obtain ottenere

occupation *(work)* il lavoro

ocean l'oceano *(m)*

October ottobre

octopus il polpo

odd *(strange)* strano(a)

of di
a bottle of wine una bottiglia di vino
a glass of water un bicchiere d'acqua
made of... fatto di...

off *(machine, etc)* spento(a) *(milk, food)* andato(a) a male

this meat is off questa carne è andata a male

office l'ufficio *(m)*

often spesso
how often? ogni quanto?

oil l'olio *(m)*

oil filter il filtro dell'olio

oil gauge l'indicatore del livello dell'olio *(m)*

ointment la pomata

OK! va bene!

old vecchio(a)
how old are you? quanti anni ha?
I'm ... years old ho ... anni

old age pensioner il/la pensionato(a)

olive oil l'olio d'oliva *(m)*

olives le olive

on *(light, engine)* acceso(a) *(tap)* aperto(a)
on the table sulla tavola
on time in orario

once una volta
at once subito

one-way *(street)* a senso unico

onions le cipolle

only solo(a)

open aperto(a)

to open aprire

opera l'opera *(f)*

operation l'operazione *(f)*

operator *(telephone)* il/la centralinista

opposite di fronte a
   opposite the hotel
   di fronte all'albergo
   quite the opposite
   al contrario
optician's l'ottico *(m)*
or o
orange *(colour)* arancione
orange *(fruit)* l'arancia *(f)*
orange juice il succo
   d'arancia
orchestra l'orchestra *(f)*
order l'ordine *(f)*
   out of order fuori servizio
to order *(food, etc)* ordinare
oregano l'origano *(m)*
organic biologico(a)
to organize organizzare
ornament il soprammobile
other l'altro(a)
   the other one l'altro
   have you any others?
   ce ne sono altri?
our il/la nostro(a)
   our car la nostra macchina
   our hotel il nostro albergo
out *(light)* spento(a)
   he/she's out è fuori
   he's gone out è uscito
outdoor *(pool, etc)* all'aperto
outside: it's outside è fuori
oven il forno
ovenproof dish la pirofila
over *(on top of)* sopra

to overbook accettare
   troppe prenotazioni
to overcharge far pagare
   troppo
overdone *(food)* troppo
   cotto(a)
overdose l'overdose *(f)*
to overheat surriscaldare
to overload sovraccaricare
to oversleep non svegliarsi
   in tempo
to overtake sorpassare
to owe dovere
   I owe you... le devo...
   you owe me... mi deve
owner il/la proprietario(a)
oxygen l'ossigeno *(m)*

P

pace il passo
pacemaker il pacemaker
to pack *(suitcase)* fare la valigia
package il pacco
package tour il viaggio
   organizzato
packet il pacchetto
padded envelope la busta
   imbottita
paddling pool la piscina per
   bambini
padlock il lucchetto
Padua Padova
page la pagina

P

paid pagato(a)
I've paid ho pagato
pain il dolore
painful doloroso(a)
painkiller l'analgesico (m)
to paint (wall, etc) verniciare
(picture) dipingere
painting (picture) il quadro
pair il paio
palace il palazzo
pale pallido(a)
pan (saucepan) la pentola
(frying pan) la padella
pancake la crêpe
panties le mutandine
pants le mutande
panty liner il proteggislip
paper la carta
paper hankies i fazzolettini
di carta
paper napkins i tovaglioloni
di carta
paragliding il parapendio
paralysed paralizzato(a)
parcel il pacco
pardon? scusi?
I beg your pardon mi scusi
parents i genitori
park il parco
to park parcheggiare
parking disk il disco orario
parking meter il parchimetro
parking ticket (fine) la multa
per sosta vietata

parmesan il parmigiano
grated parmesan
il parmigiano grattugiato
part la parte
partner (business) il/la socio(a)
(boy/girlfriend) il/la
compagno(a)
party (celebration) la festa
(political) il partito
pass (mountain) il valico
(bus, train) la tessera
passenger il/la passeggero(a)
passport il passaporto
passport control il controllo
passaporti
pasta la pasta
pastry la pasta
(fancy cake) il pasticcino
path il sentiero
patient (in hospital) il/la
paziente
pavement il marciapiede
to pay pagare
I want to pay vorrei
pagare
where do I pay? dove pago?
payment il pagamento
payphone il telefono pubblico
peace la pace
peaches le pesche
peak rate la tariffa nelle ore
di punta
peanut allergy l'allergia alle
arachidi (f)

162

pearls le perle

pears le pere

peas i piselli

pedal il pedale

pedalo il pedalò

pedestrian il pedone

pedestrian crossing il passaggio pedonale

to pee fare la pipì

to peel (fruit) sbucciare

peg (for clothes) la molletta (for tent) il picchetto

pen la penna

pencil la matita

penfriend l'amico(a) di penna

penicillin la penicillina

penis il pene

penknife il temperino

pension la pensione

pensioner il/la pensionato(a)

people la gente

pepper (spice) il pepe (vegetable) il peperone

per per
per day al giorno
per hour all'ora
per week alla settimana
per person a persona
100 km per hour 100 km all'ora

perfect perfetto(a)

performance la rappresentazione

perfume il profumo

perhaps forse

period (menstrual) le mestruazioni

perm la permanente

permit il permesso

person la persona

personal organizer l'agenda elettronica (f)

personal stereo il walkman®

pet l'animale domestico (m)

pet food il cibo per gli animali domestici

pet shop il negozio di animali domestici

petrol la benzina
4-star petrol la super
unleaded petrol la benzina senza piombo

petrol cap il tappo del serbatoio

petrol tank il serbatoio della benzina

petrol pump la pompa della benzina

petrol station la stazione di servizio

pharmacy la farmacia

phone il telefono
by phone per telefono

to phone telefonare

phonebook l'elenco telefonico (m)

phonebox la cabina telefonica

P

phonecard la scheda
telefonica
photocopy la fotocopia
I need a photocopy mi
serve una fotocopia
to photocopy fotocopiare
photograph la foto
to take a photo fare una
foto
phrase book il manuale di
conversazione
piano il pianoforte
to pick *(fruit, flowers)* cogliere
(to choose) scegliere
pickpocket il borseggiatore
pickle i sottaceti
picnic il picnic
to have a picnic fare un
picnic
picnic hamper il cestino
per il picnic
picnic rug il plaid
picnic table il tavolo da picnic
picture *(painting)* il quadro
(photo) la foto
pie *(sweet)* la torta
(savoury) il pasticcio
piece il pezzo
pier il pontile
pig il maiale
pill la pillola
to be on the pill prendere
la pillola
pillow il guanciale ; il cuscino
pillowcase la federa

pilot il pilota
pin lo spillo
pink rosa
pipe *(water, etc)* il tubo
(smoker's) la pipa
pity: what a pity! che
peccato!
pizza la pizza
place il luogo
place of birth il luogo
di nascita
plain *(obvious)* chiaro(a)
(unflavoured) naturale
plait la treccia
plan il piano
to plan progettare
plane l'aereo *(m)*
plant la pianta
plaster *(sticking)* il cerotto
(for broken limb) l'ingessatura
plastic *(made of)* di plastica
plastic bag il sacchetto di
plastica
plate il piatto
platform *(railway)* il binario
from which platform?
da quale binario?
play *(theatre)* la commedia
to play *(games)* giocare
play area l'area giochi *(f)*
playground il parco giochi
play park il parco giochi
playroom la stanza dei
giochi

pleasant piacevole

please per favore

pleased: *pleased to meet you* piacere

plenty l'abbondanza *(f)*

pliers le pinze

plug *(electrical)* la spina *(for sink)* il tappo

to plug in attaccare

plum la prugna ; la susina

plumber l'idraulico *(m)*

plumbing l'impianto idraulico *(m)*

plunger lo sturalavandini

p.m. del pomeriggio

poached *(egg)* in camicia *(fish)* bollito(a)

pocket la tasca

points *(in car)* le puntine

poison il veleno

poisonous velenoso(a)

police la polizia

policeman/woman il poliziotto/la donna poliziotto

police station il commissariato ; la questura

polish *(for shoes)* il lucido *(for furniture)* la cera

pollen il polline

polluted inquinato(a)

pony il pony

pony trekking le escursioni a cavallo

pool *(swimming)* la piscina

pool attendant il bagnino

poor povero(a)

pope il papa

pop socks i gambaletti

pork la carne di maiale

port *(seaport, wine)* il porto

porter il portiere *(for luggage)* il facchino

portion la porzione

Portugal il Portogallo

Portuguese portoghese

possible possibile

post: *by post* per posta

to post *(letters, etc)* imbucare

postbox la buca delle lettere

postcard la cartolina

postcode il codice postale

poster il poster

postman/woman il/la postino(a)

post office la posta ; l'ufficio postale *(m)*

to postpone rimandare

pot *(cooking)* la pentola

potato la patata
baked potato la patata al forno
boiled potatoes le patate lesse
fried potatoes le patate fritte
mashed potatoes il purè di patate

P

roast potatoes le patate arrosto

potato masher
lo schiacciapatate

potato peeler il pelapatate

potato salad l'insalata di patate *(f)*

pothole la buca

pottery la terracotta

pound *(money)* la sterlina

to pour versare

powder: *in powder form* in polvere

powdered milk il latte in polvere

power *(electricity)* l'elettricità

power cut l'interruzione di corrente *(f)*

pram la carrozzina

to pray pregare

to prefer preferire

pregnant incinta
I'm pregnant sono incinta

to prepare preparare

to prescribe ordinare

prescription la ricetta

present *(gift)* il regalo

preservative il conservante

president il presidente

pressure: *tyre pressure* la pressione dei pneumatici
blood pressure la pressione del sangue

pretty carino(a)

price il prezzo

price list il listino prezzi

priest il prete

print *(photo)* la foto

printer la stampante

prison il carcere ; la prigione

private privato(a)

prize il premio

probably probabilmente

problem il problema

professor il professore/ la professoressa

programme il programma

prohibited proibito(a)

promise la promessa

to promise promettere

to pronounce pronunciare
how's it pronounced? come si pronuncia?

protein la proteina

Protestant protestante

to provide fornire

public pubblico(a)

public holiday la festa nazionale

pudding il dessert

to pull tirare

to pull over *(car)* accostare

pullover il pullover ; il maglione

pump la pompa

puncture la gomma a terra

ENGLISH–ITALIAN

puncture repair kit il kit per riparare le gomme

puppet il burattino

puppet show lo spettacolo di burattini

purple viola

purse il borsellino

to push spingere

pushchair il passeggino

to put *(to place)* mettere

to put back rimettere

pyjamas il pigiama

Q

quality la qualità

quantity la quantità

quarantine la quarantena

to quarrel litigare

quarter: *a quarter* un quarto

quay il molo

queen la regina

question la domanda

queue la coda

to queue fare la coda

quick veloce

quickly velocemente

quiet *(place)* tranquillo(a)
a quiet room una stanza tranquilla

quilt la trapunta

quite *(rather)* abbastanza

it's quite expensive è abbastanza caro(a)
quite the opposite al contrario

quiz show il gioco a quiz

R

rabbit il coniglio

rabies la rabbia

race *(sport)* la gara

race course l'ippodromo *(m)*

racket *(tennis, etc)* la racchetta

radiator *(car)* il radiatore
(heater) il termosifone

radio la radio

railcard la tessera di riduzione ferroviaria

railway station la stazione dei treni

rain la pioggia

to rain piovere
it's raining piove

raincoat l'impermeabile *(m)*

rake il rastrello

rape lo stupro

raped violentata
I've been raped sono stata violentata

rare *(unique)* raro(a)
(steak) al sangue

rash *(skin)* l'orticaria *(f)*

rate *(cost)* la tariffa

R

rate of exchange il cambio

raw crudo(a)

razor il rasoio

razor blades le lamette

to read leggere

ready pronto(a)
  to get ready prepararsi

real vero(a)

to realize rendersi conto di

rearview mirror lo specchietto retrovisore

receipt la ricevuta

receiver (phone) il ricevitore

reception (desk) la reception

receptionist l'addetto(a)

to recharge (battery) ricaricare

recipe la ricetta

to recognize riconoscere

to recommend raccomandare

to record (programme) registrare

to recover (from illness) rimettersi

to recycle riciclare

red rosso(a)

to reduce ridurre

reduction la riduzione

to refer to (for information) rivolgersi a

refill (pen) il ricambio
  (lighter) la bomboletta di gas

refund il rimborso

to refuse rifiutare

regarding riguardo a

region la regione

register il registro

to register (letter) assicurare
  (car) immatricolare
  (for class) iscriversi

registered letter la lettera

registration form il modulo d'iscrizione

to reimburse rimborsare

relation (family) il/la parente

relationship il rapporto

to remain restare ; rimanere

to remember ricordare
  I don't remember non mi ricordo

remote control il telecomando

removal firm la ditta di traslochi

to remove togliere

rent l'affitto (m)

to rent (house) affittare
  (car) noleggiare

rental (house) l'affitto (m)
  (car) il nolo

repair la riparazione

to repair riparare

to repeat ripetere

to reply rispondere

report il resoconto

to report (crime) denunciare

request la richiesta

to request richiedere
to rescue salvare
reservation la prenotazione
to reserve prenotare
reserved prenotato(a)
resident residente
resort la località di vacanza
rest *(repose)* il riposo
(remainder) il resto
to rest riposarsi
restaurant il ristorante
restaurant car il vagone
ristorante
retired: *I'm retired* sono in
pensione
to return *(go back)* ritornare
(to give back) restituire
return ticket il biglietto di
andata e ritorno
to reverse fare marcia
indietro
to reverse the charges fare
una telefonata al carico del
destinatario
reverse charge call
la chiamata a carico del
destinatario
reverse gear la retromarcia
rheumatism il reumatismo
rib la costola
rice il riso
rich ricco(a)
ride *(in a car)* il giro in
macchina

to ride a horse andare a
cavallo
right *(correct)* giusto(a)
right la destra
at/to the right a destra
on the right sulla destra
right of way la precedenza
to ring *(bell)* suonare
(phone) squillare
it's ringing suona
ring l'anello *(m)*
ring road la circonvallazione
ripe maturo(a)
river il fiume
road la strada
road map la carta stradale
road sign il cartello stradale
roadworks i lavori stradali
roast arrosto(a)
roll *(bread)* il panino
rollerblades i rollerblades
romantic romantico(a)
roof il tetto
roof-rack il portabagagli
room *(hotel)* la camera
(space) lo spazio
double room la camera
doppia
family room la camera
per famiglia
single room la camera
singola
room number il numero
di camera

R

room service il servizio in camera
root la radice
rope la corda
rose la rosa
rosé wine il vino rosato
rotten (food) marcio(a)
rough (sea) mosso(a)
round rotondo(a)
roundabout la rotatoria
row (in theatre, etc) la fila
to row (boat) remare
rowing boat la barca a remi
rubber (eraser) la gomma da cancellare (material) la gomma
rubber band l'elastico (m)
rubber gloves i guanti di gomma
rubbish la spazzatura
rubella la rosolia
rucksack lo zaino
rug (carpet) il tappeto
ruins le rovine
ruler (to measure) il righello
to run correre
rush hour l'ora di punta (f)
rusty arrugginito(a)

S

sad triste
saddle la sella

safe (for valuables) la cassaforte
safe (medicine, etc) senza pericolo
is it safe? è senza pericolo?
safety la sicurezza
safetybelt la cintura di sicurezza
safety pin la spilla di sicurezza
to sail andare in barca
sailboard la tavola da windsurf
sailing la vela
sailing boat la barca a vela
saint il/la santo(a)
salad l'insalata (f)
green salad l'insalata verde
mixed salad l'insalata mista
potato salad l'insalata di patate
tomato salad l'insalata di pomodori
salad dressing il condimento per l'insalata
salami il salame
salary lo stipendio
sales (reductions) i saldi
salesman/woman il/la commesso(a)
sales rep il/la rappresentante
salt il sale

salt water l'acqua salata (f)

salty salato(a)

same stesso(a)

sample il campione

sand la sabbia

sandals i sandali

sandwich il panino ;
il tramezzino
toasted sandwich il toast

sanitary towels gli assorbenti

Sardinia la Sardegna

satellite dish l'antenna
parabolica (f)

satellite TV la televisione
via satellite

Saturday il sabato

sauce la salsa
tomato sauce la salsa di
pomodoro

saucepan la pentola

saucer il piattino

sauna la sauna

sausage la salsiccia

to save (life) salvare
(money) risparmiare

savoury (not sweet) salato(a)

to say dire

scales (weighing) la bilancia

scarf la sciarpa
(headscarf) il foulard

scenery il paesaggio

schedule il programma
(timetable) l'orario (m)

school la scuola

primary school la scuola
elementare
secondary school il liceo

scissors le forbici

score il punteggio

to score (goal) segnare

Scot lo/la scozzese

Scotland la Scozia

Scottish scozzese

scouring pad la paglietta

screen lo schermo

screen wash il liquido
lavavetri

screw la vite

screwdriver il cacciavite
phillips screwdriver il
cacciavite a stella

scuba diving le immersioni
subacquee

sculpture la scultura

sea il mare

seacat il catamarano

seafood i frutti di mare

seam (of dress) la cucitura

to search cercare

sea sickness il mal di mare

seaside: at the seaside
al mare

season (of year) la stagione
(holiday) il periodo delle
vacanze
in season di stagione

seasonal stagionale

seasoning il condimento

season ticket l'abbonamento
seat *(chair)* la sedia
(theatre, plane, etc) il posto
seatbelt la cintura di sicurezza
seaweed le alghe
second *(time)* il secondo
second secondo(a)
second class la seconda classe
second-hand di seconda mano
secretary la segretaria
security guard la guardia giurata
sedative il sedativo
to see vedere
to seize afferrare
self-catering con uso di cucina
self-employed autonomo(a)
self-service il self-service
to sell vendere
do you sell...? vende...?
sell-by date la data di scadenza
Sellotape® lo Scotch®
to send mandare ; spedire ; inviare
senior citizen l'anziano(a)
sensible pratico(a)
separated separato(a)
separately: to pay separately pagare separatamente

September settembre
septic tank la fossa settica
serious grave
(not funny) serio(a)
to serve servire
service *(in church)* la funzione
(in restaurant) il servizio
is service included? il servizio è incluso?
service charge il servizio
service station la stazione di servizio
set menu il menù turistico
settee il divano
several alcuni(e)
to sew cucire
sewerage la fognatura
sex *(gender)* il sesso
(intercourse) i rapporti sessuali
shade l'ombra *(f)*
in the shade all'ombra
to shake *(bottle)* agitare
shallow basso(a)
shampoo lo shampoo
shampoo and set lo shampoo e messa in piega
to share dividere
sharp *(razor, blade)* affilato(a)
to shave farsi la barba
shaving cream la crema da barba
shawl lo scialle
she ella ; lei

sheep la pecora

sheet *(bed)* il lenzuolo

shelf la mensola

shell *(seashell)* la conchiglia

shellfish i frutti di mare

sheltered riparato(a)

to shine brillare

shingles *(illness)* il fuoco di sant'Antonio

ship la nave

shirt la camicia

shock *(mental)* lo shock *(electric)* la scossa

shock absorber l'ammortizzatore *(m)*

shoe la scarpa

shoelaces i lacci delle scarpe

shoe polish il lucido per scarpe

shoe repairer il calzolaio

shoe shop il negozio di calzature

shop il negozio

to shop andare a fare compere

shop assistant il/la commesso(a)

shop window la vetrina

shopping: to go shopping fare compere ; fare la spesa

shopping centre il centro commerciale

shore la riva

short corto(a) *(person)* basso(a)

short circuit il corto circuito

short cut la scorciatoia

shortage la carenza

shorts i calzoncini corti

short-sighted miope

shoulder la spalla

to shout gridare

show *(theatre)* lo spettacolo

to show mostrare

shower la doccia *(rain)* il rovescio
    to take a shower fare la doccia

shower cap la cuffia da doccia

shower gel il bagnoschiuma

to shrink restringersi

shrub l'arbusto *(m)*

shut *(closed)* chiuso(a)

shutter l'imposta *(f)*

shuttle service la navetta

Sicily la Sicilia

sick *(ill)* malato(a) *(nauseous)* nauseato(a)
    I feel sick mi sento male

side il lato

side dish il contorno

sidelight la luce di posizione

sidewalk il marciapiede

sieve il setaccio

sightseeing tour il giro turistico

sign il segno
(on road) il segnale

to sign firmare

signature la firma

signpost il segnale

silk la seta

silver l'argento (m)

similar to simile a

since (time) da

to sing cantare

single (unmarried) non sposato(a)
(not double) singolo(a)
(ticket) di (sola) andata

single bed il letto a una piazza

single room la camera singola

sink il lavandino

sir Signore

sister la sorella

sister-in-law la cognata

to sit sedersi
please, sit down prego, si accomodi

size (of clothes) la taglia
(of shoes) il numero

to skate (on ice) pattinare sul ghiaccio

skateboard lo skateboard

skates (ice) i pattini da ghiaccio
(roller) i pattini a rotelle

to ski sciare

skis gli sci

ski boots gli scarponi da sci

ski instructor il/la maestro(a) di sci

ski jump il trampolino

ski lift lo ski-lift

ski pass lo skipass

ski pole/stick la racchetta da sci

ski run la pista

ski suit la tuta da sci

skin la pelle

skirt la gonna

sky il cielo

sledge la slitta

to sleep dormire

to sleep in dormire fino a tardi

sleeper (on train) la cuccetta

sleeping bag il sacco a pelo

sleeping car il vagone letto

sleeping pill il sonnifero

slice (piece of) la fetta

sliced bread il pancarrè

slide (photo) la diapositiva

to slip scivolare

slippers le pantofole

slow lento(a)

to slow down rallentare

slowly lentamente

small piccolo(a)
smaller (than) più piccolo (di)

smell l'odore (m)
  bad smell il puzzo
  nice smell il profumo
to smell (bad) puzzare
  to smell of avere odore di
smile il sorriso
to smile sorridere
smoke il fumo
to smoke fumare
  I don't smoke non fumo
  can I smoke? posso fumare?
smoke alarm l'allarme
  antincendio (m)
smoked (food) affumicato(a)
smokers (sign) fumatori
smooth liscio(a)
snack lo spuntino
  to have a snack fare lo
  spuntino
snake il serpente
  (grass) la biscia
snake bite il morso di vipera
to sneeze starnutire
snorkel il boccaglio
snow la neve
to snow: it's snowing nevica
snowboard lo snowboard
**snowboarding: to go
  snowboarding** andare a
  fare lo snowboard
snow chains le catene da
  neve
snow tyres i pneumatici
  da neve

snow plough lo spazzaneve
snowed up isolato(a) a
  causa della neve
soap il sapone
soap powder il detersivo in
  polvere
sober sobrio(a)
socket (electric) la presa
socks i calzini
soda water l'acqua di selz (f)
sofa il divano
sofa bed il divano letto
soft soffice ; morbido(a)
soft drink la bibita
software il software
soldier il soldato
sole (of foot, shoe) la suola
soluble solubile
some di (del/della)
  (a few) alcuni/alcune
someone qualcuno
something qualcosa
sometimes qualche volta
son il figlio
son-in-law il genero
song la canzone
soon presto
  as soon as possible il più
  presto possibile
sore throat il mal di gola
sorry: I'm sorry! mi scusi!
sort il tipo
  what sort? che tipo?

S

soup la minestra

sour aspro(a) ; agro(a)

soured cream la panna acida

south il sud

souvenir il souvenir

spa la stazione termale

space lo spazio
(parking) il posteggio

spade il badile

Spain la Spagna

Spanish spagnolo(a)

spanner la chiave inglese

spare parts i pezzi di ricambio

spare room la stanza degli ospiti

spare tyre la gomma di scorta

spare wheel la ruota di scorta

sparkling frizzante
sparkling water l'acqua gassata
sparkling wine il vino frizzante

spark plugs le candele

to speak parlare
do you speak English? parla inglese?

special speciale

specialist lo/la specialista

speciality la specialità

speech il discorso

speed la velocità

speedboat il motoscafo

speed limit il limite di velocità
to exceed the speed limit superare il limite di velocità

speeding l'eccesso di velocità *(m)*

speeding ticket la multa per eccesso di velocità

speedometer il tachimetro

to spell scrivere
how's it spelt? come si scrive?

to spend spendere

spice le spezie

spicy piccante

spider il ragno

to spill rovesciare

spin-dryer la centrifuga

spine la spina dorsale

spirits *(alcohol)* i liquori

splinter la scheggia

spoke *(of wheel)* il raggio

sponge la spugna

spoon il cucchiaio

sport lo sport

sports centre il centro sportivo

sports shop il negozio di articoli sportivi

spot *(stain)* la macchia
(place) il posto

sprain la slogatura

spring *(season)* la primavera
(metal) la molla

square *(in town)* la piazza
squash *(game)* lo squash
to squeeze premere ; stringere
squid il calamaro
stadium lo stadio
staff il personale
stage *(theatre)* il palcoscenico
stain la macchia
stained glass il vetro colorato
stain remover lo smacchiatore
stairs le scale
stale *(bread)* raffermo(a)
stalls *(in theatre)* la platea
stamp il francobollo
to stand stare in piedi
star la stella
starfish la stella marina
to start cominciare
starter *(food)* l'antipasto *(m)*
  (in car) il motorino d'avviamento
station la stazione
stationer's la cartoleria
statue la statua
stay il soggiorno
  enjoy your stay! buona permanenza!
to stay *(remain)* rimanere
  I'm staying at the Grand Hotel sono al Grand Hotel
steak la bistecca
to steal rubare

steamed al vapore
to steam cuocere a vapore
steel l'acciaio *(m)*
steep: *is it steep?* è in salita?
steeple il campanile
steering wheel il volante
step *(stair)* il gradino
stepdaughter la figliastra
stepfather il patrigno
stepmother la matrigna
stepson il figliastro
stereo lo stereo
sterling la sterlina
steward lo steward
stewardess la hostess
to stick *(with glue)* incollare
  (door) incepparsi
sticking plaster il cerotto
still *(motionless)* fermo(a)
  (water) naturale
  (yet) ancora
sting la puntura
to sting pungere
stitches i punti
stockings le calze
stolen rubato(a)
stomach lo stomaco ; la pancia
stomachache il mal di pancia
stone la pietra
to stop *(come to a halt)* fermarsi
  (stop doing something) smettere

S

stop sign lo stop
store *(shop)* il negozio
storey il piano
storm la tempesta ; il temporale
story il racconto
straightaway subito
straight on diritto
strange strano(a)
straw *(drinking)* la cannuccia
strawberries le fragole
stream il ruscello
street la strada
street map la piantina
strength *(of person)* la forza *(of wine)* la gradazione alcolica
stress lo stress
strike *(of workers)* lo sciopero
string lo spago
striped a strisce
stroke *(medical)* l'ictus *(m)*
  to have a stroke avere un ictus
strong forte
  strong coffee il caffè ristretto
  strong tea il tè forte
stuck bloccato(a)
student lo studente/ la studentessa
student discount lo sconto per studenti
stuffed farcito(a)

stung punto(a)
stupid stupido(a)
subscription l'abbonamento *(m)*
subtitles i sottotitoli
subway *(train)* la metropolitana *(passage)* il sottopassaggio
suddenly all'improvviso
suede la pelle scamosciata
sugar lo zucchero
sugar-free senza zucchero
to suggest proporre
suit *(man's)* l'abito *(m)* *(woman's)* il tailleur
suitcase la valigia
sum *(of money)* la somma
summer l'estate *(f)*
summer holidays le vacanze estive
summit il vertice
sun il sole
to sunbathe prendere il sole
sunblock la protezione solare totale
sunburn la scottatura solare
Sunday la domenica
sunglasses gli occhiali da sole
sunny: *it's sunny* c'è il sole
sunrise l'alba *(f)*
sunroof *(car)* il tettuccio apribile
sunscreen la crema solare protettiva

sunset il tramonto

sunshade l'ombrellone (m)

sunstroke l'insolazione (f)

suntan l'abbronzatura (f)

suntan lotion la crema
abbronzante

supermarket il supermercato

supper (dinner) la cena

supplement il supplemento

to supply fornire

sure sicuro(a) ; certo(a)
I'm sure sono sicuro(a)

to surf fare il surf
to surf the net navigare
in internet

surfboard la tavola da surf

surgery (surgical treatment)
la chirurgia

surname il cognome
my surname is... di
cognome mi chiamo...

surprise la sorpresa

suspension (in car)
la sospensione

to survive sopravvivere

to swallow inghiottire

to swear (bad language) dire
le parolacce

to sweat sudare

sweater il maglione

sweatshirt la felpa

sweet (not savoury) dolce

sweetener il dolcificante

sweets le caramelle

to swell gonfiare

to swim nuotare

swimming pool la piscina

swimsuit il costume da
bagno

swing l'altalena (f)

Swiss svizzero(a)

switch l'interruttore (m)

to switch off spegnere

to switch on accendere

Switzerland la Svizzera

swollen gonfio(a)

synagogue la sinagoga

syringe la siringa

T

table la tavola

tablecloth la tovaglia

tablet (pill) la pastiglia

table tennis il ping pong

table wine il vino da tavola

tailor il sarto

to take (carry) portare
(to grab, seize) prendere
how long does it take?
quanto tempo ci vuole?

takeaway (food) da asporto

to take off decollare

to take out (of bag) tirar
fuori

talc il borotalco

to talk parlare

T

tall alto(a)

tampons gli assorbenti interni

tangerine il mandarino

tank la cisterna
  (car) il serbatoio
  (fish) l'acquario *(m)*

tap il rubinetto

tap water l'acqua del rubinetto *(f)*

tape il nastro

tape measure il metro a nastro

tape recorder il registratore

target lo scopo

tart la crostata

taste il sapore

to taste assaggiare ; provare
  can I taste some? ne posso assaggiare un pò?

tax la tassa ; l'imposta *(f)*

taxi il taxi

taxi driver il/la tassista

taxi rank il posteggio dei taxi

tea il tè
  herbal tea la tisana
  fruit tea il tè alla frutta
  lemon tea il tè al limone
  tea with milk il tè al latte

tea bag la bustina di tè

tea pot la teiera

to teach insegnare

teacher l'insegnante *(m/f)*

team la squadra

tear *(in material)* lo strappo

teaspoon il cucchiaino

teat *(on bottle)* la tettarella

tea towel lo strofinaccio per i piatti

teenager il/la teenager

teeth i denti

telegram il telegramma

telephone il telefono

to telephone telefonare

telephone box la cabina telefonica

telephone call la telefonata

telephone card la scheda telefonica

telephone directory l'elenco telefonico *(m)*

telephone number il numero di telefono

television la televisione

to tell dire

temperature la temperatura
  to have a temperature avere la febbre

temporary provvisorio(a)

tenant l'inquilino(a)

tendon il tendine

tennis il tennis

tennis ball la pallina da tennis

tennis court il campo da tennis

tennis racket la racchetta da tennis

tent la tenda

tent peg il picchetto

terminal *(airport)* il terminal

terrace la terrazza

terracotta la terracotta

to test *(try out)* provare

testicles i testicoli

tetanus jab l'antitetanica *(f)*

than di

to thank ringraziare

thank you grazie
  thanks very much molte
  grazie

that quel/quella/quello
  that one quello là

the *(sing)* il/lo/la
  (plural) i/gli/le

theatre il teatro

theft il furto

their il/la loro

them loro ; li ; le

there *(over there)* lì

there is/there are c'è/ci
  sono

thermometer il termometro

these questi/queste
  these ones questi qui

they loro ; essi/esse

thick spesso(a)

thief il/la ladro(a)

thigh la coscia

thin sottile
  (person) magro(a)

thing la cosa
  my things la mia roba

to think pensare

thirsty: to be thirsty avere
  sete

this questo/questa
  this one questo(a)

those quei/quelle/quegli
  those ones quelli(e)

thread il filo

throat la gola

throat lozenges le pastiglie
  per la gola

through attraverso

to throw away buttare via

thumb il pollice

thunder il tuono

thunderstorm il temporale

Thursday il giovedì

thyme il timo

ticket *(bus, train, etc)*
  il biglietto
  (entry fee) il biglietto
  d'ingresso
  a single ticket un biglietto
  di (sola) andata
  a return ticket un biglietto
  di andata e ritorno
  tourist ticket il biglietto
  turistico
  book of tickets il
  blocchetto di biglietti

ticket inspector il
  controllore

ticket office la biglietteria

tidy ordinato(a)

to tidy up fare ordine

T

tie la cravatta
tight stretto(a)
tights i collant ;
la calzamaglia
tile *(floor)* la piastrella
till *(cash desk)* la cassa
till *(until)* fino a
till 2 o'clock fino alle due
time il tempo
(of day) l'ora *(f)*
this time questa volta
what time is it? che ore
sono?
do you have the time?
ha l'ora?
timetable l'orario *(m)*
tin *(can)* la scatola ; la lattina
tinfoil la carta stagnola
tin-opener l'apriscatole *(m)*
tip *(to waiter, etc)* la mancia
to tip *(waiter)* dare la mancia
tired stanco(a)
tissues i fazzoletti di carta
to a
to London a Londra
to the airport all'aeroporto
toadstool il fungo velenoso
toast *(to eat)* il pane tostato
(raising glass) il brindisi
tobacco il tabacco
tobacconist's il tabaccaio
today oggi
toe il dito del piede
together insieme

toilet la toilette
toilet for disabled la toilette
per i disabili
toilet brush lo spazzolino
del gabinetto
toilet paper la carta igienica
toiletries gli articoli per
l'igiene
token *(phone, etc)* il gettone
toll *(motorway)* il pedaggio
tomato il pomodoro
tinned tomatoes i pelati
tomato juice il succo di
pomodoro
tomato purée il concentrato
di pomodoro
tomato sauce la salsa di
pomodoro
tomorrow domani
tomorrow morning domani
mattina
tomorrow afternoon
domani pomeriggio
tomorrow evening domani
sera
tongue la lingua
tonic water l'acqua tonica *(f)*
tonight stasera
tonsilitis la tonsillite
too *(also)* anche
too big troppo grande
too small troppo piccolo(a)
too hot troppo caldo(a)
too noisy troppo rumoroso(a)
tool l'attrezzo *(m)*

toolkit gli attrezzi

tooth il dente

toothache il mal di denti

toothbrush lo spazzolino da denti

toothpaste il dentifricio

toothpick lo stuzzicadenti

top: *the top floor* l'ultimo piano *(m)*

top la cima
(clothing) la maglietta
on top of sopra di

topless topless

torch *(flashlight)* la pila

torn strappato(a)

total il totale

to touch toccare

tough *(meat)* duro(a)

tour il giro
guided tour la visita guidata

tour guide la guida turistica

tour operator l'operatore turistico *(m)*

tourist il/la turista

tourist information le informazioni turistiche

tourist office l'ufficio turistico *(m)*

tourist route l'itinerario turistico *(m)*

tourist ticket il biglietto turistico

to tow rimorchiare

towbar la barra di rimorchio

tow rope il cavo da rimorchio

towel l'asciugamano *(m)*

tower la torre

town la città

town centre il centro città

town hall il municipio

town plan la piantina

toxic tossico(a)

toy il giocattolo

toy shop il negozio di giocattoli

tracksuit la tuta sportiva

traditional tradizionale

traffic il traffico

traffic jam l'ingorgo *(m)*

traffic lights il semaforo

traffic warden il vigile

trailer il rimorchio

train il treno
the next train il prossimo treno
the first train il primo treno
the last train l'ultimo treno

trainers le scarpe da ginnastica

tram il tram

tranquillizer il tranquillante

to transfer trasferire

to translate tradurre

translation la traduzione

to travel viaggiare

travel agent's l'agenzia di viaggi *(f)*

travel documents
i documenti di viaggio

travel guide la guida

travel insurance
l'assicurazione di viaggio (f)

travel sickness (sea) il mal
di mare
(air) il mal d'aria
(car) il mal d'auto

traveller's cheques
i traveller's (cheque)

tray il vassoio

tree l'albero (m)

trip la gita ; il viaggio

trolley il carrello

trouble i problemi

trousers i pantaloni

truck il camion

true vero(a)

trunk (luggage) il baule

trunks (swimming) i calzoncini
da bagno

to try provare

to try on (clothes, etc) provare

t-shirt la maglietta

Tuesday il martedì

tumble dryer l'asciugatrice (f)

tunnel la galleria

Turin Torino

to turn (handle, wheel) girare
to turn around girarsi

to turn off (light, etc)
spegnere
(tap) chiudere

to turn on (light, etc)
accendere
(tap) aprire

turquoise (colour) turchese

tweezers le pinzette

twice due volte ; il doppio

twin beds i letti gemelli

twins i gemelli

to type battere a macchina

typical tipico(a)

tyre la gomma ;
il pneumatico

tyre pressure la pressione
delle gomme

U

ugly brutto(a)

ulcer (stomach) l'ulcera (f)
(mouth) l'afta (f)

umbrella l'ombrello (m)
(sunshade) l'ombrellone (m)

uncle lo zio

uncomfortable scomodo(a)

unconscious svenuto(a)

under sotto

undercooked poco cotto(a)

underground (metro)
la metropolitana

underpants le mutande

underpass il sottopassaggio

to understand capire
I don't understand non
capisco

do you understand? capisce?

underwear la biancheria intima

to undress spogliarsi

unemployed disoccupato(a)

to unfasten slacciare

United Kingdom il Regno Unito

United States gli Stati Uniti

university l'università *(f)*

unleaded petrol la benzina senza piombo ; la benzina verde

unlikely improbabile

to unlock aprire

to unpack disfare la valigia

unpleasant sgradevole

to unplug staccare

to unscrew svitare

until fino a

unusual raro(a)

up: to get up alzarsi

upside down sottosopra

upstairs di sopra

urgent urgente

urine l'urina *(f)*

us ci ; noi

to use usare

useful utile

usual solito(a)

usually di solito

U-turn l'inversione a U *(f)*

vacancy *(in hotel)* la camera libera

vacant libero(a)

vacation la vacanza

vaccination la vaccinazione

vacuum cleaner l'aspirapolvere *(m)*

vagina la vagina

valid valido(a)

valley la valle

valuable di valore

valuables gli oggetti di valori

value il valore

valve la valvola

van il furgone

vase il vaso

VAT l'IVA *(f)*

vegan vegetaliano(a)
I'm vegan sono vegetaliano(a)

vegetables le verdure

vegetarian vegetariano(a)
I'm vegetarian sono vegetariano(a)

vehicle il veicolo

vein la vena

Velcro® il velcro®

vending machine il distributore automatico

venereal disease la malattia venerea

V

Venice Venezia
ventilator il ventilatore
very molto
vest la canottiera
vet il/la veterinario(a)
via passando per
to video *(from TV)* registrare su videocassetta
video il video
video camera la videocamera
video cassette/tape la videocassetta
video game il videogioco
video recorder il videoregistratore
view la vista
villa la villa
village il paese
vinegar l'aceto *(m)*
vineyard la vigna
viper la vipera
virus il virus
visa il visto
visit la visita
to visit visitare
visiting hours l'orario delle visite *(m)*
visitor il visitatore/la visitatrice
vitamin la vitamina
voice la voce
volcano il vulcano

volleyball la pallavolo
voltage il voltaggio
to vomit vomitare
voucher il buono

W

wage il salario ; la paga
waist la vita
waistcoat il gilè
to wait (for) aspettare
waiter/waitress il cameriere, la cameriera
waiting room la sala d'aspetto
to wake up svegliare
Wales il Galles
walk la passeggiata
to walk andare a piedi
walking boots gli scarponcini
walking stick il bastone
Walkman® il walkman®
wall il muro ; la parete
wallet il portafoglio
to want volere
  I want... voglio...
  we want... vogliamo...
war la guerra
ward *(hospital)* il reparto
wardrobe l'armadio *(m)*
warm caldo(a)
  it's warm fa caldo

to warm up *(milk, etc)*
riscaldare

warning triangle il triangolo
d'emergenza

to wash lavare
(to wash oneself) lavarsi

wash and blow dry lo
shampoo e messa in piega

washbasin il lavandino

washing machine la lavatrice

washing powder il detersivo
in polvere

washing-up bowl la bacinella

washing-up liquid
il detersivo per i piatti

wasp la vespa

wasp sting la puntura di
vespa

waste bin il bidone della
spazzatura

watch l'orologio *(m)*

to watch guardare

watchstrap il cinturino
dell'orologio

water l'acqua *(f)*
bottled water l'acqua in
bottiglia *(f)*
drinking water l'acqua
potabile
mineral water l'acqua
minerale
sparkling water l'acqua
gassata
still water l'acqua naturale

water heater lo scaldabagno

watermelon l'anguria *(f)*

waterproof impermeabile

to water-ski fare lo sci nautico

watersports gli sport
acquatici

waterwings i braccioli
salvagente

waves *(on sea)* le onde

waxing *(hair removal)*
la ceretta

way in l'entrata *(f)* ;
l'ingresso *(m)*

way out l'uscita *(f)*

we noi

weak *(person)* debole
(tea, coffee, etc) leggero(a)

to wear portare

weather il tempo

weather forecast le
previsioni del tempo

website il sito web

wedding il matrimonio

wedding anniversary
l'anniversario di
matrimonio *(m)*

wedding present il regalo
di matrimonio

wedding ring la fede

Wednesday mercoledì

week la settimana
last week la settimana
scorsa
next week la prossima
settimana

per week alla settimana
this week questa settimana
during the week durante
la settimana
weekday il giorno feriale
weekend il fine settimana
next weekend il prossimo
fine settimana
this weekend questo fine
settimana
weekly settimanale
weekly pass l'abbonamento
settimanale *(m)*
to weigh pesare
weight il peso
welcome benvenuto
well bene
well *(for water)* il pozzo
well-done *(steak)* ben
cotto(a)
wellington boots gli stivali
di gomma
Welsh gallese
west ovest
wet bagnato(a)
wetsuit la muta
what cosa
what is it? cos'è?
wheat il grano
wheel la ruota
wheelchair la sedia a rotelle
wheel clamp il ceppo
bloccaruote

when quando
where dove
which qual/quale
while mentre
in a while fra poco
whipped cream la panna
montata
whisky l'whisky *(m)*
white bianco(a)
who chi
whole tutto
wholemeal bread il pane
integrale
whose: whose is it? di chi è?
why perché
wide largo(a) ; ampio(a)
widow la vedova
widower il vedovo
width la larghezza
wife la moglie
wig la parrucca
to win vincere
wind il vento
windbreak *(camping)* il
frangivento
windmill il mulino a vento
window la finestra
(shop) la vetrina
(car) il finestrino
windscreen il parabrezza
windscreen wiper il
tergicristallo

to windsurf fare il windsurf

windy: *it's windy* c'è vento

vine il vino
red wine il vino rosso
white wine il vino bianco
dry wine il vino secco
sweet wine il vino dolce
rosé wine il vino rosato
sparkling wine il vino
frizzante
house wine il vino della
casa

vine list la lista dei vini

ving (of bird) l'ala (f)
(of car) la fiancata

ving mirror lo specchietto
laterale

vinter l'inverno (m)

vire il filo

with con
with ice con ghiaccio
with milk con latte
with sugar con zucchero

without senza
without ice senza ghiaccio
without milk senza latte
without sugar senza
zucchero

vitness il/la testimone

woman la donna

wonderful meraviglioso(a)

wood (material) il legno
(forest) il bosco

wooden di legno

wool la lana

word la parola

work il lavoro

to work (person) lavorare
(machine, car, etc) funzionare
it doesn't work non
funziona

work permit il premesso
di lavoro

world il mondo

worried preoccupato(a)

worse peggio

worth (value) il valore
it's worth £5 vale cinque
sterline

to wrap up (parcel) incartare

wrapping paper la carta
di regalo

wrinkles le rughe

wrist il polso

to write scrivere
please write it down
lo scriva per favore

writing paper la carta
da lettere

wrong sbagliato(a)
what's wrong? cosa c'è?

wrought iron il ferro
battuto

X

x-ray la radiografia

to x-ray radiografare

Y

yacht lo yacht
year l'anno *(m)*
 this year quest'anno
 next year l'anno prossimo
 last year l'anno scorso
yearly *(every year)*
 annualmente
yellow giallo(a)
Yellow Pages le pagine
 gialle®
yes sì
yesterday ieri
yet: *not yet* non ancora
yoghurt lo yogurt
 plain yoghurt lo yogurt
 naturale
yolk il tuorlo
you lei ; tu ; voi
young giovane
your il/la suo(a) ; il/la tuo(a) ;
 il/la vostro(a)

Z

zebra crossing le strisce
 pedonali
zero lo zero
zip la cerniera
zone la zona
zoo lo zoo
zoom lens lo zoom

A

a at ; in

abbaglianti *mpl* full-beam headlights

abbiamo... we have...
non abbiamo... we don't have...

abbigliamento *m* clothes

abbonamento *m* subscription ; season ticket

abbronzatura *f* suntan

abito *m* dress ; man's suit

aborto *m* abortion
aborto spontaneo miscarriage

abuso *m* misuse

a.C. B.C.

accamparsi to camp

accanto (a) beside ; next (to)

acceleratore *m* accelerator

accendere to turn on ; to light
accendere i fari switch on your headlights

accendino *m* cigarette lighter

accensione *f* ignition

accento *m* accent *(pronunciation)*

acceso(a) on *(light, engine)*

accesso *m* access
divieto di accesso no access

accettazione *f* reception
accettazione bagagli check-in

accomodarsi to make oneself comfortable
si accomodi do take a seat

accompagnare to accompany

accordo *m* agreement

acetone *m* nail polish remover

ACI *m* Automobile Association

acqua *f* water
acqua calda hot water
acqua corrente running water
acqua distillata distilled water
acqua gassata sparkling water
acqua minerale mineral water
acqua naturale still water
acqua potabile drinking water

acquisto *m* purchase

addetto(a) authorized

adesso now

adulto(a) adult

aereo *m* plane ; aircraft

aeroplano *m* airplane

aeroporto *m* airport

affari *mpl* business
per affari on business

affittare to rent ; to let
affitasi for rent

affitto *m* lease ; rent

affogare to drown

agenda *f* diary

A

agenzia f agency
  agenzia di viaggi travel
  agent
  agenzia immobiliare estate
  agent
aggredire to attack
aglio m garlic
ago m needle
  ago ipodermico
  hypodermic needle
agosto m August
AIDS m AIDS
aiutare to help
aiuto! help!
alba f dawn
albergo m hotel
albero m tree ; mast
albicocca f apricot
alcolici mpl alcoholic drinks
alcolico(a) alcoholic
alcool m alcohol
alcuni(e) some ; a few
alcuno(a) any ; some
alimentari mpl groceries
allacciare to fasten (seatbelt,
  etc)
allarme m alarm
  allarme antincendio fire
  alarm
allergia f allergy
allergico(a) a allergic to
alloggio m accommodation
alluvione f flood
Alpi fpl Alps
alpinismo m climbing
alt stop

altezza f height
alto(a) high ; tall
  alta stagione high season
  alta marea high tide
altro(a) other
  altri passaporti other
  passports
alzarsi to get up ; to stand
  up
amabile sweet (wine)
amare to love (person)
amarena f sour black cherry
amaro(a) bitter (taste)
ambasciata f embassy
ambiente m environment
ambulanza f ambulance
ambulatorio m surgery ;
  out-patients
America f America
americano(a) American
amico(a) m/f friend
ammalato(a) ill
amministratore delegato m
  managing director
ammontare m total amount
ammortizzatore m shock
  absorber
amo m bait
amore m love
analasi del sangue f blood
  test
analcolico m soft drink
analcolico(a) non-alcoholic
analgesico m painkiller
ananas m pineapple
anatra f duck

anca f hip

anche too ; also ; even

ancora still ; yet ; again
  ancora un po'? a little more?
  non ancora not yet

ancora f anchor

andare to go
  andare a cavallo to ride a horse
  andare a piedi to go on foot
  andare bene to fit (clothes)
  andare in macchina to go by car

andata: *andata e ritorno* return (ticket)
  di (sola) andata single (ticket)

andiamo! let's go!
  andiamo a... we're going to...

anestetico m anaesthetic

angina pectoris f angina

anguria f watermelon

anice m aniseed

animale m animal
  animale domestico pet

annata f vintage ; year
  vino d'annata vintage wine

anniversario m anniversary

anno m year
  buon anno! happy New Year!

annuale annual

annullamento m cancellation

annullare to cancel

annuncio m announcement ; advert

antibiotico m antibiotic

anticipo m advance (loan)
  in anticipo in advance ; early

anticoncezionale m contraceptive

antifurto m burglar alarm

antigelo m antifreeze ; de-icer

antipasto m starter ; hors d'œuvre

antisettico m antiseptic

antistaminico m anihistamine

anziano(a) m/f senior citizen

ape f bee

aperitivo m apéritif

aperto(a) open
  all'aperto open-air

appartamento m flat ; apartment

appendicite f appendicitis

appuntamento m appointment ; date

apribottiglie m bottle opener

aprile m April

aprire to open ; to turn on (tap)

apriscatole m tin-opener

arachide f peanut

arancia f orange

aranciata f orange squash

arancione orange (colour)

A

area f area
  area di servizio service area
argento m silver
aria condizionata f air-conditioning
armadio m cupboard ; wardrobe
arrabbiato(a) angry
arredato(a) furnished
arrestare to arrest
arrivare to arrive
arrivederci goodbye
arrivo m arrival
  arrivi nazionali domestic arrivals
  arrivi internazionali international arrivals
arrosto m roast
arte f art ; craft
articolo m article
  articoli da dichiarare goods to declare
  articoli da regalo gifts
artigiano(a) m/f craftsperson
artista m/f artist
artrite f arthritis
ascensore m lift ; elevator
ascesso m abscess
asciugamano m towel
asciugare to dry
asciugatrice f tumble dryer
ascoltare to listen (to)
asma f asthma
aspettare to wait (for) ; to expect

aspirapolvere m vacuum cleaner
aspirina f aspirin
assaggiare to taste
asse m axle (car)
  asse da stiro ironing board
assegno m cheque
assicurato(a) insured
assicurazione f insurance
assistente m/f assistant
assistenza f assistance ; aid
associazione f society
assorbenti mpl sanitary towels
  assorbenti interni tampons
ATM public transport service
attaccare to attach ; to attack ; to fasten
attacco m fit (seizure)
  attacco cardiaco heart attack
attendere to wait for
attento(a) careful
attenzione f caution
  fare attenzione to be careful
atterraggio m landing (of plane)
atterrare to land (plane)
attestare to declare
attore m actor
attracco m mooring ; berth
attraente attractive
attraversare to cross

attraverso through
attrazione f attraction
attrezzatura f equipment
attrezzo m tool
attrice f actress
auguri! happy birthday! ; best wishes!
aumentare to increase
Australia f Australia
australiano(a) Australian
austriaco(a) Austrian
autentico(a) genuine
autista m/f driver
auto f car
autobus m bus
autofficina f garage (for repairs)
autoforniture fpl car parts and accessories
autonoleggio m car hire
autore m author
autorimessa f garage
autorizzazione f authorization
autostop m hitchhiking
autostrada f motorway
autunno m autumn
avanti in front ; forward(s)
  avanti! come in!
avere to have
  avere bisogno di to need
  avere fame to be hungry
  avere sete to be thirsty
avvertire to warn
avvisare to inform ; to warn

avviso m notice ; advertisement
azienda f business ; firm
  azienda di soggiorno local tourist board
azzardo m risk ; hazard
azzurro(a) light blue

B

babbo m daddy
  Babbo Natale Father Christmas
baciare to kiss
bacinella f washing-up bowl
bacio m kiss
baci! love and kisses (in letter)
baffi mpl moustache
bagagli mpl luggage
bagagliaio m boot (of car)
bagaglio m luggage
  bagaglio a mano hand luggage
bagnarsi to bathe ; to get wet
bagnino m lifeguard
bagno m bath ; bathroom
balcone m balcony
ballare to dance
balletto m ballet
ballo m dance
balneazione f bathing
  divieto di balneazione no swimming
balsamo m hair conditioner

B

bambino(a) m/f child ; baby
bambini mpl children
  per bambini for children
bambola f doll
banana f banana
banca f bank
bancarella f stall ; stand
banchina f platform ; quay
banco m counter ; desk
  banco informazioni
  enquiry desk
Bancomat® m cash
  dispenser
banconota f banknote
bandiera f flag
bar m bar ; café
barattolo m tin ; jar
barba f beard
barbiere m barber
barca f boat
barista m/f barman/barmaid
basso(a) low ; short
  bassa marea low tide
basta that's enough
battello m boat
batteria f battery *(car)*
  batteria scarica flat
  battery
baule m trunk *(luggage)*
bavaglino m bib
bello(a) beautiful ; fine ;
  lovely
benda f bandage
bene well ; all right ; OK
benvenuto welcome

benzina f petrol
  fare benzina to get petrol
bere to drink
bevanda f drink
biancheria f linen *(for beds,
  table)*
  biancheria intima
  underwear
bianco(a) white ; blank
  lasciate in bianco leave
  blank
biberon m baby's bottle
bibita f soft drink
  bibite soft drinks
bicchiere m glass *(for
  drinking)*
bici f bike *(pushbike)*
bicicletta f bicycle
bidet m bidet
bidone m bin ; dustbin ; can
biglietteria f ticket office
biglietto m ticket ; note ; card
  biglietto d'auguri
  greetings card
  biglietto da visita business
  card
bin. abbreviation of **binario**
binario m platform
biologico(a) organic
biondo(a) blond *(person)*
biro f biro
birra f beer
  birra alla spina draught
  beer
  birra bionda lager
  birra chiara lager
birreria f bar ; pub

biscotto m biscuit

bisogno m need
avere bisogno di to need

bistecca f steak

bloccare to block
bloccare un assegno
to stop a cheque

blocchetto di biglietti m
book of tickets

blocco m block ; notepad

blu blue

blue jeans mpl jeans

boa f buoy

bocca f mouth

boccaglio m snorkel

bocce fpl bowls (game)

bolletta f bill

bollire to boil

bollitore m kettle

bomba f bomb

bombola del gas f gas
cylinder

bombolone m doughnut

borotalco m talc

borsa f bag ; handbag ;
briefcase
borsa della spazzatura
bin liner
borsa termica cool-box
(for picnic)

borseggiatore m pickpocket

borsellino m purse

bosco m wood ; forest

bottega f shop

botteghino m box office

bottiglia f bottle

bottone m button

boxer mpl boxer shorts

braccialetto m bracelet

braccio m arm

braccioli mpl armbands
(swimming)

braciola f steak ; chop

brindisi m toast (raising glass)

brioche f croissant

britannico(a) f British

bronchite f bronchitis

bruciare to burn

bruciore di stomaco m
heartburn

brutto(a) bad (weather, news) ;
ugly

buca delle lettere f
postbox

bucato m washing ; laundry
bucato in lavatrice
machine wash
bucato a mano hand
washing

buco m hole ; leak

buono(a) good
buon appetito! enjoy your
meal!
buon compleanno! happy
birthday!
buon giorno good
morning/ afternoon
buona notte good night
buona sera good
afternoon/evening
a buon mercato cheap

buono m voucher ; coupon ;
token

B

burattino *m* puppet
burrasca *f* storm
burro *m* butter
burro di cacao *m* lip salve
bussare to knock (on door)
busta *f* envelope
bustina di tè *f* tea bag
buttare via to throw away

C

cabina *f* beach hut ; cabin
  cabina telefonica
  phonebox
cacciavite *m* screwdriver
cadere to fall
caffè *m* coffee (espresso)
  caffè corretto espresso
  with spirit such as grappa
  caffè macchiato espresso
  with a little warm milk
  caffè solubile instant
  coffee
  caffellatte milky coffee
caffettiera *f* espresso-
  maker
calamita *f* magnet
calciatore *m* football player
calcio *m* football ; kick
calcolatrice *f* calculator
caldo(a) hot
calendario *m* calendar
calle *f* street (in Venice
  dialect)
callo *m* corn (on foot)
calmante *m* painkiller

calmo(a) calm
calpestare to tread on
calvo(a) bald
calza *f* stocking ; sock
calzamaglia *f* tights
calzature *fpl* shoeshop
calze *fpl* stockings
calzini *mpl* socks
calzolaio *m* shoe mender's
calzoleria *f* shoeshop
calzoncini corti *mpl* shorts
  calzoncini da bagno
  swimming trunks
cambiamento *m* change
cambiare to change
  cambiare autobus/treno
  to change bus/train
  cambiare soldi to change
  money
  cambiarsi to change one's
  clothes
cambio *m* exchange ; gear
camera *f* room (in house,
  hotel)
  camera da letto bedroom
  camera doppia double
  room
  camera libera vacancy
  (in hotel)
  camera per famiglia family
  room
  camera singola single
  room
  camere vacancies
cameriera *f* chambermaid
cameriere *m* waiter
camiceria *f* shirt shop

camicetta f blouse
camicia f shirt
  camicia da notte
  nightdress
camion m lorry
camminare to walk
camoscio m chamois
campagna f countryside ;
  campaign
campanello m bell
campeggiare to camp
campeggio m camping ;
  campsite
  campeggio libero free
  campsite
camping gas m gas da
  campeggio
campione m sample ;
  champion
campo m field ; court
  campo da tennis tennis
  court
  campo di calcio football
  pitch
  campo di golf golf course
  campo sportivo sports
  ground
camposanto m cemetery
Canada m Canada
canadese Canadian
canale m canal ; channel
cancellare to erase ;
  to cancel
cancellazione f cancellation
cancro m cancer
candeggina f bleach
candela f candle ; spark plug

candida f thrush *(candida)*
cane m dog
canile m kennel
canna da pesca f fishing rod
cannuccia f straw *(for drinking)*
canoa f canoe
canottaggio m rowing
canottiera f vest
canotto m dinghy *(rubber)*
cantante m/f singer
cantare to sing
cantiere m building site
cantina f cellar ; wine cellar
canzone f song
capelli mpl hair
capire to understand
  capisce? do you
  understand?
  non capisco I don't
  understand
capitale f capital *(city)*
capitolo m chapter
capo m head ; leader ; boss
Capodanno m New Year's
  day
capogruppo m group
  leader
capolavoro m masterpiece
capolinea m terminus
capoluogo m county town
capotreno m guard *(on train)*
cappella f chapel
cappello m hat
cappotto m overcoat

cappuccino m cappuccino
capra f goat
carabiniere m policeman
caraffa f carafe
caramelle fpl sweets
carbone m coal ; charcoal
carburante m fuel
carburatore m carburettor
carcere m prison
caricare to charge (battery)
carico m load ; shipment ; cargo
carino(a) pretty ; lovely ; nice
carne f meat
carnevale m carnival
caro(a) dear ; expensive
carote fpl carrots
carrello m trolley
carriera f career
carro m cart
  carro attrezzi breakdown van
carrozza f carriage
  carrozze cuccette couchettes
  carrozza letto sleeper
carrozzeria f bodywork
carrozzina f pram
carta f paper ; card ; map
  carta assegni cheque card
  alla carta à la carte
  carta d'argento senior citizen's rail card
  carta di credito credit card
  carta famiglia family rail card
  carta d'identità identity card
  carta igienica toilet paper
  carta d'imbarco boarding card
  carta stradale road map
  carta verde green card
carte da gioco fpl playing cards
cartella f briefcase ; folder
cartello m sign ; signpost
cartine fpl cigarette papers
cartoccio m paper bag
cartoleria f stationer's
cartolina f postcard
casa f house ; home
  a casa at home
casalinga f housewife
casalinghi mpl household articles
cascata f waterfall
casco m helmet
casella postale f post-office box
casinò m casino
caso: in caso di in case of
cassa f till ; cash desk
  cassa chiusa position closed
cassaforte f safe (for valuables)
cassetta f cassette
  cassetta delle lettere letterbox
cassetto m drawer

cassiere(a) m/f cashier ; teller

castello m castle

catena f chain ; mountain range
  catene (da neve) snow chains

cattedrale f cathedral

cattivo(a) bad ; nasty ; naughty

cattolico(a) Catholic

causa f cause ; case *(lawsuit)*
  a causa di because of

cavalcare to ride *(horse)*

cavallo m horse

cavatappi m corkscrew

cavo m cable
  cavo da rimorchio tow rope

cavolfiore m cauliflower

CD m CD

c'è there is

cedro m cedar ; lime *(fruit)*

CE f EC

celibe single *(not married)*

cellulare m mobile phone

cena f dinner *(evening meal)*

cenare to have dinner

cenone m New Year's Eve dinner

centesimo m cent

centimetro m centimetre

cento hundred

centrale central

centralino m switchboard

centro m centre
  centro città city centre
  centro commerciale shopping centre
  centro storico old town

ceppo bloccaruote m wheel clamp

cera f wax *(for furniture)*

ceramica f ceramics ; pottery

cercare to look for

ceretta f waxing *(hair removal)*

cerini mpl matches

cerniera f zip

cerotto m sticking plaster

certificato m certificate
  certificato di nascita birth certificate

cervello m brain

cestino m basket ; waste paper bin

che what ; who ; which
  che gusto? what flavour?
  che ore sono? what time is it?

cherosene m paraffin

chi? who?
  di chi è? whose is it?

chiamare to call
  chiamare per telefono to phone

chiamarsi to be called *(name)*
  come si chiama? what's your name?

chiamata f call *(telephone)*

C

chiave f key
chiave inglese spanner
chiedere to ask ; to ask for
chiesa f church
chilo m kilo
chilogrammo m kilogram
chilometraggio m mileage (in km)
chilometro m kilometre
chiodo m nail (metal)
chirurgia f surgery (operations)
chitarra f guitar
chiudere to close ; to turn off (tap)
chiudere a chiave to lock
chiuso(a) closed
chiuso per turno closed for weekly day off
chiuso per ferie closed for holidays
chiusura centralizzata f central locking (car)
ciabatta f flat bread ; slipper
ciao! hi! ; bye!
cibo m food
cielo m sky
ciliegia f cherry
cinghia della ventola f fan belt
cintura f belt
cintura di sicurezza seatbelt
cinturino dell'orologio m watchstrap

cioccolato m chocolate
cipolla f onion
circo m circus
circolare to move (traffic)
circolazione f traffic
circonvallazione f ring road
cisterna f cistern ; tank
cisti f cyst
cistite f cystitis
CIT f Italian Tourist Agency
citofono m intercom
città f city ; town
cittadino(a) citizen
classe f class
clavicola f collar bone
cliente m/f customer
climatizzato(a) air-conditioned
clinica f clinic
cocco m coconut
cocomero m watermelon
coda f tail ; queue
codice m code
codice a barra barcode
codice postale postcode
codice stradale highway code
cofano m bonnet (car)
cognata f sister-in-law
cognato m brother-in-law
cognome m surname
di cognome mi chiamo... my surname is...
coincidenza f connection (train, etc)

colazione f breakfast ; lunch

collana f necklace

collant mpl tights

collega m/f colleague

colletto m collar

collina f hill

collo m neck ; package

colluttorio m mouthwash

colomba f dove ; Easter cake

colore m colour

Colosseo m Coliseum

colpa f fault
non è colpa mia it's not my fault

coltello m knife

combustibile m fuel

come like ; as ; how
come? how? *(in what way)*
come si chiama? what's your name?
come si pronuncia? how is it pronounced?
come si scrive? how is it spelt?
come sta? how are you?
come va? how's it going?

cominciare to begin

commesso(a) m/f assistant ; clerk

commissariato m police station

commozione cerebrale f concussion

comodo(a) comfortable

compagnia f company
compagnia aerea airline

compilare to fill in *(form)*

compleanno m birthday

completo(a) no vacancies ; full

comporre to dial *(number)*

comprare to buy

compreso(a) included

compressa f tablet

computer m computer

comune m town hall ; commune

con with
con bagno with bathroom
con filtro filter-tipped
con ghiaccio with ice

concerto m concert

conchiglia f seashell

condimento m seasoning ; dressing *(for food)*

conducente m/f driver *(taxi, bus)*

confermare to confirm

confine m boundary ; border

congelatore m freezer

congratulazioni! congratulations!

congresso m conference

cono m cone
cono gelato ice-cream cone

conoscere to know *(to be acquainted with)*

consegna f consignment ; delivery

conservante m preservative

consigliare to advise

consiglio m advice

consumare to use up
da consumarsi entro best before

consumazione f drink

contanti mpl cash
pagare in contanti to pay cash

contatore m electricity meter

contento(a) happy

continuare to continue

conto m account ; bill
conto corrente current account
conto dettagliato itemised bill
conto in banca bank account

contorno m vegetable side dish

contrabbando m smuggling

contratto m contract

contravvenzione f fine

contro against ; versus

controllare to check

controllo m check ; control
controllo passaporti passport control

controllore m ticket collector

convalida f date stamp

convalidare to validate *(ticket)*

convincere to persuade

coperta f blanket

coperto m place setting ; cover charge

copertura f cover *(insurance)*

coppa gelato f ice cream served in goblet/tub

coppia f couple *(two people)*

copriletto m bedspread

coraggioso(a) brave

corda f rope

cornetto m ice cream cone

corpo m body

corrente f current *(electric, water)*
corrente d'aria draught

correre to run

corridoio m corridor

corriere m courier

corsa f race ; journey
corsa semplice single fare

corsia f lane ; hospital ward ; route
corsia di emergenza hard shoulder
corsia di sorpasso outside lane

corso m course ; avenue
corso dei cambi exchange rates
corso intensivo crash course

cortile m courtyard

corto(a) short

cos'è? what is it?
cos'è successo? what happened?

cosa f thing
cosa? what?

coscia f thigh

così so ; thus (in this way)

cosmetici mpl cosmetics

costa f coast
  Costa Azzurra French Riviera

costare to cost

costoletta f chop

costoso(a) expensive

costruire to build

costume m custom ; costume
  costume da bagno swimsuit

cotone m cotton
  cotone idrofilo cotton wool

cotto(a) cooked
  poco cotto(a) medium rare (steak)

cotton fioc® m cotton bud

crampi mpl cramps

cravatta f tie

credere to believe

credito m credit
  non si fa credito no credit given

crema f cream ; custard
  crema da barba shaving cream

crescere to grow

crespella f fried pastry twist

cric m jack (for car)

crisi epilettica f epileptic fit

cristallo m crystal
  di cristallo made of crystal

croccante f crisp

croce f cross

crocevia m crossroads

crociera f cruise

crollo m collapse

cronaca f news

cruciverba m crossword puzzle

crudo(a) raw

cuccetta f couchette ; sleeper

cucchiaino m teaspoon

cucchiaio m spoon ; tablespoon

cucina f cooker ; kitchen ; cooking
  cucina a gas gas cooker

cucinare to cook

cucire to sew

cuffia f bathing cap

cuffie fpl earphones

cugino(a) m/f cousin

culla f cradle

cuocere to cook
  cuocere a vapore to steam
  cuocere alla griglia to grill

cuoco m chef

cuoio m leather

cuore m heart

cupola f dome

curva f bend ; corner

cuscino m cushion

custode m caretaker

custodia f case ; holder

cyber-café m internet cafe

D

da from ; by ; with ; worth
  da asporto take-away
  dall'Inghilterra from
  England
  dalla Scozia from Scotland
  da vedere worth seeing
  da 100 euro worth
  100 euros
danneggiare to spoil ;
  to damage
danno *m* damage
dappertutto everywhere
dare to give
  dare su to overlook ;
  to give onto
  dare la precedenza give
  way
  dare da mangiare to feed
  dare la mancia to tip
  (waiter, etc)
data *f* date
  data di nascita date of birth
  data di scadenza sell-by
  date
dati *mpl* data
dattero *m* date (fruit)
davanti a in front of ;
  opposite
dazio *m* customs duty
d.C. A.D.
debito *m* debt
decaffeinato(a)
  decaffeinated
decollare to take-off
decollo *m* takeoff
delizioso(a) delicious

dente *m* tooth
dentiera *f* dentures
dentifricio *m* toothpaste
dentro in ; indoors ; inside
deodorante *m* deodorant
  deodorante per ambienti
  air freshener
deposito bagagli *m* left-
  luggage
descrivere to describe
descrizione *f* description
desiderare to want ;
  to desire
destinazione *f* destination
destra *f* right
detergente *m* cleanser
detersivo *m* detergent
  detersivo in polvere soap
  powder
  detersivo per i piatti
  washing-up liquid
detrazione *f* deduction
dettagli *mpl* details
deviazione *f* detour ;
  diversion
di of ; some
  di cristallo/plastica made
  of crystal/plastic
  di Giovanni Giovanni's
  di lusso luxury (hotel, etc)
  di mattina in the morning
  di pomeriggio in the
  afternoon
  di moda fashionable
  di notte at night
  di stagione in season
  di valore of value ;
  valuable

diabete m diabetes
diabetico(a) diabetic
diaframma m cap (diaphragm)
dialetto m dialect
diamante m diamond
diapositiva f slide (photo)
diarrea f diarrhoea
dicembre m December
dichiarare to declare
dichiarazione f declaration
dieta f diet
  essere a dieta to be on a diet
dietro behind ; after
  dietro di behind
difetto m fault
difficile difficult
diga f dam ; dyke
digerire to digest
digestivo m after-dinner liqueur
dimenticare to forget
Dio m God
dipinto(a) painted
diramazione f fork (in road)
dire to say ; to tell
diretto(a) direct
  treno diretto through train
direttore m manager ; director
direzione f management ; direction
dirigere to manage (be in charge of)

diritto(a) straight
  sempre diritto straight on
disabile disabled (person)
disastro m disaster
dischetto m floppy disk ; diskette
disco m disk ; record
  disco orario parking disk
discoteca f disco
disdire to cancel
disegno m drawing
disfare la valigia to unpack
disinfettante m disinfectant
disoccupato(a) unemployed
dispiacere: mi dispiace I'm sorry
disponibile available
distaccare to detach ; to unplug
distante far ; distant
distanza f distance
distorsione f sprain
distributore m dispenser
  distributore di benzina petrol station
disturbare to disturb
disturbo m trouble
dito m finger
  dito del piede toe
ditta f firm ; company
diurno(a) day(time)
divano m sofa ; divan
  divano letto sofa bed
diversi(e) several ; various
diverso(a) different
divertente funny (amusing)

D

divertimento m entertainment ; fun

divertirsi to enjoy oneself

dividere to share

divieto forbidden
divieto di sorpasso no overtaking
divieto di sosta no parking

divisa f uniform

divorziato(a) divorced

dizionario m dictionary

DOC abbreviation of denominazione di origine controllata *(guarantee of wine quality)*

doccia f shower

docente m/f lecturer

DOCG abbreviation of denominazione di origine controllata e garantita *(guarantee of wine quality)*

documenti mpl papers *(passport)*

dogana f customs

dolce sweet *(not savoury)* ; mild

dolce m sweet ; dessert ; cake

dolcelatte m creamy blue cheese

dolcificante m sweetener

dolciumi mpl sweets

dollari mpl dollars

dolore m pain ; grief

doloroso(a) painful

domanda f question

domandare to ask *(a question)*

domani tomorrow
domani mattina tomorrow morning
domani pomeriggio tomorrow afternoon
domani sera tomorrow evening/night

domattina tomorrow morning

domenica Sunday

donna f woman
donne Ladies ; women

dopo after ; afterward(s)

dopobarba m aftershave

dopodomani the day after tomorrow

doppio(a) double

dormire to sleep

dove? where?

dovere to have to

droga f drugs *(narcotics)*

drogheria f grocery shop

duepezzi m two-piece suit

duomo m cathedral

durante during

durare to last

duro(a) hard ; tough ; harsh

E

e and

E east *(abbreviation)*

è is (to be)

ebreo(a) Jewish

ecc. etc.

eccedenza f excess ; surplus

eccesso m excess
  eccesso di velocità
  speeding

eccezionale exceptional

eccezione f exception

ecco here is/are

economico(a) cheap

edicola f newsstand ; kiosk

edificio m building

effetto m effect
  effetti personali
  belongings

egregio(a) dear *(in formal letter)*

elastico m rubber band

elenco m list
  elenco telefonico phone
  directory

elettricista m/f electrician

elettricità f electricity

elettrico(a) electric(al)

elettrodomestici mpl
  electrical goods

emergenza f emergency

emicrania f migraine

emorroidi fpl haemorrhoids

enoteca f wine shop ; wine
  bar

ente m corporation ; body

entrambi(e) both

entrare to come/go in ;
  to enter

entrata f entrance

  entrata abbonati season
  ticket holders' entrance
  entrata libera free
  admission

epatite f hepatitis

epilessia f epilepsy

epilettico(a) epileptic

equitazione f horse-riding

erba f grass

ernia f hernia

errore m mistake

esame m examination

esatto(a) exact ; accurate

esaurimento nervoso m
  nervous breakdown

esaurito(a) exhausted ;
  out of print
  tutto esaurito sold out

esca m fishing bait

escluso(a) excluding

escursione f excursion

esente exempt
  esente da dogana duty-
  free

esempio example
  per esempio for example

esercizio m exercise ;
  business

esigenza f requirement

esperto(a) expert ;
  experienced

esplosione f explosion

esportare to export

esposto(a) exposed
  esposto(a) a nord north-
  facing

E

espresso *m* express train ; coffee

espresso(a) express *(parcel, etc)*

essere to be
 essere assicurato(a) to be insured
 essere capace (di) to be able to
 essere d'accordo to agree
 essere nato(a) to be born

est *m* east

estate *f* summer

esterno(a) outside ; external

estero(a) foreign
 all'estero abroad

estintore *m* fire extinguisher

estivo(a) summer

età *f* age

etichetta *f* luggage tag ; label

euro euro

eurocheque *m* Eurocheque

Europa *f* Europe

eventuale possible

evitare to avoid

F

fa ago
 un anno fa a year ago

fabbrica *f* factory

fabbricare to manufacture

faccia *f* face

facile easy

fagiano *m* pheasant

fallire to fail

fallito(a) bankrupt

fallo *m* foul *(football)*

falso(a) fake

fame *f* hunger
 avere fame to be hungry

famiglia *f* family

familiare family ; familiar

famoso(a) famous

fanale *m* light

fanalino dello stop *m* brake light

fango *m* mud

farcito(a) stuffed ; filled

fare to do ; to make
 fare attenzione to be careful
 fare la spesa to go shopping

farfalla *f* butterfly

fari *mpl* headlights

farina *f* flour

farmacia *f* chemist's ; pharmacy
 farmacie di turno duty chemists

farmaco *m* drug *(medicine)*

faro *m* headlight ; lighthouse

fascia *f* band ; bandage

fastidio: *non mi dà fastidio* I don't mind

fatelo da voi *m* DIY

fatto a mano hand-made

fatto di ... made of ...

fattoria *f* farm ; farmhouse

fattura *f* invoice

favore m favour
 per favore please

fax m fax

fazzoletto m handkerchief
 fazzoletto di carta tissue

febbraio February

febbre f fever
 avere la febbre to have
 a temperature
 febbre da fieno hay fever

fede f wedding ring

federa f pillowcase

fegato m liver

felice happy

felpa f sweatshirt

femmina f female

feriale workday (Monday-
Saturday)

ferie fpl holiday(s)
 essere in ferie to be on
 holiday

ferire to injure

ferita f wound ; injury ; cut

ferito(a) injured

fermare to stop

fermata f stop
 fermata dell'autobus bus
 stop

fermo(a) still ; off (machine)
 stare fermo to stay still

ferro da stiro m iron (for
clothes)

ferrovia f railway

festa f festival ; holiday ;
party
 festa nazionale public
 holiday

festivo(a) sundays/public
holiday

fetta f slice

fiamma f flame

fiammifero m match

fico m fig

fidanzato(a) engaged
(to marry)

fieno m hay

fiera f fair (trade)

figlia f daughter

figlio m son

fila f line (row, queue)
 fare la fila to queue

filiale f branch ; subsidiary

film m film (at cinema)

filo m thread ; wire
 filo interdentale dental floss

filtro m filter
 filtro dell'olio oil filter

finanza f finance
 Guardia di finanza
 Customs and Excise

fine f end
 fine settimana weekend
 fine stagione end of
 season

finestra f window

finestrino m window (car, train)

finire to finish

finito(a) finished

fino(a) fine ; elegant

fino a until ; as far as
 fino alle due till 2 o'clock

fior di latte m cream (ice
cream flavour)

F

fiori *mpl* flowers
fiorista *m/f* florist
Firenze Florence
firma *f* signature
firmare to sign
 firmare il registro to sign register
fiume *m* river
focaccia *f* flat salted bread
foglia *f* leaf *(of tree, etc)*
fogna *f* sewer ; drain
folla *f* crowd
folle mad
 in folle in neutral *(car)*
fon *m* hairdryer
fondo *m* back *(of room)* ; bottom
fontana *f* fountain
fonte *f* source
foratura *f* puncture
forbici *fpl* scissors
 forbicine nail scissors
forchetta *f* fork *(for eating)*
foresta *f* forest
forfora *f* dandruff
formaggio *m* cheese
fornaio *m* baker
fornello *m* stove ; hotplate
fornitore *m* supplier
forno *m* oven
 forno a microonde microwave
forse perhaps
forte strong ; loud ; high *(speed)*

fortunato(a) lucky
forza *f* strength ; force
foto *f* photo
fotocopia *f* photocopy
fotocopiare to photocopy
fototessera *f* passport-type photo
foulard *m* headscarf
fra between ; among(st)
 fra 2 giorni in 2 days
 fra poco in a while
fragile breakable
fragola *f* strawberry
frana *f* landslide
francese French
francese *m* French *(language)*
Francia *f* France
francobollo *m* stamp
frappé *m* milk shake
fratello *m* brother
frattura *f* fracture
frazione *f* village
freccia *f* indicator *(car)* ; arrow
freddo(a) cold
frenare to brake
freno *m* brake
 freno a mano handbrake
frequente frequent
fretta *f* hurry
 avere fretta to be in a hurry
friggere to fry
frigorifero *m* refrigerator
frittata *f* omelette
fritto(a) fried

frizione f clutch *(car)*

frizzante fizzy ; sparkling

fronte f forehead ; front
  di fronte a facing ;
  opposite

frontiera f frontier ; border

frullato m milkshake

frutta f fruit
  frutta secca dried fruit

frutti di mare mpl seafood

fruttivendolo m
  greengrocer

FS Italian State Railways

fuga f escape ; leak *(gas)*

fuggire to escape

fulmine m lightning

fumare to smoke
  non fumo I don't smoke

fumatori smokers

fumo m smoke

funerale m funeral

funghi mpl mushrooms
  funghi porcini boletus
  mushrooms
  funghi secchi dried
  mushrooms

funicolare f funicular railway

funzionare to work
  (mechanism)
  non funziona it doesn't
  work

fuoco m fire ; focus
  fuochi d'artificio fireworks

fuori outside ; out
  fuori servizio out of order

furgone m van

furto m theft

fuseaux mpl leggings

fusibile m fuse

futuro m future

G

gabinetto m lavatory
  gabinetto biologico
  chemical toilet
  gabinetto medico doctor's
  surgery

galleria f tunnel ; gallery ;
  arcade ; circle *(theatre)*
  galleria d'arte art gallery

Galles m Wales

gallese Welsh

gamba f leg

gara f race *(sport)*

garanzia f guarantee ;
  warranty

gas m gas

gasolio m diesel

gassato(a) fizzy

gassosa f lemonade

gastrite f gastritis

gatto m cat

gay gay *(person)*

gel per capelli m hair gel

gelateria f ice-cream shop

gelatina f jelly

gelato m ice cream

gelo m frost

geloso(a) jealous

G

gemelli *mpl* twins ; cufflinks
genere *m* kind *(type)* ; gender
genero *m* son-in-law
genitori *mpl* parents
Genova *f* Genoa
gentile kind *(person)*
Germania *f* Germany
gesso *m* chalk ; plaster *(for limb)*
gettare to throw
 non gettare rifiuti no dumping
gettone *m* token
 gettone di presenza attendance fee
ghiaccio *m* ice
ghiacciolo *m* ice lolly
giacca *f* jacket
giallo *m* thriller *(book or film)*
giallo(a) yellow ; amber *(light)*
giardiniere *m* gardener
giardino *m* garden
gilè *m* waistcoat
gin *m* gin
 gin tonic gin and tonic
ginocchio *m* knee
giocare to play ; to gamble
giocattolo *m* toy
gioco *m* game
 gioco a quiz quiz show
gioielleria *f* jeweller's
gioielli *mpl* jewellery
gioielliere *m* jeweller
giornalaio *m* newsagent

giornale *m* newspaper
giornalista *m/f* journalist
giornata *f* day
giorno *m* day
 giorni feriali Monday-Saturday
 giorni festivi Sundays/holidays
giovane young
giovedì *m* Thursday
girare to turn ; to spin
 girarsi to turn around
girasole *m* sunflower
girella *f* scrunchie
giro *m* tour ; turn
 fare un giro a piedi to go for a stroll
 giro turistico sightseeing tour
gita *f* trip ; excursion
 gita in barca boat trip
 gita in pullman coach trip
giù down ; downstairs
giubbotto salvagente *m* life jacket
giudice *m* judge
giugno *m* June
giusto(a) fair ; right *(correct)*
gli the ; to him/it
globale inclusive *(costs)*
goccia *f* drop *(of liquid)* ; drip
gola *f* throat ; gorge
golfo *m* gulf
gomito *m* elbow
gomma *f* rubber ; tyre
 gomma a terra flat tyre
 gomma da cancellare eraser

gommone m dinghy (inflatable)

gonfiare to inflate

gonfio(a) swollen

gonfiore m lump (swelling)

gonna f skirt

gradazione f content (of alcohol)

gradevole pleasant

gradino m step ; stair

Gran Bretagna f Great Britain

grana f parmesan cheese

granaio m barn

granchio m crab

grande large ; great ; big

grande magazzino m department store

grandine f hail

granita f water ice (flavoured)

grappa f strong spirit (often drunk with coffee)

grasso(a) fat ; greasy

gratis free of charge

grattacielo m skyscraper

grattugia f grater

grattugiato(a) grated

gratuito(a) free of charge
il servizio è gratuito service included

grave serious

grazie thank you

gridare to shout

grigio(a) grey

griglia f grill
alla griglia grilled

grissini mpl breadsticks

grosso(a) big ; thick

grucce fpl crutches

gruccia f coat hanger

gruppo m group
gruppo sanguigno blood group

guadagnare to earn

guanciale m pillow

guanto m glove
guanto da forno oven glove
guanto di spugna facecloth
guanti di gomma rubber gloves

guardacoste m coastguard

guardare to look (at) ; to watch

guardaroba m cloakroom

guardia f guard
Guardia di finanza Customs and Excise

guasto out of order

guerra f war

guida f guide (person or book) ; directory
guida a sinistra left-hand drive
guida telefonica telephone directory
guida turistica tour guide

guidare to drive ; to steer

guidatore m driver

guinzaglio m lead (for dog)

gustare to taste ; to enjoy

gusto m flavour

ha...? do you have...?
  ha l'ora? do you have the time?
hamburger m burger
herpes m cold sore ; herpes
ho... I have...
  ho ... anni I'm ... years old
  ho bisogno di... I need...
  ho fame I'm hungry
  ho fretta I'm in a hurry
  ho sete I'm thirsty
hostess f stewardess

I

i the
identificare to identify
idratante m moisturizer
idraulico m plumber
ieri yesterday
il the
imbarcarsi to embark
imbarcazione f boat
imbarco m boarding
  carta d'imbarco boarding card
imbottigliato(a) bottled
imbucare to post (letter, etc)
immediatamente at once
immergere to dip (into liquid)
immersioni subacquee fpl scuba diving
immondizie fpl rubbish

immunizzazione f immunisation
impanato coated in breadcrumbs
imparare to learn
impasto m mixture
imperatore m emperor
impermeabile m raincoat
impero m empire
impiego m use ; employment
impiegato(a) m/f employee ; white-collar worker
importante important
importare to import ; to matter
  non importa it doesn't matter
importo m (total) amount
impossibile impossible
imposta f tax (on income) ; shutter
  imposta sul valore aggiunto (IVA) value-added tax (VAT)
improbabile unlikely
in in ; to
  in Spagna to Spain
  in vacanza on holiday
inalatore m inhaler
inadempienza f negligence
incantevole charming
incaricarsi di to take charge of
incartare to wrap up (parcel)
incassare to cash (a cheque)
incendio m fire

inchiostro m ink

incidente m accident

incinta pregnant

incluso(a) included ; enclosed

incontrare to meet

incontro m meeting (by chance)

incrocio m crossroads ; junction

indicatore m indicator ; gauge
indicatore del livello dell'olio oil gauge

indicazioni fpl directions

indice m index ; contents

indietro backwards ; behind

indirizzo m address

infarto m heart attack

infatti in fact ; actually

infermeria f infirmary

infermiera f nurse

infezione infection

infiammabile inflammable

infiammazione f inflammation

influenza f flu

informare to inform
informarsi (di) to inquire (about)

informazioni fpl information

ingessatura f plaster cast

Inghilterra f England

inghiottire to swallow

inglese English

ingorgato(a) blocked (pipe, sink)

ingorgo m blockage ; hold-up
ingorgo stradale traffic jam

ingresso m entry/entrance
ingresso gratuito free entry

iniezione f injection

inizio m start

innocuo(a) harmless

inondazione m flood

inoltre besides

inquinato(a) polluted

insalata f salad
insalata di patate potato salad
insalata di pomodori tomato salad
insalata mista mixed salad
insalata verde green salad

insegnante m/f teacher

insegnare to teach

inserire to insert
inserire le banconote una per volta insert banknotes one at a time

insettifugo m insect repellent

insetto m insect

insieme together

insieme m outfit

insolazione f sunstroke

insulina f insulin

interessante interesting

internazionale international

Internet m Internet

interno *m* inside ; extension *(phone)*

intero(a) whole

interpretazione *f* interpretation

interprete *m/f* interpreter

interruttore *m* switch

intervallo *m* half-time ; interval

intervento *m* operation

inversione *f* U-turn

intervista *f* interview

intestato(a) a registered in the name of

intimi donna *mpl* ladies' underwear

intorno around

intossicazione alimentare *f* food-poisoning

introdurre to introduce

inutile unnecessary ; useless

invalido(a) disabled ; invalid

invece di instead of

invernale winter

inverno *m* winter

investire to knock down *(car)*

inviare to send

invitare to invite

invito *m* invitation

io I

ipermercato *m* hypermarket

ipermetrope long-sighted

Irlanda *f* Ireland
  Irlanda del Nord Northern Ireland

irlandese Irish

iscritto *m* member
  per iscritto in writing

iscriversi a to join *(club)*

iscrizione *f* inscription ; enrolment

isola *f* island

istituto *m* institute

istruttore(trice) *m/f* instructor

istruzioni *fpl* instructions

Italia *f* Italy

italiano(a) Italian

itinerario *m* route
  itinerario turistico scenic route

itterizia *f* jaundice

IVA *f* VAT

J

jolly *m* joker *(cards)*

L

la the ; her ; it ; you

là there
  per di là that way

labbra *fpl* lips

lacca *f* lacquer ; hair spray

ladro *m* thief

lago *m* lake

L

lamette *fpl* razor blades
lampada *f* lamp
lampadina *f* lightbulb
lampone *m* raspberry
lana *f* wool
largo(a) wide ; broad
lasciare to leave ; to let *(allow)*
lassativo *m* laxative
lassù up there
latte *m* milk
  latte a lunga conservazione long-life milk
  latte di soia soya milk
  latte fresco fresh milk
  latte in polvere powdered milk
  latte intero whole milk
  latte scremato skimmed milk
  latte parzialmente scremato semi-skimmed milk
lattuga *f* lettuce
lavabile washable
lavaggio *m* washing
  lavaggio auto car wash
  per lavaggi frequenti for frequent use
lavanderia *f* laundry *(place)*
  lavanderia automatica launderette
lavandino *m* sink
lavare to wash
  lavare a secco to dry-clean
lavarsi to wash *(oneself)*

lavasecco *m* dry-cleaner's
lavastoviglie *f* dishwasher
lavatrice *f* washing machine
lavorare to work *(person)*
lavoro *m* job ; occupation ; work
  lavori stradali road works
  lavori in corso road works
le *(feminine plural)* ; them ; to her ; to you
legge *f* law
leggere to read
leggero(a) light *(not heavy)* ; weak
legno *m* wood *(material)*
lei she ; her ; you
lentamente slowly
lente *f* lens *(of glasses)*
  lente d'ingrandimento magnifying glass
  lenti a contatto contact lenses
lento slow
lenzuolo *m* sheet *(bed)*
lesbica lesbian
lesione *f* injury
lettera *f* letter
  lettera raccomandata registered letter
lettino *m* cot
letto *m* bed
  letto a una piazza single bed
  letto matrimoniale double bed
  letti gemelli twin beds
  letti a castello bunk beds

ITALIAN-ENGLISH

219

L

lettore CD m CD player
lì there *(over there)*
libero(a) free/vacant
libreria f bookshop
libretto m booklet
  libretto degli assegni cheque book
libro m book
licenza f licence ; permit
  licenza di caccia hunting permit
  licenza di pesca fishing permit
limetta per le unghie f nail file
limite m limit ; boundary
  limite di velocità speed limit
limone m lemon
linea f line ; route
  linea aerea airline
lingua f language ; tongue
lino m linen
liquido m liquid
  liquido dei freni brake fluid
  liquido lavavetri screen wash
  liquido per lenti a contatto contact lens solution
liquore m liqueur
liquori mpl spirits *(alcohol)*
liscio(a) straight ; smooth
lista f list
  lista dei vini wine list
listino prezzi m price list

litro m litre
livello m level
lo him ; it
locale local
locale m room ; place ; local train
  locale notturno nightclub
località di vacanza f resort
locanda f inn
Londra f London
lontano(a) far
lozione f lotion
  lozione solare suntan lotion
lucchetto m padlock
  lucchetto della bici bike lock
luce f light
lucertola f lizard
luglio m July
lui him
lumaca f snail
luna f moon
  luna di miele honeymoon
luna park m funfair
lunedì m Monday
lunghezza f length
lungo(a) long
  lungo la strada along the street
  a lungo for a long time
lungomare m promenade ; seafront
luogo m place
  luogo di nascita place of birth

upo m wolf

usso m luxury
  di lusso luxury (hotel, etc)

M

na but

nacchia f stain ; mark

nacchina f car ; machine
  macchina a noleggio hire
  car
  macchina fotografica
  camera
  macchina sportiva sports
  car

macedonia f fruit salad

macellaio m butcher's

macinato(a) ground (coffee,
  meat)

madre f mother

magazzino m warehouse

maggio m May

maggiore larger ; greater ;
  largest ; older ; oldest

maglietta f t-shirt

maglione m jumper ;
  sweater

magro(a) thin (person) ;
  low-fat ; lean (meat)

mai never ; ever

maiale m pig ; pork

mal see male

malato(a) ill ; sick

malattia f disease
  malattia venerea venereal
  disease

male badly (not well)

male m pain ; ache
  mal d'aria air sickness
  mal d'auto car sickness
  mal d'orecchi earache
  mal di denti toothache
  mal di gola sore throat
  mal di mare sea sickness
  mal di pancia
  stomachache
  mal di testa headache

maltempo m bad weather

mamma f mum(my)

mancia f tip (to waiter, etc)

mandare to send
  mandare per fax to fax

mangiare to eat
  mangiare fuori to eat out

manica f sleeve
  la Manica the English
  Channel

mano f hand
  fatto(a) a mano handmade

Mantova f Mantua

manuale di conversazione
  m phrase book

manzo m beef

marca f brand (make)

marcia f gear (car) ; march

marciapiede m pavement

mare m sea ; seaside
  Mare del Nord North Sea

margarina f margarine

margherita f daisy

marina f navy

marito m husband

marmellata f jam

M

marmellata d'arance
marmalade

marrone m brown ;
chestnut

marsupio m bumbag ;
money belt

martedì m Tuesday
martedì grasso Shrove
Tuesday

martello m hammer

marzo m March

maschera f mask ; fancy
dress

maschile masculine ; male

massimo(a) maximum

masticare to chew

materassino m airbed ; lilo

materasso m mattress

materiale m material

matrigna f stepmother

matrimonio m wedding

mattina f morning
di mattina in the morning

matto(a) mad

mazza f mallet
mazze da golf golf clubs

meccanico m mechanic ;
repair shop

medicina f medicine

medico m doctor

Mediterraneo m
Mediterranean

medusa f jellyfish

meglio better ; best
meglio di better than

mela f apple

melanzana f aubergine ;
eggplant

melone m melon

membro m member

meningite f meningitis

meno less ; minus

mensa f canteen

mensile monthly

mensilmente monthly

mensola f shelf

menta f mint

mento m chin

mentre while ; whereas

menù m menu
menù alla carta à la carte
menu
menù a prezzo fisso set-
price menu
menù turistico set menu

meraviglioso(a) wonderful

mercatino dell'usato m flea
market

mercato m market

merce f goods

merci fpl freight ; goods

mercoledì m Wednesday

merenda f snack

meridionale southern

mese m month

messa f mass *(in church)*

messaggio m message

mestruazioni fpl period
(menstrual)

metà f half
metà prezzo half-price

metro m metre

M

metro a nastro tape
measure
metropolitana f under-
ground ; metro
mettere to put ; to put on
(clothes)
mettersi in contatto con
to contact
mezzanotte f midnight
mezzi mpl means ; transport
mezzo m middle
mezzo(a) half
mezza pensione half board
mezzogiorno m midday ;
noon
il Mezzogiorno the south
of Italy
mezz'ora f half an hour
mi me ; to me ; myself
mia my
miele m honey
migliorare to improve
migliore better ; best
Milano Milan
miliardo m billion
milione m million
mille thousand
millimetro m millimetre
minestra f soup
minimo m minimum
ministro m minister (political)
minorenne underage
minori mpl minors
minuto m minute
mio my
miscela f blend

misto(a) mixed
mittente m/f sender
MM metro ; underground
mobili mpl furniture
moda f fashion
moderno(a) modern
modo m way ; manner
modulo m form (document)
modulo d'iscrizione
registration form
moglie f wife
molletta f clothes peg
molletta per capelli
hairgrip
molo m jetty ; quay ; pier
molti(e) many
molte grazie thanks very
much
molto much ; a lot ; very
molto tempo for a long
time
molta gente lots of people
monastero m monastery
moneta f coin ; currency
montagna f mountain
monumento m monument
mordere to bite (animal)
morire to die
morsicare to bite (insect)
morsicato(a) bite (from
insect)
morso(a) bitten
morto(a) dead
mosca f fly
moscerino m midge ; gnat
moschea f mosque

mosso(a) rough *(sea)* ; ruffled
mostra f exhibition
mostrare to show
moto f motorbike
motore m engine ; motor
motorino m moped
motorino d'avviamento m starter motor
multa f fine *(to be paid)*
municipio m town hall
muro m wall
museo m museum
musica f music
muta f wetsuit
mutande fpl underpants
mutandine fpl knickers ; panties

N

N north *(abbreviation)*
nafta f diesel
Napoli Naples
nascita f birth
naso m nose
nastro m tape ; ribbon
nato(a) born
nauseato(a) nauseous
nave f ship
nave-traghetto f ferry
nazionale national ; domestic *(flight)*
nazionalità f nationality
nazione f nation

né ... né neither ... nor
nebbia f fog
necessario(a) necessary
negativo m negative *(photo*
negozio m shop
nero(a) black
nessuno(a) no ; nobody ; none
netto m net
    al netto di IVA net of VAT
neve f snow
nevicare to snow
niente nothing
    niente da dichiarare nothing to declare
nipote m/f nephew/niece
nipotina f granddaughter
nipotino m grandson
noce f walnut
nocivo(a) harmful
nodo m knot ; bow
    nodo ferroviario junction *(railway)*
noi we
noleggiare to hire
noleggio m hire
    noleggio auto car hire
    noleggio barche boat hire
    noleggio bici bike hire
    noleggio sci ski hire
nolo m hire
nome m name ; first name
    nome da ragazza maiden name
non not
    non ancora not yet
    non c'é there isn't

non funziona it doesn't work
non capisco I don't understand
non pericoloso(a) safe
non-fumatore m/f non-smoker
nonna f grandmother
nonno m grandfather
nord m north
nostro(a) our
notare to notice
notizie fpl news
notte f night
 notte di San Silvestro New Year's Eve
 di notte at night
novembre m November
nubile single *(woman)*
nulla nothing ; anything
nullo(a) void *(contract)*
numero m number ; size *(of shoe)*
 numero di camera room number
 numero del conto account number
 numero di telefono phone number
nuòra f daughter-in-law
nuotare to swim
Nuova Zelanda f New Zealand
nuovo(a) new
 di nuovo again
nuvoloso(a) cloudy

O

o or
O west *(abbreviation)*
obbligatorio(a) compulsory
oceano m ocean
occasione f opportunity ; bargain
occhiali mpl glasses
 occhiali da sci skiing goggles
 occhiali da sole sunglasses
occhio m eye
occupato(a) busy/engaged
odore m smell
offerta f offer
officina f workshop ; repair shop
oggetto m object
oggi today
ogni each ; every
 ogni giorno every day ; daily
 ogni quanto? how often?
 ogni tanto occasionally
olio m oil
 olio solare suntan oil
 olio di girasole sunflower oil
 olio d'oliva olive oil
olive fpl olives
oltre beyond ; besides
ombra f shade
 all'ombra in the shade
ombrello m umbrella
ombrellone m sun umbrella
ombretto m eye shadow

o

omogemeizzati mpl baby food

omosessuale homosexual

onde fpl waves

onestà f honesty

onesto(a) honest

opera f opera

operatore turistico m tour operator

operazione f operation (surgical)

opuscolo m brochure

ora now

ora f hour
 ora di punta rush hour
 che ore sono? what's the time?

orario m timetable
 in orario on time
 orario di apertura opening hours
 orario di cassa banking hours
 orario visite visiting hours

ordinare to order ;
 to prescribe

ordine f order (in restaurant)

ordinato(a) tidy

orecchini mpl earrings

orecchio m ear

orecchioni mpl mumps

oreficeria f jeweller's

orina f urine

ormeggiare to moor

ormeggio m mooring

oro m gold
 placcato oro gold-plated

orologeria m watchmaker's

orologio m clock ; watch

orticaria f rash (skin)

ortografia f spelling

ospedale m hospital

ospite m/f guest ; host/hostess

osso m bone

ostello m hostel
 ostello della gioventù youth hostel

osteria f inn

ottenere to get ; obtain
 ottenere la linea to get through (on phone)

ottimo(a) excellent

ottobre m October

otturazione f filling (in tooth)

ovest m west

P

pacchetto m packet

pacco m package ; parcel

padella f frying-pan

Padova Padua

padre m father

padrone(a) m/f owner

paesaggio m scenery ; countryside

paese m country (nation) ; village

pagare to pay ; to pay for

pagato(a) paid

pagina f page

paio m pair

palazzo m building ; block of flats ; palace

palestra f gym

palla f ball

pallina f ball (small)
  pallina da golf golf ball
  pallina da tennis tennis ball

pallone m football

pandoro m Italian Christmas cake

pane m bread ; loaf
  pane integrale wholemeal bread
  pane carré sandwich bread
  pane e coperto cover charge
  pane di segale rye bread

pannettone m Italian Christmas cake

panetteria f baker's

pangrattato m breadcrumbs

panificio m bakery

panino m bread roll
  panino imbottito sandwich

paninoteca f sandwich bar

panna f cream

panno m cloth ; fabric

pannolini mpl nappies

pantaloni mpl trousers
  pantaloni corti shorts

pantofole fpl slippers

papa m pope

papà m daddy

parabrezza m windscreen

paraurti m bumper (on car)

parcheggiare to park

parcheggio m car park
  parcheggio custodito supervised car-park
  parcheggio libero free parking
  parcheggio sotterraneo underground car park

parchimetro m parking meter

parco m park
  parco nazionale national park

parente m/f relation ; relative

Parigi f Paris

parlare to speak ; to talk

parmigiano m parmesan
  parmigiano grattugiato grated parmesan

parola f word

parolaccia f swear word

parrucchiere(a) m/f hairdresser

parte f share ; part ; side

partenza f departures
  partenze internazionali international departures
  partenze nazionali domestic departures

partire to depart ; to leave

partita f match ; game
  partita di calcio football match

passaggio m passage ; lift (in car)
  dare un passaggio to give a lift

P

passaporto m passport
passeggiata f walk ; stroll
passeggino m pushchair
passo m pace ; pass (mountain)
   passo carrabile keep clear
   passo chiuso pass closed
   fare quattro passi to go for a stroll
pasticcino m cake (small, fancy)
pastiglia f tablet (pill)
pasto m meal
pastorizzato pasteurised
patata f potato
patatine fpl crisps
   patatine frite chips
patente f permit ; driving licence
patrigno m stepfather
pavimento m floor
paziente m/f patient
pecora f sheep
pedaggio m toll (motorway)
pedale m pedal
pedalò m pedalboat
pedicure m chiropodist
pedoni mpl pedestrians
peggio worse
pelati mpl tinned tomatoes
pelle f skin ; hide ; leather
pellegrino m pilgrim
pelletterie fpl leather goods
pellicola f film (for camera)
   pellicola a colori colour film

pellicola in bianco e nero black and white film
pelo m fur
pene m penis
penicillina f penicillin
penisola f peninsula
penna f pen
pensare to think
pensione f guesthouse
   pensione completa full board
   mezza pensione half board
   pensione familiare bed and breakfast
pentola f saucepan
pepe m pepper (spice)
per for ; per ; in order to
   per esempio for example
   per favore please
   per via aerea air mail
pera f pear
perché why ; because ; so that
percorso m walk ; journey ; route
   percorso panoramico scenic route
perdere to lose ; to miss (train, etc)
perdita f leak (of gas, liquid)
pericolante unsafe
pericolo m danger
pericoloso(a) dangerous
   non pericoloso(a) safe
periferia f outskirts ; suburbs

permanente continua parking restrictions still apply

permanenza f stay ; residency

permesso m licence ; permit
permesso! excuse me! *(to get by)*
permesso di soggiorno residence permit

permettere to allow

perso(a) lost *(object)* ; missed *(train, plane, etc)*

persona f person

personale m staff

pesante heavy

pesare to weigh

pesca f angling ; fishing ; peach
divieto di pesca no fishing

pescare to fish

pesce m fish

pescivendolo m fishmonger's

peso m weight

pettine m comb

petto m chest ; breast
petto di pollo chicken breast

pezzo m piece ; cut *(of meat)*

piacere to please
le piace? do you like it?
piacere! pleased to meet you!

piangere to cry *(weep)*

piano slowly ; quietly

piano m floor *(of building)* ; plan

pianta f map ; plan ; plant

pianterreno m ground floor

piantina f street map

piatto m dish ; course ; plate
primo piatto first course

piazza f square *(in town)*

piazzale m large square

piazzola (di sosta) f lay-by

piccante spicy ; hot

picchetto m tent peg

piccolo(a) little ; small

piede m foot
a piedi on foot

pieno(a) full

pietra f stone

pigiama m pyjamas

pigro(a) lazy

pila f battery ; torch

pillola f pill

pinne fpl flippers

pino m pine

pinze fpl pliers

pinzette fpl tweezers

pioggia f rain

piombo m lead *(metal)*

piovere to rain

piscina f swimming pool
piscina per bambini paddling pool

pista f track ; race track
pista da ballo dance floor
pista da sci ski run

P

più more ; most ; plus
  più di more than
  più economico(a) cheaper
  più tardi later
piumino *m* duvet
pizzeria *f* pizza restaurant
pizzico *m* pinch ; sting
pizzo *m* lace
plastica *f* plastic
  di plastica made of plastic
pneumatico *m* tyre
po' a little *(shortened form of poco)*
pochi(e) few
poco(a) little ; not much
  un po' a little
poi then
polizia *f* police
  polizia stradale traffic police
poliziotto *m* policeman
polizza *f* policy
pollo *m* chicken
polmone *m* lung
poltrona *f* armchair ; seat in stalls
pomata *f* ointment
pomeriggio *m* afternoon
  di pomeriggio in the afternoon
pomodoro *m* tomato
pompa *f* pump
pompelmo *m* grapefruit
ponte *m* bridge ; deck
  ponte macchine car deck
pontile *m* jetty ; pier

porcellana *f* china
porta *f* door ; gate ; goal
  porta di sicurezza emergency exit
portabagagli *m* luggage rack ; porter *(at airport, station, etc)*
portacenere *m* ashtray
portafoglio *m* wallet
portare to carry/bring ; to wear
portiere *m* porter *(doorkeeper)* ; goalkeeper
portineria *f* caretaker's lodge
porto *m* port ; harbour
  porto di scalo port of call
Portogallo *m* Portugal
porzione *f* portion ; helping
posate *fpl* cutlery
posologia *f* dosage
possiamo we can
  non possiamo we cannot
posso I can
  non posso I cannot
posta *f* post office ; mail
  posta elettronica e-mail
  posta raccomandata registered mail
posteggio *m* car park
  posteggio taxi taxi rank
posto *m* place ; job ; seat
  posti in piedi standing room
  posti a sedere seating capacity
  posti prenotati reserved seats

potabile ok to drink

potere to be able

pranzo m lunch

pré-maman m maternity dress

preavviso m advance notice

precotto(a) ready-cooked

predeterminare l'importo desiderato select required amount

preferire to prefer

preferito(a) favourite

prefisso m prefix ; area code
prefisso telefonico dialling code

pregare to pray
si prega... please...

prego don't mention it!

prelievo m collection ; sample

premere to push ; to press

premio m prize

prendere to take ; to catch (bus, etc)
prendere il sole to sunbathe
prendere in prestito to borrow

prenome m first name

prenotare to book ; to reserve

prenotato(a) reserved

prenotazione f reservation

preoccupato(a) worried

preparare to prepare ; to get ready

presa f socket (electric)

preservativo m condom

pressione del sangue f blood pressure

prestare to lend

presto early ; soon

prete m priest

previsione f forecast
previsioni del tempo weather forecast

previsto(a) scheduled ; expected
come previsto as expected

prezzo m price
prezzo al dettaglio retail price
prezzo fisso set price
prezzo di catalogo list price
prezzo al minuto retail price
prezzo d'ingresso entrance fee

prima di before

primavera f spring (season)

primo(a) first ; top ; early
primo piano first floor
primo piatto first course

principale main

principiante m/f beginner

privato(a) private

problema m problem

professione f profession

professore m/f teacher ; professor

profondità f depth

profondo(a) deep

P

profumeria f perfume shop
progettare to plan
programma m programme ; syllabus ; schedule
proibire to ban ; to prohibit
proibito(a) forbidden ; prohibited
prolunga f extension (electrical)
promettere to promise
pronto(a) ready
  pronto! hello! (on telephone)
  pronto soccorso casualty
proprietario(a) m/f owner
proprio(a) own
prossimamente coming soon
prossimo(a) next
proteggislip m panty liner
protesi dell'anca f hip replacement
protestante Protestant
provare to try ; to test (try out) ; to try on (clothes)
provvisorio(a) temporary
prugna f plum
PTP abbreviation of **Posto Telefonico Pubblico**
pubblicità f advertisement
pubblico m audience ; public
pulce f flea
pulito(a) clean
pulizia f cleaning
  pulizia del viso facial
pullman m coach

pulmino m minibus
punteggio m score
puntine fpl points
punto m point ; stitch ; full stop
  punto d'incontro meeting place
puntura f bite ; sting ; injection
puzzle m jigsaw
puzzo m bad smell

Q

qua here
quaderno m exercise book
quadro m picture ; painting
qual(e) what ; which ; which one
qualche some
  qualche volta sometimes
qualcosa something ; anything
qualcuno someone ; somebody
qualificato(a) qualified
qualità f quality
qualsiasi any
qualunque any
quando? when?
quanto(a)? how much?
  quanti(e)? how many?
quartiere m district
quarto m quarter
  quarto d'ora quarter of an hour

quattro four

quei those ; those ones

quel(la) that ; that one

quelli(e) those ; those ones

quello(a) that ; that one

questi(e) these ; these ones

questo(a) this ; this one

questura f police station

qui here

quindi then ; therefore

quindici giorni fortnight

quotidiano m daily (paper)

quotidiano(a) daily

R

rabarbaro m rhubarb

rabbia f anger ; rabies

racchetta f racket ; bat
racchetta da neve snowshoe
racchetta da sci ski pole

raccomandare to recommend

racconto m story

radiatore m radiator

radio f radio

radiografia f x-ray

raffreddore m cold (illness)
raffreddore da fieno hay fever

ragazza f young woman ; girlfriend
ragazza alla pari au pair

ragazzo m young man ; boyfriend

RAI f Italian State Broadcasting

rallentare to slow down

rapido m express train

rapido(a) high-speed ; quick

rasoio m razor
rasoio elettrico electric razor

reato m crime

recarsi alla cassa pay at cash desk

recentemente recently

reclamo m complaint

recupero monete returned coins

regalo m present ; gift

reggiseno m bra

regione f region ; district ; area

registrare to record

registratore m cassette player

registro m register

Regno Unito m United Kingdom

regolamento m regulation

regolare regular ; steady

remare to row (boat)

rendersi conto di to realize

rene m kidney

reparto m department ; ward

restare to stay ; to remain

R

restituire to return ; to give back

restituzione f return ; repayment

resto m remainder ; change (money)

restringersi to shrink

rete f net ; goal
rete portabagagli rack (luggage)

retro m back
vedi retro please turn over

retromarcia f reverse gear

reumatismo m rheumatism

ricambio m spare part ; refill

ricaricare to recharge (battery)

ricetta f prescription ; recipe

ricevere to receive ; to welcome

ricevitore m receiver (phone)

ricevuta f receipt

richiedere to require

richiesta f request

riciclare to recycle

riconoscere to recognize

riconoscimento m identification

ricordare to remember
non mi ricordo I don't remember

ricordo m souvenir ; memory

ricorrere a to resort to

ricoverare to admit (to hospital)

ridere to laugh

ridurre to reduce

riduttore m adaptor

riduzione f reduction

riempire to fill

rientro m return ; return home

rifare to do again ; to repair

rifiutare to refuse

rifiuti mpl rubbish ; waste

rifugio m mountain inn ; shelter

righello m ruler (for measuring)

rigore m penalty (football)

riguardo m care ; respect
riguardo a... regarding...

rilasciato(a) a issued at

rimandare to postpone

rimanere to stay ; to remain

rimborsare to reimburse

rimborso m refund

rimessa f remittance ; garage

rimettere to put back

rimettersi to recover (from illness)

rimorchiare to tow

rimorchio m trailer
a rimorchio on tow

rimozione f removal ; towing away

Rinascimento m Renaissance

rinfreschi mpl refreshments

ringraziare to thank

rinnovare to renew

rinunciare to give up

riparare to repair

riparato(a) sheltered ; repaired

riparazione f repair

ripetere to repeat

ripido(a) abrupt ; steep

ripiegare to fold

ripieno m stuffing

riposarsi to rest

riposo m rest (repose)

risalita f reascent

risarcimento m compensation

riscaldamento m heating

riscaldare to heat up (food)

rischio m risk

risciacquare to rinse

riscuotere to collect ; to cash

riserva f reserve ; reservation
riserva di caccia private hunting
riserva naturale nature reserve

riservare to reserve

riservato(a) reserved

riso m rice ; laugh

risotto m rice cooked in stock

risparmiare to save (money)

rispondere to answer ; to reply

risposta f answer

ristorante m restaurant

ritardo m delay

ritirare to withdraw

ritiro m retirement ; withdrawal
ritiro bagagli baggage reclaim

ritornare to return (go back)

ritorno m return

riunione f meeting

riuscita f result ; outcome

riva f bank ; shore

riviera f riviera

rivista f magazine ; revue

rivolgersi a to refer to (for info)

roba f stuff ; belongings

roccia f rock

rognoni mpl kidneys

romanico(a) Romanesque

romanzo m novel
romanzo rosa romantic novel

rompere to break

rondine f swallow (bird)

rosa pink

rosa f rose

rosmarino m rosemary

rosolia f German measles ; rubella

rossetto m lipstick

rosso(a) red

rosticceria f shop selling cooked food

rotonda f roundabout

rotondo(a) round

R

rotto(a) broken
roulotte f caravan
rovesciare to spill ; to knock over
rovine fpl ruins
rtd delay
rubare to steal
rubinetto m tap
rubrica f address book
ruggine f rust
rughe fpl wrinkles
rullino m roll of film
rum m rum
rumore m noise
rumoroso(a) noisy
ruota f wheel
  ruota di scorta spare wheel
rupe f mountain cliff
ruscello m stream
russare to snore

S

S south *(abbreviation)*
sabato Saturday
sabbia f sand
saccarina f saccharin
sacchetto m small bag
  sacchetto di carta paper bag
  sacchetto di plastica plastic bag
sacco a pelo m sleeping bag
sacerdote m priest

sagra f local food festival
sala f hall ; auditorium
  sala da pranzo dining room
  sala d'aspetto waiting room
  sala partenze departure lounge
salame m salami
salario m wage
salato(a) salted ; savoury
saldare to settle *(bill)* ; to weld
saldi sale
saldo m payment ; balance
sale m salt
salire to rise ; to go up
  salire in to get in *(vehicle)*
salita f climb ; slope
  in salita uphill
salmone m salmon
  salmone affumicato smoked salmon
salone m lounge ; salon
salotto m living room ; lounge
salsa f sauce
salsiccia f sausage
saltare to jump
saltato(a) sautéed
salumeria f delicatessen
salumi mpl cured pork meats
salute f health
  salute! cheers!
saluto m greeting
salvagente m life belt

salvare to rescue ; to save *(life)*

salvavita m circuit breaker

salve! hello!

salvia f sage *(herb)*

salvietta f serviette

salviettine per bambini fpl baby wipes

salvo except ; unless

sandali mpl sandals

sangue m blood
al sangue rare *(steak)*

sanguinare to bleed

sapere to know

sapone m soap

sapore m flavour ; taste

saporito(a) tasty

Sardegna f Sardinia

sarto m tailor

sartoria f tailor's ; dressmaker's

sasso m stone

sauna f sauna

sbagliato(a) wrong

sbaglio m mistake

sbarco m landing *(boat)*

sbrigare to hurry

scadente low *(standard, quality)*

scadenza f expiry

scadere to expire *(ticket, etc)*

scaduto(a) out-of-date ; expired

scala f scale ; ladder ; staircase

scala anticendio fire escape
scala mobile escalator

scalare to climb

scaldabagno m water heater

scaldare to heat up

scale fpl stairs

scalino m step

scalo m stopover

scaloppina f veal escalope

scarico(a) flat *(battery)*

scarpa f shoe
scarpe da ginnastica trainers

scarponcini mpl walking boots

scarponi da sci mpl ski boots

scatola f box ; tin

scegliere to choose

scelta f range ; selection ; choice

scendere to go down
scendere da to get off *(bus, etc)*

scheda f slip *(of paper)* ; card
scheda telefonica phonecard

schiena f back *(of body)*

sci m ski ; skiing
sci di fondo cross-country skiing
sci nautico water-skiing

scialuppa di salvataggio f lifeboat

sciare to ski

sciarpa f scarf

S

sciogliere to melt

sciopero m strike

sciovia f ski-lift

scivolare to slip

scomodo(a) inconvenient ; uncomfortable

scomparire to disappear

scompartimento m compartment

scongelare to defrost

sconto m discount
  sconti reductions

scontrino m ticket ; receipt ; chit

scopa f broom (brush)

scorso(a) last

scossa f shock (electric)

scottatura f burn
  scottatura solare sunburn

Scozia f Scotland

scozzese Scottish

scrivania f desk

scrivere to write ; to spell

scultura f sculpture

scuola f school
  scuola di sci ski school
  scuola materna nursery school

scuro(a) dark (colour)

scusare to excuse ; to forgive

scusarsi to apologise

scusi? pardon?

se if ; whether

sé oneself

seconda f second gear

238

secondo m second (time) ; main course (meal)

secondo(a) second ; according to
  seconda classe second class
  di seconda mano secondhand

sede f head office

sedersi to sit down

sedia f chair
  sedia a rotelle wheelchair
  sedia a sdraio deckchair

sedile per bambini m baby-seat (car)

seggiolone m highchair

seggiovia f chair-lift

segnale m signal ; road sign

segnare to score (goal)

segreteria telefonica f answering machine

seguente following

seguire to follow ; to continue

sella f saddle

selvatico(a) wild

semaforo m traffic lights

semifreddo m dessert made with ice cream

seminterrato basement

semplice plain ; simple

sempre always ; ever
  per sempre for ever

senso unico one-way street
  senso vietato no entry

sentiero m path ; footpath

sentire to hear

sentirsi to feel

senza without

separato(a) separated

sera f evening

serbatoio m tank (car)
serbatoio dell'acqua cistern

serio serious (not funny)

serpente m snake

serratura f lock

servire to serve

servizio m service ; report (in press)
servizio al tavolo waiter service
servizio compreso service included

servizi mpl facilities ; bathroom

sesso m sex

seta f silk

sete f thirst
avere sete to be thirsty

settembre m September

settentrionale northern

settimana f week
settimana bianca week's skiing holiday

settimanale weekly

sfida f challenge

sfuso(a) loose ; on tap (wine)

sganciare to lift receiver

sì yes

Sicilia f Sicily

sicurezza f safety ; security

sicuro(a) sure

sidro m cider

Sig. Mr abbreviation of Signor

Sig.ra Mrs/Ms abbreviation of Signora

sigaretta f cigarette

sigaro m cigar

Sig.na Miss abbreviation of Signorina

Signor: il Signor Grandi Mr Grandi

signora f lady ; madam ; Mrs ; Ms
signore ladies

signore m gentleman ; sir
signori gents

signorina f young woman ; Miss

silenzio m silence

simile a similar to

simpatico(a) pleasant ; nice

sindacato m trade union

sindaco m mayor

singolo(a) single

sinistra f left

sistemare to arrange

sito m site
sito web website

skipass m skipass

slacciare to unfasten ; to undo

slavina f snowslide ; landslide

slegato(a) loose (not fastened)

slogatura f sprain

smarrito(a) missing *(thing)*

smettere to stop doing something

soccorso *m* assistance ; help
soccorso alpino mountain rescue

socio *m* associate ; member

soggiorno *m* stay ; sitting room

soldi *mpl* money

sole *m* sun ; sunshine

solito: *di solito* usually

sollevare to raise ; to relieve

sollievo *m* relief

solo(a) alone ; only

solubile soluble
caffè solubile instant coffee

sonnifero *m* sleeping pill

sono I am (to be)

sopra on ; above ; over
di sopra upstairs

sopracciglia *fpl* eyebrows

sopravvivere to survive

sorella *f* sister

sorpassare to overtake *(in car)*

sorpresa *f* surprise

sorridere to smile

sorriso *m* smile

sospeso(a) suspended ; postponed

sosta *f* stop
divieto di sosta no parking

sott'acqua underwater

sotterraneo(a) underground

sotto underneath ; under ; below

Spagna *f* Spain

spagnolo(a) Spanish

spalla *f* shoulder

sparire to disappear

spazzatura *f* rubbish

spazzola *f* brush
spazzola per capelli hairbrush
spazzolino da denti toothbrush

speciale special

specialità *f* speciality

specialmente especially

spedire to send ; to dispatch

spegnere to turn off ; to put out

spendere to spend *(money)*

spento(a) turned off ; out *(light, etc)*

sperare to hope

spese *fpl* shopping ; expenses

spesso often

spettacolo *m* show ; performance

spezzatino *m* stew

spiaggia *f* beach ; shore
spiaggia privata private beach

spiccioli *mpl* small coins ; change
non ho spiccioli I've no change

spiegare to explain

spina f bone *(of fish)* ; plug *(electric)*

spingere to push

spirale f coil *(IUD)*

spogliatoio m dressing room

sporco(a) dirty

sportello m counter ; window

sportivo(a) informal *(clothes)*

sposarsi to get married

sposato(a) married
  non sposato(a) single

spugna f sponge

spuma f hair mousse

spumante m sparkling wine

spuntino m snack

squadra f team

squillare to ring *(phone)*

Srl Ltd

stabilimento m factory

stadio m stadium

stagione f season
  di stagione in season

stalla f stable

stampatello m block letters

stanco(a) tired

stanza f room
  stanza da bagno bathroom
  stanza dei giochi playroom

stare to be
  stare attento(a) a... beware of..
  stare bene to be well
  stare in piedi to stand

  come sta? how are you?

stasera tonight ; this evening

Stati Uniti mpl United States

stazione f station ; resort
  stazione balneare seaside resort
  stazione dell'autobus bus station
  stazione di servizio petrol station
  stazione ferroviaria train station

stella f star

sterlina f sterling ; pound

stesso(a) same

stirare to iron

stitichezza f constipation

stitico(a) constipated

stivali mpl boots

storia f history

storico(a) historic(al)
  centro storico old town

strada f road ; street
  strada chiusa road closed
  strada panoramica scenic route
  strada sbarrata road closed
  strada statale main road
  strada senza uscita no through road

stradina f lane

straniero(a) foreign ; foreigner

strano(a) strange

stupido(a) stupid

S

su on ; onto ; over ; about ; up

sua his ; her(s) ; its ; your(s)

subito at once ; immediately

succedere to happen

succo m juice
succo d'arancia orange juice
succo di frutta fruit juice
succo di mela apple juice
succo di pomodoro tomato juice

succursale m branch (of bank, etc)

sud m south

sue his ; her(s) ; its ; your(s)

suo(i) his ; her(s) ; its ; your(s)

suocera f mother-in-law

suocero m father-in-law

suola f sole (of foot, shoe)

suonare to ring ; to play

suono m sound

superare to exceed ; to overtake

supermercato m supermarket

supplemento m supplement

supposta f suppository

surf m surf

surgelato(a) frozen

sveglia f alarm clock/call

svegliare to wake up

svenire to faint

sviluppare to develop (photos)

Svizzera f Switzerland

svizzero(a) Swiss

svolta f turn

T

tabaccaio m tobacconist's

tacco m heel

tachimetro m speedometer

taglia f size (of clothes)

tagliare to cut

tailleur m women's suit

tallone m heel

tangenziale f by-pass

tanti(e) so many

tanto(a) so much ; so

tappo m cork ; plug ; cap
tappo del serbatoio petrol cap

tardi late

targa f numberplate (car)

tariffa f tariff ; rate
tariffa economica cheap rate
tariffa festiva rate on holidays
tariffa ore di punta peak rate

tartufo m truffle

tasca f pocket

tassa f tax

tasso m rate
tasso di cambio exchange rate

tavola f table ; plank ; board
tavola calda hot snacks

tavola da surf surfboard
tavola a vela windsurfing board

taxi m taxi

tazza f cup

tè m tea
tè al latte tea with milk
tè al limone lemon tea
tè freddo iced tea

teatro m theatre ; drama

tedesco(a) German

telecomando m remote control

telefonare to (tele)phone

telefonata f phone call

telefonino m mobile phone

telefono m telephone
telefono pubblico payphone

televisione f television

telone impermeabile m groundsheet

temperatura f temperature

temperino m penknife

tempesta f storm

tempio m temple

tempo m weather ; time

temporale m thunderstorm

tenda f curtain ; tent

tendine m tendon

tenere to keep ; to hold

tenore m tenor (singer)

tenore alcolico m alcohol content

tergicristallo m windscreen wiper

terminal m terminal (airport)

termometro m thermometer

termosifone m heater

terra f earth ; ground

terrazza f terrace

terremoto m earthquake

terza f third gear

terzi mpl third party

terzo(a) third

tessera f pass ; season ticket

tesserino m pass (bus, train)

tessuto m fabric

testa f head

testicoli mpl testicles

tettarella f dummy (for baby)

tetto m roof

tettuccio apribile m sunroof (car)

Tevere m Tiber

thermos m thermos flask

thriller m thriller

timone m rudder

tirare to pull

toccare to touch ; to feel
non toccare do not touch

togliere to remove ; to take away

toilette f toilet

tonno m tuna

topo m mouse

Torino m Turin

tornare to return ; to come/go back

torneo m tournament

toro m bull

torre f tower
torrone m nougat
torta f cake ; tart ; pie
Toscana f Tuscany
tosse f cough
tossico(a) toxic
tossire to cough
totale m total (amount)
tovaglia f tablecloth
tovagliolo m napkin
tra between ; among(st) ; in
tradizionale traditional
tradurre to translate
traduzione f translation
traffico m traffic
traghetto m ferry
tramezzino m sandwich
trampolino m diving board ;
  ski jump
tranquillante m tranquillizer
tranquillo(a) quiet (place)
trasferire to transfer
trasporto m transport
trattoria f restaurant
traveller's cheque mpl
  traveller's cheque
traversata f crossing ; flight
treno m train
  treno merci goods train
triangolo d'emergenza m
  warning triangle
tribuna f stand (stadium)
tribunale m law court
trimestre m term (school)
triste sad

tritare to mince ; to chop
troppi(e) too many
troppo too much ; too
trovare to find
trucco m make-up
tu you (familiar)
tubo m pipe ; tube
  tubo di scappamento
  exhaust
tuffarsi to dive
turno m turn ; shift
  di turno on duty
tuta sportiva f tracksuit
tutti (e) all ; everybody
  tutte le direzioni all
  routes
tutto everything ; all

U

ubriaco(a) drunk
uccello m bird
uccidere to kill
UE European Union
ufficio m office ; church
  service
  ufficio informazioni
  information bureau
  ufficio oggetti smarriti
  lost
  property office
  ufficio postale post office
ufficio turistico tourist
  office
uguale equal ; even
ulcera f ulcer

ultimo(a) last

un a ; an ; one

unghia f nail *(finger, toe)*

unione f union
Unione Europea European Union

Unità Sanitaria Locale local health centre

università f university

uno(a) a ; an ; one

uomo m man
uomini gents

uova mpl eggs

uovo m egg
uovo di Pasqua Easter egg
uovo sodo hard-boiled egg

uragano m hurricane

urgente urgent

usare to use

uscire to go/come out

uscita f exit/gate
uscita di sicurezza emergency exit

USL *abbreviation of* **Unità Sanitaria Locale**

uso m use

utile useful

uva f grapes

V

va bene all right *(agreed)*

vacanza f holiday(s)
vacanze estive summer holidays

vaccinazione f vaccination

vagina f vagina

vaglia m money order

vagone m carriage ; wagon
vagone letto sleeper
vagone ristorante restaurant car

valanga f avalanche

valico m pass *(mountain)*

valido(a) valid
valido fino a... valid until...

valigia f suitcase

valore m value; worth
di valore valuable

valuta f currency

valvola f valve

varicella f chickenpox

vasetto m jar

vaso m vase

vassoio m tray

vecchio(a) old

vedere to see

vedova f widow

vedovo m widower

vegetaliano(a) vegan

vegetariano(a) vegetarian

veicolo m vehicle

vela f sail ; sailing

veleno m poison

velenoso(a) poisonous

veloce quick

velocemente quickly

velocità f speed

vena f vein

V

vendere to sell
  vendesi for sale
vendita f sale
  vendita al minuto retail
  vendita a rate hire
  purchase
venerdì m Friday
venerdì santo m Good
  Friday
Venezia f Venice
venire to come
ventaglio m fan *(hand-held)*
ventilatore m electric fan
vento m wind
verde green
verdura f vegetables
verità f truth
vermut m vermouth
vernice f paint
verniciare to paint
vero(a) true ; real ; genuine
versamento m payment ;
  deposit
versare to pour
vertice m summit
vescica f blister
vespa f wasp
vestaglia f dressing gown
vestirsi to get dressed
vestiti mpl clothes
vestito m dress
vetrina f shop window
vetro m glass *(substance)*
via f street ; by *(via)*
  per via aerea by air mail

viaggiare to travel
viaggiatore m traveller
viaggio m journey ; trip ;
  drive
  viaggio d'affari business
  trip
  viaggio organizzato
  package tour
viale m avenue
vicino (a) near ; close by
vicolo m alley ; lane
  vicolo cieco cul-de-sac
videocamera f videocamera
videocassetta f
  videocassette
videogioco m computer
  game
videoregistratore m video
  recorder
vietato forbidden
  vietato accendere fuochi
  do not light fires
  vietato fumare no smoking
  vietato l'ingresso no entry
  vietato ingresso veicoli
  no entry for vehicles
  vietato scendere no exit
vigili del fuoco fire brigade
vigilia f eve
  Vigilia di Natale Christmas
  Eve
vigna f vineyard
vincere to win
vino m wine
  vino bianco white wine
  vini da pasto table wines
  vino da tavola table wine

vini pregiati quality wines
vino rosso red wine
violentare to rape
virus *m* virus
visita *f* visit
  visite guidate guided
  tours
visitare to visit
vista *f* view
visto *m* visa
vita *f* life ; waist
  vita notturna night life
vitamina *f* vitamin
vite *f* vine ; screw
vivere to live
vivo(a) live ; alive
voce *f* voice
volante *m* steering wheel
volare to fly
voler dire to mean *(signify)*
volere to want
volo *m* flight
  volo di linea scheduled
  flight
  volo charter charter flight
volta *f* time
  una volta once
  due volte twice
voltaggio *m* voltage
vomitare to vomit
vongola *f* clam
vostro(a) your ; yours
vulcano *m* volcano
vuoto(a) empty

Z

zanzara *f* mosquito
zanzaria *f* mosquito net
zia *f* aunt
zio *m* uncle
zona *f* zone
  zona blu restricted parking
  zone
  zona pedonale pedestrian
  zone
zucchero *m* sugar
zucchini *mpl* courgettes
zuppa *f* soup
  zuppa inglese type of trifle

GRAMMAR

NOUNS

In Italian all nouns are either *masculine* or *feminine*. Where in English we say **the apple** and **the book**, in Italian it is **la mela** and **il libro** because **mela** is *feminine* and **libro** is *masculine*. The gender of nouns is shown in the *article* (**il**, **la**, **un**, **una**, etc.):

THE:

masc. sing.	**il**	*fem. sing.*	**la**
	l' (+vowel)		**l'** (+vowel)
	lo (+z, gn, pn, ps, x, s+consonant)		

masc. plur.	**i**	*fem. plur.*	**le**
	gli (+vowel, +z, gn, pn, s+consonant)		

A, AN:

masc.	**un**	*fem.*	**una**
	uno (+z, gn, pn, s+consonant)		**un'** (+vowel)

NOTE: definite articles (**il**, **la**, **i**, **le**, etc.) used after the prepositions **a** (**to**, **at**), **da** (**by**, **from**), **su** (**on**), **di** (**of**, **some**) and **in** (**in**, **into**) contract as follows:

a + il	= al	da + il	= dal	su + il	= sul
a + lo	= allo	da + lo	= dallo	su + lo	= sullo
a + l'	= all'	da + l'	= dall'	su + l'	= sull'
a + la	= alla	da + la	= dalla	su + la	= sulla
a + i	= ai	da + i	= dai	su + i	= sui
a + gli	= agli	da + gli	= dagli	su + gli	= sugli
a + le	= alle	da + le	= dalle	su + le	= sulle

di + il	= del	in + il	= nel
di + lo	= dello	in + lo	= nello
di + l'	= dell'	in + l'	= nell'
di + la	= della	in + la	= nella
di + i	= dei	in + i	= nei
di + gli	= degli	in + gli	= negli
di + le	= delle	in + le	= nelle

g. **alla** casa (**to the** house)   **sul** tavolo (**on the** table)

NOUNS: FORMATION OF PLURALS

For most nouns, the singular ending changes as follows:

masc. sing.	masc. plur.	example	
o	i	libr**o**	libr**i**
e	i	padr**e**	padr**i**
a	i	artist**a**	artist**i**

NOTE: nouns ending in e can be either masculine or feminine. In the plural they all end in i, e.g.

la television**e**	le television**i**
il mar**e**	i mar**i**

NOTE: most nouns ending in co and go become chi and ghi in the plural to keep the c and g hard sounding. Some exceptions occur in the masculine, e.g. **ami**co – **ami**ci.

fem. sing.	fem. plur.	example	
a	e	mel**a**	mel**e**
e	i	madr**e**	madr**i**

NOTE: nouns ending in ca and ga become che and ghe in the plural to keep the c and g hard sounding.
Nouns ending in cia and gia often becomes ce and ge to keep the c and g soft sounding.

ADJECTIVES

Adjectives normally follow the noun they describe in Italian, e.g. **la mela rossa (the red apple)**

Some common exceptions which precede the noun are:
bello beautiful, **breve** short, **brutto** ugly, **buono** good, **cattivo** bad, **giovane** young, **grande** big, **lungo** long, **nuovo** new, **piccolo** small, **vecchio** old
e.g. **una bella giornata (a beautiful day)**

Italian adjectives have to reflect the gender of the noun they describe. To make an adjective *feminine*, an a replaces the o of the *masculine*, e.g. **rosso - rossa**. Adjectives ending in e, e.g. **giovane**, can be either *masculine* or *feminine*. The plural forms of the adjective change in the way described for nouns (above).

MY, YOUR, HIS, HER

These words also depend on the gender and number of the noun they accompany, and not on the sex of the 'owner'.

	with masc. sing. noun	with fem. sing. noun	with masc. plur. noun	with fem. plur. noun
my	il mio	la mia	i miei	le mie
your (polite)	il suo	la sua	i suoi	le sue
your (plural)	il vostro	la vostra	i vostri	le vostre
his/her	il suo	la sua	i suoi	le sue

PRONOUNS

SUBJECT

I	io
you	lei
he	lui / egli
she	lei / ella
it (masc.)	esso
it (fem.)	essa
we	noi
you	voi
they	loro
(things:masc)	essi
(things:fem.)	esse

OBJECT

me	mi
you	la
him	lo / l' (+vowel)
her	la / l' (+vowel)
it (masc.)	lo / l' (+vowel)
it (fem.)	la / l' (+vowel)
us	ci
you	vi
them (masc.)	li
them (fem.)	le

The object pronouns shown above are also used to mean to me, to us, etc., except:

to him / to it	= gli
to her / to it / to you	= le
to them	= loro

Pronoun objects (other than **loro**) usually precede the verb:

lo vedo	but	**scriverò loro**
I see him		I will write to them

When used with an infinitive (the verb form given in the dictionary), the pronoun follows and is attached to the infinitive less its final e:

voglio comprarlo (comprare)   I want to buy it

Subject pronouns (**io**, **tu**, **egli**, etc.) are often omitted before verbs, since the verb ending generally distinguishes the person:

parlo	<u>I</u> speak
parliamo	<u>we</u> speak
parlono	<u>they</u> speak

Lei is the polite form for **you**; **voi** is the plural form. **Tu**, the familiar form for **you**, should only be used with people you know well, or children.

VERBS

There are three main patterns of endings for verbs in Italian – those ending **are**, **ere** and **ire** in the dictionary. Two examples of the **ire** verbs are shown, since two distinct groups of endings exist. Subject pronouns are shown in brackets because these are often not used:

	PARL<u>ARE</u>	TO SPEAK	VEND<u>ERE</u>	TO SELL
(io)	parlo	I speak	vendo	I sell
(tu)	parli	you speak	vendi	you sell
(lui/lei)	parla	(s)he speaks	vende	(s)he sells
(noi)	parliamo	we speak	vendiamo	we sell
(voi)	parlate	you speak	vendete	you sell
(loro)	parlano	they speak	vendono	they sell

	DORM<u>IRE</u>	TO SLEEP	FIN<u>IRE</u>	TO FINISH
(io)	dormo	I sleep	finisco	I finish
(tu)	dormi	you sleep	finisci	you finish
(lui/lei)	dorme	(s)he sleeps	finisce	(s)he finishes
(noi)	dormiamo	we sleep	finiamo	we finish
(voi)	dormite	you sleep	finite	you finish
(loro)	dormono	theysleep	finiscono	they finish

IRREGULAR VERBS

Among the most important irregular verbs are the following:

	ESSERE	**TO BE**	**AVERE**	**TO HAVE**
(io)	**sono**	I am	**ho**	I have
(tu)	**sei**	you are	**hai**	you have
(lui/lei)	**è**	(s)he is	**ha**	(s)he has
(noi)	**siamo**	we are	**abbiamo**	we have
(voi)	**siete**	you are	**avete**	you have
(loro)	**sono**	they are	**hanno**	they have

	ANDARE	**TO GO**	**FARE**	**TO DO**
(io)	**vado**	I go	**faccio**	I do
(tu)	**vai**	you go	**fai**	you do
(lui/lei)	**va**	(s)he goes	**fa**	(s)he does
(noi)	**andiamo**	we go	**facciamo**	we do
(voi)	**andate**	you go	**fate**	you do
(loro)	**vanno**	they go	**fanno**	they do

	POTERE	**TO BE ABLE**	**VOLERE**	**TO WANT**
(io)	**posso**	I can	**voglio**	I want
(tu)	**puoi**	you can	**vuoi**	you want
(lui/lei)	**può**	(s)he can	**vuole**	(s)he wants
(noi)	**possiamo**	we can	**vogliamo**	we want
(voi)	**potete**	you can	**volete**	you want
(loro)	**possono**	they can	**vogliono**	they want

PAST TENSE

To form the simple past tense, **I spoke/I have spoken**, **I sold/I have sold**, etc. combine the present tense of the verb **avere – to have** with the past participle of the verb, e.g.

| | ho parlato | **I spoke/I have spoken** |
| | ho venduto | **I sold/I have sold** |

PARLARE *(past)*

ho parlato	**I spoke**
hai parlato	**you spoke**
ha parlato	**(s)he spoke**
abbiamo parlato	**we spoke**
avete parlato	**you spoke**
hanno parlato	**they spoke**

VENDERE *(past)*

ho venduto	**I sold**
hai venduto	**you sold**
ha venduto	**(s)he sold**
abbiamo venduto	**we sold**
avete venduto	**you sold**
hanno venduto	**they sold**

DORMIRE *(past)*

ho dormito	**I slept**
hai dormito	**you slept**
ha dormito	**(s)he slept**
abbiamo dormito	**we slept**
avete dormito	**you slept**
hanno dormito	**they slept**